Italy since 1989

Events and Interpretations

Vittorio Bufacchi

and

Simon Burgess

Revised Edition

palgrave

First edition in hardcover 1998
Reprinted (with new Preface and minor alterations) 2001

First published in paperback 2001 by
PALGRAVE
Houndmills, Basingstoke, Hampshire RG21 6XS and
175 Fifth Avenue, New York, N. Y. 10010
Companies and representatives throughout the world

PALGRAVE is the new global academic imprint of
St. Martin's Press LLC Scholarly and Reference Division and
Palgrave Publishers Ltd (formerly Macmillan Press Ltd).

ISBN 0–333–63402–0 hardback (*outside North America*)
ISBN 0–312–21050–7 hardback (*in North America*)
ISBN 0–333–93071–1 paperback (*worldwide*)

This book is printed on paper suitable for recycling and made from fully managed and sustained forest sources.

A catalogue record for this book is available from the British Library.

The Library of Congress has cataloged the hardcover edition as follows:
Bufacchi, Vittorio, 1957–
　　Italy since 1989 : events and interpretations / Vittorio Bufacchi and Simon Burgess.
　　　p. cm.
　　Includes bibliographical references and index.
　　ISBN 0–312–21050–7
　　　1. Italy—Politics and government—1976–1994. 2. Italy—Politics and government—1994– 3. Political corruption—Italy. 4. Berlusconi, Silvio, 1936– 5. Dini, Lamberto. I. Burgess, Simon M. II. Title.
　　DG581.B84 1997
　　320.945'09'049—dc21
　　　　　　　　　　　　　　　　　　　　　　97–24013
　　　　　　　　　　　　　　　　　　　　　　CIP

10　9　8　7　6　5　4　3　2　1
10　09　08　07　06　05　04　03　02　01

Printed in Great Britain by Antony Rowe Ltd, Chippenham, Wiltshire

To Corinne
and
to Fulvio and Marisa Bufacchi

Contents

List of Tables and Figures

Tables

Figures

Preface to the 2000 Reprint

'Instant' analysis is a hazardous enterprise. Even the most tentative observations are liable to be confounded by new developments. Apparent patterns dissolve into trendless fluctuation. Progression often proves to be illusory. This is particularly the case in surveying the latest changes in the Italian polity, involving the move from a notoriously static to a more open, and therefore unpredictable, political order. The structures of particratic rule, characterised by the colonising of economy and society by the political parties (see the Introduction and Chapter 4 below) may have been eroded, yet enough of the old habits and practices survive for the transition to remain 'unfinished'.[1] Attempts to address the most pressing problems – reshaping the governing institutions, instilling a sense of public morality and reinventing the relationship between the citizen and the state – can easily fall victim to false remedy, so that 'the forms change, but not the substance, the rhetoric evolves but it is still rhetoric, the lies vary but they remain lies'.[2] It is at least evident, for this reason, that the settlement which eventually emerges will not be determined by high-sounding democratic declarations but by competing calculations of partisan advantage.

This short preface is at best a timid attempt to update the original text by trying to make sense of the period between spring 1996 and autumn 1999. We pick up the story where the text of the first edition ends, with the election of Romano Prodi and the centre-left 'Olive Tree' alliance. Italian politics is like an Italian opera, full of characters interweaving in a plot which is often impossible to follow. We endeavoured to introduce all the leading players, and explain the rudimentary aspects of the storyline, in the original text. For this reason we strongly recommend all readers to postpone the reading of this preface until after having read the rest of the book. The brave may proceed at their own peril.

PRODI'S GOVERNMENT (APRIL 1996–OCTOBER 1998)

The coming to power of the 'Olive Tree' alliance in April 1996 was doubly significant. For the first time, the main party of the left, the Democratic Party of the Left (PDS) made up the bulk of the representatives of the new majority, overcoming its historical imprisonment in opposition. As the incoming Prime Minister Romano Prodi commented, just as Berlusconi had managed to 'unfreeze' the right in 1994, he (Prodi) had 'unfrozen' the left.[3] Because the alliance was essentially an anti-Berlusconi coalition, many of its supporters regarded the outcome as retrospectively validating Berlusconi's eviction from office (caused by the defection of the Northern League) in early 1995. The experience of the alternation of power underlined the truth of the dictum – of Samuel P. Huntington – that it takes two turnovers of government in order to consolidate a regime change.[4]

As in 1994, the 1996 election involved the voters in directly choosing a government, an impression somewhat fortuitously borne out once again by the final results.[5] The 'Olive Tree' had to rely on the 35 Deputies and 10 Senators of a party outside the alliance, Communist Refoundation (RC), for an overall majority in both chambers of parliament. Prodi's cabinet team, moreover, was dominated by non-political figures, including Carlo Azeglio Ciampi (treasury and budget), Lamberto Dini (foreign affairs) and the crusading magistrate Antonio di Pietro[6] (public works). Nevertheless Prodi confidently expected that the alliance would be unified enough to serve for the full five-year term. For far too long Italy had been an industrial giant but a political pygmy, Prodi declared: 'this we want to change'.

Prodi pinned his modernising ambitions on Italy meeting the Maastricht convergence criteria for European monetary union. Relying on the competent advice of Ciampi, Prodi's first Budget for 1997 imposed a total reduction of L.63 000b, mainly funded by spending cuts and a one-off 'Eurotax', designed to reduce the budget deficit to the target figure of 3 per cent of GDP by the end of the year. The lira also re-entered the ERM. Accused of 'fiscal dictatorship' by the opposition, the Prime Minister was adamant that unless Italy qualified for the single currency the country would be unable to defend itself against international speculators. The public finances were given a further boost by proceeds from the privatising of Telecom Italia and the sale of shares in ENI, the state energy and chemicals conglomerate. Even so, the national debt still stood at approximately 123 per cent of GDP, more than twice the Maastricht limit, prompting fears from other European countries that Italy's financial laxity might undermine the whole EMU project. To allay such misgivings, the 1998 Budget package set out plans for a further reduction of the deficit and the debt over the coming three years, backed up by guarantees from Ciampi about continuing to enforce strict monetary discipline. In the space of one year, the deficit was miraculously lowered by four percentage points, to 2.7 per cent of GDP. According to the PDS, the government had saved the country from the real risk of bankruptcy. In May 1998, following the introduction of a stability pact pressed for by Germany (envisaging heavy fines for countries breaching the agreed targets), Italy was named among those eligible for the first wave of monetary union, even though it had fulfilled only four out of the five requirements laid down at Maastricht.

This striking success was almost immediately offset by the breakdown of all-party talks on constitutional reform. A 70-member parliamentary Bicameral Committee, chaired by the leader of the PDS, Massimo D'Alema, began work in February 1997. Its stated task was to consider the merits of adopting either a French-style, semi-presidential arrangement, dominated by a directly elected head of state, or opting instead for a German-style system which would strengthen the prime minister's executive authority. The committee also examined proposals for removing the remaining proportional element in the voting system, streamlining the legislative process by strengthening the Chamber of Deputies and (one of the promises made by the PDS during the election campaign) preparing the way for devolution of power to the regions. After several weeks of haggling, the committee, by 51 votes to 9, decided to endorse a presidentialist model, but one leaving extensive scope for policy making (especially economic) in the hands of the prime minister. Berlusconi's support for this compromise was reportedly secured by a pledge to leave his ownership of three television channels untouched. In deference to the small centre parties, the

25 per cent of seats elected by proportional voting were to be retained, counterbalanced by a topping-up of seats awarded to the largest party or coalition after an election, thus ensuring a working parliamentary majority.

These deliberations had an effect in hastening the realignment of all political forces across the ideological spectrum. In February 1998, D'Alema orchestrated the merging of the PDS with some ex-Socialists and a number of tinier movements (including the Social Christians, and the Labour Federation) in the newly-created *Democratici di Sinistra* (DS, or Left Democrats).[7] The reason behind this transformation was, in part, to legitimize a further shift of the centre-left towards the centre, in an attempt to take away votes from the many centrist parties who were desperately trying to carve out a space for themselves between the left-wing 'Olive Tree' alliance and the right-wing *Polo per le Libertá* (Pole for Freedom).

On the centre-right, in July 1998 a new party was born, the Democratic Union for the Republic (UDR). The brainchild of Francesco Cossiga, the former president, a life Senator and an increasingly influential, if incalculable, power broker, the UDR came into being when some forty MPs were lured away from other parties, mostly from the CDU, but also from CCD and Forza Italia.

On the right, the Pole for Freedom appeared to be in crisis. Silvio Berlusconi (Forza Italia) was struggling to win the argument about curbing the powers of magistrates, at a time of intensified judicial inquiries into his business dealings.[8] His main political ally in the Pole for Freedom, Gianfranco Fini (National Alliance), tried to take advantage of Berlusconi's moment of weakness by challenging his leadership. Berlusconi responded by announcing to *Panorama* magazine in April 1998 that he no longer supported the propositions adopted by the Bicameral Committee. All attempts to revive the agreement failed.

The collapse of institutional reform was not a make-or-break issue for Prodi's government. It was, on the other hand, a portent. In a vote in June 1998 on expanding NATO to include the Czech Republic, Hungary and Poland, Communist Refoundation (RC) refused to line up behind Prodi, who was only rescued from defeat by Cossiga's UDR. After verifying that RC support for the 'Olive Tree' was intact,

Prodi then carried a motion of confidence in the Chamber of Deputies in July. However, the RC leader Bertinotti stopped short of the show of full support that Prodi wanted.

The Budget for 1999 soon became the next main point of contention between Prodi and Bertinotti. Meeting the target of 2.0 per cent for the public deficit required austere measures on all fronts, but especially on pensions (Italy spends 15.7 per cent of GDP on pensions as compared to an EU average of 12.1 per cent). Bertinotti not only refused to endorse a cut in the state pension scheme, but insisted among other concessions on the setting up of a job creation agency in the south. Prodi stood his ground, counting on some RC MPs splitting off from Bertinotti. In a critical further vote of confidence on 9 October, Prodi lost by 313 votes to 312, bringing to an end – after 876 days – the second longest government of the postwar period.

D'ALEMA STEPS UP

Prodi had always maintained that, were he to lose his majority, he would never preside over a reconstructed government. President Scalfaro, sounding out parliamentary opinion, per-suaded him otherwise. The opposition, clamouring for fresh elections now that the original centre-left coalition had broken up, denounced Prodi as a 'charlatan'. Prodi, who had hitherto rejected any permanent dealings with the UDR, was offered a life-line by Cossiga, upon the following conditions: a request before parliament for his support; an admission that the electoral majority of April 1996 had ceased to exist; and the right to veto cabinet appointments. Prodi rejected the offer. The price he was being asked to pay was too high.

Rather than install another stop-gap administration of tech-nocrats, Scalfaro turned to D'Alema, inviting him to try where Prodi had failed. In a move to secure a solid majority in both the Chamber of Deputies and the Senate, now that the 'Olive Tree' alliance could no longer count on the support of Bertinotti's RC, D'Alema quickly struck a bargain with the tricky Cossiga (UDR) and with Armando Cossutta, leader of the brand new Italian Communists' Party (PdCI), a splinter party that broke away from RC when Bertinotti decided to vote against Prodi's austerity budget.

D'Alema was sworn in as the head of a new government on 21 October 1998, going on to submit a cabinet list of 25 ministers (compared to 20 under Prodi) drawn from a total of eight different parties and factions. Ciampi and Dini stayed at their posts, while Giuliano Amato took on the special job of institutional reform.[9] D'Alema also appointed a record number of six women to the new cabinet. Italy had a government again – the 56th since the war – but a government brought about and formed by the old politics of parliamentary manoeuvre, in complete disregard (as had happened with the downfall of Berlusconi) of the requirements of a popular mandate. This did not prevent D'Alema from telling Italians that they might one day like to vote him into office.

Succeeding Prodi, D'Alema nevertheless vowed to continue with his predecessor's policies of economic rigour, chiefly by tackling the combined legacy of over generous state pensions, high taxation and low growth. His precarious parliamentary majority gave him little room for positive action. Nevertheless he pulled off two early achievements. In March 1999 he helped to procure Prodi's selection as the next President of the European Commission, and in May, in an uncontested ballot during a joint session of parliament, Ciampi was voted Italy's tenth Italian President. Ciampi gained 707 (71.4 per cent) of the votes cast in the first round, short-circuiting the usual, ritualised wheeling-and-dealing. If the swift election of the new President was a welcome departure from old style politicking,[10] there were also signs of nostalgia for the old political order: two of the most discredited politicians in recent years, Bettino Craxi (ex-PSI) and Giulio Andreotti (ex-DC), received respectively six and ten votes.[11] Ciampi's place at the Treasury was taken by Amato, one of whose first awkward tasks was to ask the European Union to allow Italy, contrary to all the assurances previously given, to raise its budget deficit. This was clear evidence that the sacrifices already made in order to qualify for entry into monetary union would pale by comparison with the drastic steps necessary to remain in future within the euro-zone.

D'Alema's diplomatic skills were tested to the limit by the NATO offensive against Serbia, Italy providing 13 air bases for

NATO attacks. Although the bombing campaign went on for much longer than the Prime Minister hoped, he did manage to hold his disparate coalition together. His efforts were not, having said that, rewarded by the electorate.

SPRING TIME, ELECTION TIME

Frequent elections are a feature of Italian politics and 1999 was particularly eventful. Between mid-April and mid-June three different elections, each following a different electoral system, were scheduled.

The recommendations of the parliamentary commission on institutional reform having stalled, a referendum was held in April in favour of abolishing outright the remaining 25 per cent portion of proportional voting in elections to the Chamber of Deputies. The referendum was fully endorsed and supported by all the major parties as well as many prominent opinion makers. The electorate was told, in no uncertain terms, that voting 'Yes' would put an end to the proliferation of smaller parties,[12] encourage strong government and lead to greater political stability. And yet, surprisingly, the referendum failed. Turnout only reached 49.6 per cent, 0.4 per cent short of the 50 per cent threshold for the verdict to be constitutionally binding.

Regional turnout in the referendum of April 1999

North	53.9%
Centre	54.0%
South	42.8%
Isles	40.2%

Of those who did cast their vote, 91.5 per cent (just under 21 million voters) supported the idea, but for the want of an extra 200 000 votes the proposal was lost. The 'No' strategy, suggesting doubters simply stay away, won the day. The referendum is hardly the perfect reforming instrument. As we argue in Chapter 6, it might, furthermore, be a mistake on the part of the political class to believe that Italy's problems of governance are susceptible to a 'technical solution'.

The European elections of 13 June 1999 were also a severe test for D'Alema's 'Olive Tree' alliance. The run up to the elections was, as one would expect, marred by tensions and conflicts. The key question turned on whether the parties in the 'Olive Tree' should present a joint electoral list or present separate lists. The desire to create a third coalition of centre parties, which would find space on the ideological spectrum between the Pole for Freedom and the Olive Tree, was the motivation behind exploratory talks about a possible electoral pact between the PPI and Cossiga's UDR. In a preemptive move aimed at stopping the PPI–UDR political project from materialising, ex-prime minister Prodi formed a new political party in March, Democratici per l'Ulivo (Democrats for the Olive Tree). Prodi's initiative proved to be successful.[13] His declared political goal was not only to revive the centre-left 'Olive Tree' alliance, fending off attacks from the centre, but also to take the leadership of the 'Olive Tree' away from D'Alema and return it to one of the Centre parties in the alliance.

The two main parties in the ruling 'Olive Tree' alliance, DS and PPI, both lost votes compared with the 1996 general election and the 1994 European elections. No doubt many of their votes went to Prodi's Democratici per l'Ulivo, which won 7.7 per cent of the votes and seven seats. UDEUR failed to make an impact, winning only 1.6 per cent of the votes and one seat. There were mixed fortunes amongst the opposition parties. Berlusconi's Forza Italia won more votes (25.2 per cent, up almost 5 per cent from the general election of 1996) and more seats than any other party (22). Fini's Alleanza Nazionale, in alliance with Patto Segni, did rather poorly, losing 5 per cent compared to the general elections of 1996. But the real surprise was Emma Bonino, a member of the European Commission. Her list, supported by Pannella's Radical Party, won 8.5 per cent of the votes and seven seats. After the election a number of party leaders offered their resignations, among them Franco Marini (PPI), Luigi Manconi (Greens) and Gianfranco Fini (AN).

Two weeks after the European election, there were still regional, provincial and municipal elections to be fought. Overall the centre-right did better than the centre-left. In a symbolic blow to the left, however, the DS-backed candidate

Results of the European Election in Italy (87 seats)

| | *1999 European Elections* | | *1996 General Elections* | *1994 European Elections* | |
	% votes	*seats*	*% votes*	*% votes*	*seats*
FI	25.2	22	20.6	30.6	27
DS	17.3	15	21.1	19.1	16
AN/PS	10.3	9	15.7	12.5/3.3	11/0
Lista Bonino	8.5	7	1.9	2.1	2
DU-Prodi	7.7	7	–	–	–
Lega Nord	4.5	4	10.1	6.6	6
RC	4.3	4	8.6	6.1	5
PPI	4.2	4	6.8	10.0	8
CCD	2.6	2	5.8	–	–
CDU	2.2	2	–	–	–
SDI	2.2	2	–	–	–
PdCI	2.0	2	–	–	–
Greens	1.8	2	2.5	3.2	3
UDEUR	1.6	1	–	–	–
MST	1.6	1	0.9	–	–
RI-Dini	1.1	1	4.3	–	–
Others	2.9	2	–	–	–

Note: FI = Forza Italia; DS = Democratici di Sinistra; AN = Alleanza Nazionale; PS = Patto Segni (AN and PS presented a combined list in the 1999 European elections but separate lists in the 1996 general election and 1994 European elections); Lista Bonino (in the 1996 general elections this appeared as Pannella–Sgarbi, and in the 1994 European elections as Lista Pannella);
DU-Prodi = Democratici per l'Ulivo; RC = Rifondazione Comunista; PPI = Partito Popolare Italiano (in the 1996 general elections this appeared as PPI–SVP–UD–Prodi); CCD = Centro Cristiano Democratico (in the 1996 general elections this appeared as CCD–CDU); CDU = Cristiano Democratici Uniti; SDI = Social Democratici Italiani; PdCI = Partito dei Comunisti Italiani; UDEUR = Unione Democratica per l'Europe; MST = Movimento Sociale Tricolore; RI-Dini = Rinnovamento Italiano–Dini; Others include Democratici Liberali Repubblicani Europei (1 seat in 1999 European elections) and Partito Pensionati (1 seat in 1999 European elections).

was defeated in the mayoral race in Bologna, long considered the showpiece city of left-wing rule.

DEMOCRATIC DEFICIT

Italy's budget deficit might be improving. Italy's democratic deficit has yet to be corrected. The project to create bipolar electoral competition between clearly defined parties of government and opposition, judged by the electorate for their competence and efficiency, still has much ground to gain. This applies to the left as much as the right. Prime Minister D'Alema is able to point to the threat posed by the free market to social cohesion, yet it is unclear whether all of his colleagues in the 'Olive Tree' coalition have broken with the tradition of using public spending for political spoils. The right, lacking united leadership, falls back too readily on trying to revive the Communist bogey.

Too many of the central actors currently in positions of power are recycled figures implicated in various scandals. Prodi himself is pursued, even in Brussels, by allegations about his tenure of IRI in 1982–89 and 1993–94.[14] Cossutta, whose Italian Communists' Party was invited by D'Alema to enter his government coalition, was recently revealed to have been a paid 'asset' of the Soviet Union. Cossiga is caught up in many of the unresolved mysteries of Italy's recent past, which continue to capture attention.[15] The leaders of the opposition are not faring any better. The autocratic Umberto Bossi humiliated and expelled rivals from his party, the Northern League, for challenging his authority. The leader of the so-called 'post-fascist', supposedly 'domesticated' National Alliance, Gianfranco Fini, launched an attack on the civil rights of homosexuals, arguing that they should be banned from teaching in schools.[16] And of course Berlusconi remains under investigation on various charges of corruption, a constant reminder of the way in which politics and business – so typical of the First Republic – remain entangled.

The opening of a new millennium, with another general election no more than eighteen months away, is an opportune time to take stock of Italy's achievements since War World Two. No one can doubt that over the last fifty years Italy has succeeded in establishing a solid democracy, unlike some of its Mediterranean neighbours.[17] The degree of *liberality* of its democratic system, the extent, that is, to which the authority of the state relies on popular consent rather than party mediated exploitation, is a different matter.[18] In terms of liberal pedigree, Italy's postwar performance was less than spectacular, although it was always going to be difficult for a liberal political culture to flourish in a country held hostage by three great illiberal forces: Fascism, Catholicism and Communism. One question we posed for ourselves at the outset of writing this book was whether, with the ending of the Cold War, the semblance of a truly liberal culture was starting to take shape (see the Introduction and Conclusion). The evidence is discouraging. It is a measure of the distance still to be travelled that, in the eyes of many, the growing emphasis on community values, transparency in public administration and the reassertion of the rule of law is looked upon as questionable, if not pernicious.[19] Ten years on from the groundbreaking events of 1989 with which this book begins, the 'democratic normalisation' of Italy is far from assured.

Notes

1. M. Frei, *Italy: The Unfinished Revolution*, London: Sinclair-Stevenson (1996).
2. The formula of Indro Montanelli, in the postscript of his *Storia d'Italia*, Milan: Rizzoli (1996).
3. Interview in *Le Monde*, 22 October 1997. For an account of Berlusconi's term in office, see Chapter 9 below.
4. Of course, as Mark Donovan correctly suggests in his review of the first edition of *Italy Since 1989*, in *Modern Italy*, Vol. 4, No. 1, May 1999, it is far from clear that Italy's evolving political system is consolidating itself around a two-bloc party system.
5. See I. Diamanti and M. Lazar, *Politique a L'Italienne*, Paris: PUF (1997).
6. Di Pietro resigned after six months, complaining of the endless attempts to investigate or control him. Standing as an 'Olive Tree' candidate, he won a seat in the Senate in November 1997. In 1999 he formed a brand new party, L'Italia dei Valori (Italy's Values).
7. For a detailed recounting of this change, see M. Bull, 'From PDS to Cosa 2: The Second Congress of the Democratic Party of the Left', European University Institute Working Paper, SPS No. 97/3.
8. In December 1997 Berlusconi was sentenced to 1 year and 4 months in jail for false accounting. In July 1998 he was found guilty of bribing tax inspectors (2 years and 9 months) and of making illegal payments

worth $21m. to the Socialist Party (2 years and 4 months). All of the
sentences were appealed against.

9.   Professor Amato, prime minister in 1992–93, has kindly pointed out in
     reading through our account of his premiership that the exit of the
     lira from the ERM (Chapter 3, p. 78) followed upon, and was a con-
     sequence of, the prior departure of sterling, after the British refusal to
     realign. He adds, with regard to the abortive decree on Tangentopoli
     (pp. 120–3), that the elimination of preventative detention was never
     an item on the agenda. We are grateful to Professor Amato for point-
     ing out these errors in our original text.
10. The last presidential election in 1992 took 10 days and 16 ballots to
     decide.
11. In September and October 1999, Andreotti was cleared of two
     separate charges of (a) complicity in the murder of Mino Pecorelli
     and (b) mafia association, calling into serious question the use made
     by the prosecution of the evidence of mafia *pentiti* (see Chapter 5).
12. The Italian parliament, in 1998, had representatives from one
     ex-Communist party, two Communist parties, three ex-Socialist
     parties, four ex-Christian Democrat parties, one ex-Fascist party and
     one Fascist party. No less than 18 parties were represented in the
     European Parliament.
13. The pact between PPI and UDR never materialised. At the end of
     February Cossiga officially dissolved the party he had created only
     seven months previously, although some of its MPs went on to form
     the Unione Democratica per l'Europa (Democratic Union for
     Europe).
14. The Istituto per la Ricostruzione Industriale (IRI) was established in
     1933 in order to rescue banks and firms that had collapsed during the
     depression. In the 1980s its main role was in modernising the country.
     For an account of the politics of IRI, see P. Bianchi 'The IRI in Italy:
     Strategic Role and Political Constraints', *West European Politics*, Vol. 10,
     No. 2, April 1987.
15. P. Robb, *Midnight in Sicily*, London: The Harvill Press (1998).
16. Fini found support for his homophobic views from Rocco Buttiglione,
     leader of the centre party CDU, and Gianfranco Miglio.
17. The democratic nature of the Italian polity has recently come under
     scrutiny by Stanton Burnett and Luca Mantovani in their book *The
     Italian Guillotine*, Lanham, MD: Rowman and Littlefield, 1998. Their
     central thesis is that the Milan magistrates whose investigations of
     political corruption between 1992 and 1994 led to the end of the First
     Republic were the chief architects of a 'coup d'état' orchestrated for
     the benefit of the left with the support of the mafia. We feel that
     Burnett and Mantovani indulge in what can only be described as con-
     spiracy theory. The authors' melodramatic claim that the book had to
     be published in the United States because of the *de facto* suspension of
     freedom of expression in Italy is indicative of their state of mind.
18. For a brief account of liberalism and liberal democracy, see the
     Introduction below.
19. The view taken by Joseph La Palombara, in his review of *Italy Since
     1989* in *The Political Science Quarterly*, Vol. 113, No. 4 (1998).

Preface

Writing in 1513, as he came to the end of his work *The Prince*, Niccoló Machiavelli observed:

> I asked myself whether in present-day Italy the times were propitious for recognising a new ruler, and whether the circumstances existed here which would make it possible for a prudent and capable man to introduce a new order, bringing honour to himself and prosperity to all and every Italian. Well, I believe that so many things conspire to favour a new ruler, that I cannot imagine there ever was a time more suitable than the present.[1]

It is unfortunate that almost 500 years after Machiavelli wrote these words, his recommendation remains valid, albeit it for very contrasting reasons. In 1513 Machiavelli was preoccupied with trying to rescue the Italian city-states 'from the cruel and arrogant domination of foreigners'. Today the central question is whether and how far it may be possible to liberate Italy from the abuse of power perpetrated by its own indigenous political class.

Although we have taken this uncertain (and, at the time of writing, still all too evidently incomplete) transition to a new Italy as our point of departure, we ought also to explain how this book came to be written, what it sets out to do and what it does not pretend to be. In the first place, it is aimed at English-speaking students of Italian affairs, as well as at anyone with a general interest in the political life of what used to be called *il bel paese*. The scope of the book is a narrow one, concentrating specifically on the tumultuous period since 1989. It does nothing more than attempt to complement and, where possible, build upon the excellent long-range accounts already provided by Donald Sassoon and Paul Ginsborg.[2]

Secondly, it does not provide the reader with a formal description of the constitutional mechanics of the Italian polity. Readers interested in learning about the powers of the President and of the prime minister, the organisation of parliament or the role of the judiciary would be better advised to first consult the abundance of other detailed textbooks available to an English-speaking audience.[3]

The main purpose of the present book is simply to conduct a guided tour through the phenomenal changes that have recently taken place across Italy. The speed and scale of the changes has not only meant that much of the existing and even the latest literature is in danger of becoming obsolete.[4] It is also the case that the conventional Anglo-American terms of academic discussion – the language of swings of opinion, party realignments and old clichés like the pouring of new wine into old bottles – is inadequate for conveying the full significance of what has and has not occurred; as Alfio Mastropaolo points out, all existing models have been overthrown.[5] As a result, it is not surprising to find that many scholars of Italian affairs, like Ginsborg, have been calling for a diverse, multicausal explanation that is necessary to any proper understanding of the Italian crisis.[6] While we share the view that taking into consideration a number of different spheres – economic, political, social and cultural – is necessary for a proper understanding of an historic epoch, it is important not to confuse understanding with explanations. In fact to understand an event is not to explain an event.[7] This book is an attempt to understand *and* explain the Italian crisis, which is why the approach taken is, with apologies, largely political.

The layout of the book also requires some comment. In attempting to make sense of the huge amount of source material, we have chosen the somewhat unusual arrangement of bringing together the straightforwardly descriptive and the more analytical approaches, combining them in what we hope is an interconnected whole. The historical chapters (Chapters 1, 3, 5 and 7), dealing with a narrative of the main events over the period, follow a chronological order. These were largely written by Simon Burgess. A more in-depth analysis of key moments and issues, using at a very basic level the methodology of rational choice analysis, can be found in Chapters 2, 4, 6, 8 and 11, for which Vittorio Bufacchi was primarily responsible. Both authors had a hand in drafting Chapters 9 and 10, which assess respectively the governments of Silvio Berlusconi and Lamberto Dini, as well as jointly writing the Introduction and Conclusion. This layout, while unorthodox, seemed to us to be the best way of allowing the interested reader to pick and choose from what is intended chiefly to be a work of reference.

Acknowledgement is owed to the trustees of the Arthur McDougall Fund for permission to quote from two articles which originally appeared in the journal *Representation*: 'All change: the Italian electoral referendum of April 1993' and 'The new Italy and the general election of March 1994', both in Vol.32, No.118, Summer 1994. We are grateful to the relevant publishers and editors for permission to draw on material in the following articles in the preparation of Chapter 4 ('The success of "mani pulite": luck or skill?', in R. Leonardi and R. Nanetti (eds) *Italy: Politics and Policy*, Aldershot: Dartmouth 1996) and Chapter 10 ('The Coming of Age of Italian Democracy', *Government and Opposition*, Vol.31, No.3, Summer 1996). Over the last three years, a number of friends have come to our rescue during the preparation of this book. Conversations with Paolo Trombin on the lack of a liberal tradition in Italy were precious for this project. Thanks are also due to Percy Allum, Mark Donovan, Shari Garmise, Mario Ricciardi and Federico Varese, all of whom generously read various parts of the manuscript at different stages. Any errors of fact are entirely of our own making, as is the conceit in disregarding the well-founded warning that no one who understands what is involved in theorising about the modern state would ever attempt it.[8]

VITTORIO BUFACCHI
SIMON BURGESS

Notes

1. N. Machiavelli, *The Prince*, translated by G. Bull (1961) pp.133–4.

2. D. Sassoon, *Contemporary Italy* (1986); P. Ginsborg, *A History of Contemporary Italy: Society and Politics, 1943–1988* (1990). For a shorter but more recent account, see P. McCarthy *The Crisis of the Italian State: From the Origins of the Cold War to the Fall of Berlusconi* (1995).

3. The *locus classicus* is, of course, the Italian Constitution itself. Other works of value include P. Allum, *Italy: Republic without Government?* (1973); P. Lange and S. Tarrow (eds), *Italy in Transition: Conflict and Consensus* (1980); F. Spotts and T. Wieser, *Italy: A Difficult Democracy* (1986); and J. La Palombara, *Democracy, Italian Style* (1987). Since 1986 and on a yearly basis, a volume on *Italian Politics: A Review* has

appeared, with articles discussing the major political and social issues of the previous twelve months. These volumes are essential reading for all students of Italian politics.

4. See, for example, the first-class books by D. Hine, *Governing Italy: The Politics of Bargained Pluralism* (1993), and P. Furlong, *Modern Italy: Representation and Reform* (1994), both of which were unlucky in their timing.

5. A. Mastropaolo, 'Perché é entrata in crisi la democrazia Italiana? Un'ipotesi sugli anni ottanta', in M. Caciagli *et al.* (eds), *L'Italia fra Crisi e Transizione* (1994) p.71.

6. P. Ginsborg, 'Comment expliquer la crise italienne?', in *Politix* (30) 1995, p.6. See also his 'Italian political culture in historical perspective', in *Modern Italy*, Vol.1, No.1, Autumn 1995, p.4; and 'Explaining Italy's crisis', in S. Gundle and S. Parker (eds), *The New Italian Republic* (1996).

7. For an account of the difference between understanding and explanation, see M. Hollis *The Philosophy of Social Sciences* (1995).

8. J. Dunn 'In the thicket of the theories of the state', in *Government and Opposition*, Vol.22, 1987, p.519.

List of Abbreviations

AD	(Alleanza Democratica) Democratic Alliance
AN	(Alleanza Nazionale) National Alliance
CAF	Triumvirate of Craxi–Andreotti–Forlani
CCD	(Centro Cristiano Democratico) Christian Democratic Centre
CDU	(Cristiano Democratici Uniti) Christian Democrats United
CGIL	General Confederation of Italian Labour
CISL	Italian Confederation of Workers' Union
COREL	Committee for Electoral Reform
CORID	Committee for Democratic Reform
CSM	Supreme Council of the Judiciary
CT	Corrupt transaction
CO	Corrupt official
DC	(Democrazia Cristiana) Christian Democracy
DIA	(Direzione Investigativa Anti-Mafia) Anti-mafia investigative directorate
DM	Deutschmark
DS	(Democratici di Sinistra) Left Democrats
EFIM	(Ente Per Finanziamento Dell' Industria Manifatturiera) Southern Manufacturing Industry Holdings Corporation
EMS	European Monetary System
EMU	European Monetary Union
ENEL	State Electricity Company
ENI	National Petrolium Company
ERM	Exchange Rate Mechanism
FI	Forza Italia!
GL	Green Lists
INA	(Istituto Nazional Assicurazioni) National Insurance Agency
IRI	Institute for Industrial Reconstruction
L	Lira – immediately prior to the withdrawal of the lira from the Exchange Rate Mechanism of the European Monetary System in September 1992,

	there were approximately L2,125 to the pound sterling.
MSI	(Movimento Sociale Italiano) Italian Social Movement
NL	(Lega Nord) Northern League
PCI	(Partito Communista Italiano) Italian Communist Party
PdCI	(Partito dei Comunisti Italiani) Italian Communists' Party
PDS	(Partito Democratico della Sinistra) Democratic Party of the Left
PLI	(Partito Liberale Italiano) Italian Liberal Party
PPI	(Partito Popolare Italiano) Italian People's Party
PR	(Partito Radicale) Radical Party
PRI	(Partito Repubblicano Italiano) Italian Republican Party
PSDI	(Partito Social Democratico Italiano) Italian Social Democratic Party
PSI	(Partito Socialista Italiano) Italian Socialist Party
RAI	Italian Radio and Television
RC	(Rifondazione Comunista) Communist Refoundation
SISDE	Civilian Secret Service
UDR	(Unione Democratica per la Repubblica) Democratic Union for the Republic
UDEUR	(Unione Democratica per l'Europa) Democratic Union for Europe
UIL	Union of Italian Labour
WEU	Western European Union

Introduction: Understanding Italian Politics in the 1990s

Over the course of the last ten years, and in the most surprising and dramatic of circumstances, modern Italy has undergone a remarkable transformation, the whole country living through what many native commentators have unhesitatingly described as a largely peaceful, popularly-inspired revolution.[1] Confronted by a series of challenges to the authority and competence of government common to other West European nations in the late 1980s, the Italian polity also faced particular problems of its own – including national indebtedness of colossal proportions, rampant organised crime, widespread political corruption, and institutional decay – that seemed incapable of being resolved and threatened ultimate crisis and collapse.

In chronicling the story of a death long foretold,[2] it has become acceptable to talk of the coming to an end of Italy's First Republic, originally inaugurated after World War Two with the drafting of the 1948 Constitution, and the dawning of a new Second Republic, generally thought to have been ushered in by and following the general election of March 1994. A brief re-counting of the sequence of events since 1989 certainly under-lines the impression of a disintegrating political order.

Already strongly affected by the fall of communism in Eastern Europe and the integrationist tide in the European Community, it was also apparent – by the time of the general election in the spring of 1992 – that the old Italian party system hitherto dominated by the Christian Democrats and their Socialist allies was beginning to fall apart. The assassina-tion in May–June 1992 of two prominent and popular magis-trates involved in the fight against the mafia seriously undermined the credibility of the state and the established po-litical class. These events coincided with the uncovering by in-vestigators in Milan of a complex network of deep-rooted, systematic and pervasive corruption reaching across public ad-ministration and industry, bringing further discredit upon the

1

governing elite. As large numbers of politicians and industrialists were arrested and tried in court, this affair became both
farcical and tragic, with one former prime minister, Bettino
Craxi, fleeing abroad to escape trial, several central figures
(including the well-known businessman Raul Gardini) com-
mitting suicide, and – to cap it all – the elder statesman of
postwar Italy, Giulio Andreotti, facing charges of being a
member of the mafia itself. Andreotti's trial began in
September 1996. With the existing parliament deprived of all
legitimacy, interim administrations were formed in an attempt
to tackle in earnest the mounting political, economic and
moral difficulties. In 1993, referendum-led alterations to the
electoral law opened the way to a confused phase in party politics which culminated, in March 1994, in an outright election
victory for a wholly new right-wing alliance brought together
by the media tycoon Silvio Berlusconi, who promised nothing
less than national revival and a fresh Italian economic miracle.
Unable to deliver on its promises, and racked by internal
feuds, the Berlusconi coalition – Italy's 53rd government since
the war – lasted only seven months before it too broke up in
December 1994, leaving the reality of the so-called Second
Republic very much in doubt. The first-ever victory of a
centre-left coalition, in a further general election in the spring
of 1996, promised yet another new start.

The historic importance of what has happened in Italy in the
years since 1989 is unquestionable; its revolutionary effects are
far more open to debate. Two points need to be clarified at
the outset. First of all, the transition to a Second Republic does
not imply a constitutional change as such. While there has been
much talk of more profound changes, including a shift to a
French-style presidential democracy which would require the
rewriting of the constitutional text, for the time being all
the changes have occurred at the legislative level. What distinguished the end of the old Republic was the newly introduced
electoral system (the legislation for which came into force
without requiring any amendments of a constitutional nature)
and the presumed disappearance of the unregulated,
omnipresent and all-powerful influence of the political parties
in all aspects of Italian politics and society.[3] In the second place,
referring to recent events as if they amounted to a revolution
may be too simplistic and is certainly misleading. Definitions of

revolutions differ and the concept lacks precision, but a revolution is usually conceived of as an urgent, deliberate and decisive break with the past, signalling a drastic shift in the distribution of political power, including changes in the political class.[4] The extent to which the claim of an Italian revolution actually meets these criteria has given rise in particular to two opposing outlooks, which we can call the reformist and the radical.

The reformist view is that recent changes in Italy provide a striking instance of (somewhat unexpected) democratic self-renewal. Admirers of Italy's 'difficult', 'flawed', but always special version of democracy[5] have inclined to the argument that the great unravelling is evidence of the health and vitality of the country's institutions and attitudes, and of the capacity of a supposedly 'blocked' political system to generate reform. Corruption may have been endemic, but it was not inherent to the exercise of power. The fact that extensive wrongdoing did eventually come to light is taken as proof that all failings were remediable. Under the double strain of external and internal pressures, Italy was compelled to embark on a genuine, long overdue reshaping of its democratic practices.

This optimistic interpretation (optimistic in so far as it relies on a judgement about a future outcome that remains ambiguous) is not a universally shared one. An alternative school, largely though by no means solely made up of radicals frustrated by the predicament of the Italian left, finds the much-vaunted revolution to be an incomplete, if not altogether false appellation, based on a misreading of the character of the new parties, new programmes and new leaders that came to the fore. In short, the democratising of Italy has not been anything like as profound as it might seem.[6]

In order to arrive at any overall evaluation of the old Italy and the new, and to weigh up the balance of rival arguments (which we shall return to in our conclusion), it is necessary to look more closely at some of the defining characteristics of the Italian political system, starting from the key concept of *partitocrazia*, and to examine how closely they approximate to the commonly accepted attributes of the democratic ideal. In so doing, the distinctiveness of the Italian way of governing can be clarified. The point at issue is not *whether* Italy is democratic, but *what kind* of a democracy it is, and *why* it has functioned in the way that it has.

PARTITOCRAZIA

The postwar politics of Italian democracy have been exceptional, even by Mediterranean standards, and even allowing for
Italy's sharp geographical and social cleavages. But the outstanding peculiarity of the Italian model has, by general agreement,
been the exceptionally powerful role played by the political
parties in the political system, expressed in the Italian neologism
of *partitocrazia*. Italy, it is said, has a parliament of the parties[7]
in which the informal parties, rather than the formal institutions, constitute the main vehicles through which conflict is
mediated.[8] There is pluralistic bargaining of a sort, but this is
more than counterbalanced by 'the abnormal, excessive and suf-
focating presence of parties both at the level of interest articula-
tion (hence within civil society) and in decision-making (where
parties expropriate state institutions)';[9] put at its strongest, Italy
is a republic of the parties,[10] a hegemonic party-state, based
upon the complete interpenetration of party and state.[11]

The party-state idea – although it perfectly captures the privi-
leged position of the parties in the pluralistic process[12] – is not a
well developed one, at least not in relation to the Western
democracies. Other commentators have preferred to employ
related expressions like partytocracy, partyocracy, party-power
and even rule by party, to convey a similar meaning. Mario
Calise, in a recent roundtable discussion,[13] opted instead for
particracy, arguing that this was a less Italy-specific and more
generalised rendering, and (following Sartori) that it was the
most elegant. The fact that it too carries a pejorative connot-
ation cannot, he conceded, be helped.

For Calise, the key point is whether particracy is equivalent to
the familiar notion of party government, or whether it is a different, indeed exceptional type of governmental system. According
to Pasquino, particracy and party government are synonymous.
He maintains that a minimal definition of party government requires that (i) all the most important government decisions must
be made by people chosen in elections conducted according to
party distinctions or by people nominated by and responsible to
people elected in this way; (ii) policies must be decided within
the governing party or after negotiations among parties of the
governing coalition; and (iii) the most important actors (ministers or prime ministers) must be chosen within their own parties
and must be responsible to the electorate through their parties.[14]

It cannot be denied that these working propositions applied in the postwar Italian context, but it has yet to be shown that they go to make up what is commonly meant by party government. The question is more substantial than it may appear. As Calise points out, it is wrong to treat them as equivalent terms, for the simple reason that the doctrine of party government pertains to the already recognisable idea of parliamentary rule, whereas particracy has to be considered as a unique form of government *in its own right*, a third type of system to be compared and contrasted with parliamentarianism and presidentialism.'Particracy', he continues 'is a form of government where a party holds monopolistic control over the government process, just as presidents and parliaments are supposed to do within their own regime'.[15]

The distinguishing characteristic of particracy is its strong association with an unrestricted spoils system which, though not unknown in the two other types of government, is not just incidental but functional. The spoils system allows all kinds of political resources, especially jobs in the public sector, to be parcelled out among the ruling parties, creating in the process powerful centres of power within the party structure. Calise claims that this type of party patronage is the 'true rationale' of a particratic form, because 'it brings together the electorate, the party organisation and the executive branch in the name of democratic theory'.[16]

This conception of Italian-style democracy is a thought-provoking one, especially given that most textbooks on Italian politics show an interest in democratic theory but few of them treat it with the kind of thoroughgoing analysis that it deserves.[17] It is to the implications of the particratic idea for an understanding of Italian democracy that we now turn.

CHARACTERISING ITALIAN DEMOCRACY

While attempts to give meaning to the contemporary idea of democracy have flourished in recent years, it remains a controversial notion. The most widely accepted definition of democracy is a procedural one, referring to the sanctioning of predetermined procedures which establish how collective decisions are arrived at, without prescribing any substantive ends or goals. According to this approach, a democracy lays down who is authorised to take decisions and what procedures they must follow.[18] Furthermore it ensures that the way in which laws are determined has a formal connection with popular preferences. It follows that a political system is held to be democratic if its institutional arrangements enjoy popular consent.[19] Even Robert Dahl, who is not prepared to abandon the view that democracy remains a substantive ideal, emphasises the procedural mechanisms that constitute a democracy. Thus, Dahl explains, a modern representative democracy, or 'polyarchy', is characterised by a distinguishing set of political mechanisms – the election of officials, free and fair elections, an inclusive suffrage, the right to run for office, freedom of expression, access to alternative sources of information, and the right of free association – all of which, he insists, are 'necessary to the highest feasible attainment of the democratic process in the government of a country'.[20]

While it is true that, historically, democracy and liberalism[21] appeared to be incompatible,[22] their coupling is, in the modern context, now taken for granted. Indeed, in Bobbio's terms, they are doubly interdependent, since:

> [I]f liberalism provides those liberties necessary for the proper exercise of democratic power, democracy guarantees the existence and persistence of fundamental liberties. In other words: an illiberal state is unlikely to ensure the proper workings of democracy, and conversely an undemocratic state is unlikely to be able to safeguard basic liberties. The historical proof of this interdependence is provided by the fact that when both liberal and democratic states fall they fall together.[23]

The chief result of this fusing of democracy and liberalism has been to promote a belief in limited government, which lies at the very heart of liberal concerns. In a liberal democracy, the ideals of democracy are never pursued at the expense of individual freedom, instead democracy is to be valued for its ability to foster individual human development in its richest diversity.[24] Liberal philosophy envisages a clear demarcation between the mutually exclusive spheres of private and public life, or of civil society from the realm of the state. This public–private dichotomy has Greco-Roman origins, but was most fully developed in the moral claim to equal rights first enshrined in the French and American revolutions at the end of the eighteenth century. It was liberalism that made the dichotomy between the public and the private sphere into the cornerstone of its tradition.

Although the liberal tradition in general, and the public–private divide in particular, have been the subject of pertinent criticisms, especially in feminist circles,[25] there is at least one aspect to it which is worth defending – namely, its endorsement of impartiality. If by impartiality we understand a rejection of favouritism, founded on the egalitarian premise that the well-being of all moral beings matters intrinsically,[26] then the separation of the public and the private spheres, and in particular the way in which rules and procedures are enacted in a democratic state, can be seen as an attempt to capture this commitment to impartiality towards all citizens. The public–private dichotomy helps to establish that the public sphere of action (and in particular the bureaucracy) treats all citizens impartially, with equal consideration and respect, or in other words that all citizens are treated as equal by virtue of being equal citizens.

What bearing do these modern democratic precepts have on recent Italian practice? As Calise acknowledges, a particratic spoils system does find some rudimentary democratic justification in so far as it bridges the gulf between the citizen and the state:

> While in the past a partisan use (and misuse) of governmental resources would be considered a private interference in public affairs, a particratic spoils system can be presented as a way – if not necessarily the best one – to make sure that the democratic game is respected: to the victors belong the spoils. Besides, democracy is in this case a substantial rather than a formal business. By means of an unrestricted spoils system, particracy brings to the fore its own idea of a democratic state – one where the bureaucrats as well as the domain of state intervention must be as close as possible to the electorate.[27]

This harmonising claim may, of course, have a superficial romantic appeal, but it cannot suffice as a convincing validation of particratic rule. The particratic system of government self-evidently offends against the basic postulates of liberal democracy, as defined above. The point to emphasise here is that political parties in Italy play a dominating role in all aspects of public life, be it political, social or economic. By aspiring to create a society within a society, political parties foster a holistic conception of community life. Holism refers to any approach which accounts for individual agents by appeal to some larger whole.[28] It is this holistic ingredient that is primarily responsible for the tension between particratic democracy and liberal democracy. As a result of this, one feels that democracy in Italy is built on non-liberal foundations. Of course there was a time when liberalism was the norm in Italy. At the turn of the century Italy made an effort to embrace the liberal ideology, indeed Italy produced liberal thinkers of international stature. Yet as Richard Bellamy[29] points out, Italian liberalism contrasted sharply with that of Britain and France. In other words, it was very much a case of liberalism, Italian style. For example, in the works of Benedetto Croce, Italy's best known liberal thinker, one finds more references to Hegel than to John Stuart Mill, which is a clear indication that Italian liberalism was always less individualistic and more holistic than its British counterpart.

Italy's brand of liberalism, although unorthodox, was still part of the European liberal tradition. It was the advent of fascism that killed off any hope of liberal political culture taking hold in Italy. Instead of embracing the culture of liberal democracy, Italy champions a view of democracy which belongs to the civic humanist tradition, which centres on the virtues of active citizenship and direct political participation.[30] That Italy lags behind other European states in terms of its commitment to *liberal* democracy finds some confirmation in an empirical study from the early 1970s by Robert Putnam on how politicians conceive democracy in Britain and Italy. One of the most striking cross-national differences is the fact that while in Italy 'direct popular participation' is evoked much more frequently as a defining characteristic of democracy, in Britain some respondents went as far as to reject direct popular participation as a defining characteristic of democracy. Alternatively nearly half of the British (compared to less than a quarter of the Italian) respondents refer to party competition or the existence of an alternative government as the essential of a democracy.[31] The different conceptions of democracy found in Britain and Italy is summed up by Putnam as follows: 'Locke, Mill, and Schumpeter versus Rousseau, Marx, and Mussolini – this is the contrast between Britain and Italy'.[32]

We feel that the lack of a liberal political culture in Italy is regrettable from a normative point of view. Assessing political culture in Italy has been at the centre of many debates for decades now.[33] For example there are those, like Paul Ginsborg,[34] who give Italian political culture a favourable hearing, while others, like Carlo Galli,[35] argue that Italian political culture is inadequate for modern times. Needless to say, defining and evaluating a political culture is a very complex affair, and in what follows we do not pretend to do justice to the intricacies of this question. For the purpose of this book, our only specific interest concerns the question of the repercussions of not endorsing a liberal culture on popular conceptions of democracy.

The vices of a non-liberal conception of democracy far outweigh any virtues. In the first place, the spoils system undermines any observance of impartiality. Liberal democracy not only tells us that all individuals have rights, but that we all have *equal* rights. This notion of equal rights is held to have axiomatic priority over all other values.[36] Yet it is the same notion of equality that is sacrificed under a system of power-based patronage, whereby clientelism and corruption have thrived. Whether clientelism is taken to mean that governmental resources are assigned on the basis of personal relationships,[37] or whether it refers to socially-minded clientelism (in which a more substantial share of the spoils may be given out in response to group pressures, or class demands, and often to those at the bottom of the social scale), it remains the case that an element of arbitrary choice is inescapable. Resources are not distributed by open and transparent means in accordance with impartial principles of equal respect; they are covertly skewed so as to favour certain sections or interests with a political purpose in mind. Democracy is 'flawed' by the mismanagement of power that arises from the false conception of the state as a vehicle for personal or factional advantage.[38] All political conflict is 'marketised'.[39] The inegalitarian nature of particratic patronage has been spectacularly confirmed by the evidence of illegality uncovered in the ongoing succession of bribery and corruption scandals since 1992.

But there has been a further (normatively) unappealing effect which the particratic configuration of power and patronage has had on Italian politics – its reformulating of the traditional ideological contest between right and left. Though some political theorists have shown signs of a growing discomfort with the whole idea of a political right and left, claiming that this way of thinking is increasingly inadequate[40] and out of date in an era of volatile, individualistic voting, it cannot be denied that the idea of the right and the left – with each wing typically defined in relation to its opposite – still has a strong and universal, if not indispensable, appeal.

In the liberal democratic canon, one of the most basic distinctions between right and left has turned on the extent to which it is felt that the public sphere (that is the State) has a legitimate claim to interfere in the institutions and activities of private or civil society. Many of the reforms and much of the debate in Britain and the United States in the 1980s had to do with governments trying to curb the power of the interventionist state in the name of a more liberal economy, just as, in several other European countries, greater emphasis was given to the need to maintain a high provision of welfare and public services. This left-right polarity has, for the most part, never truly applied in postwar Italian conditions. Because of the particratic form of government, the state has always been markedly interventionist, with high government spending as a proportion of gross national product, a large number of state employees, and an extensive range of state-owned industries and parallel agencies. For many years, Italy has had one of the most progressive laws on maternity leave, one of the cheapest systems of public transport, and one of the most generous state pension schemes. What this has meant is that the Italian left has been robbed of its animating principles by always finding itself in the paradoxical position of opposing statist governments. Because of the far-reaching control of the ruling political parties over civil society, the left cannot be identified by particular policies, as in other Western countries, but only by appealing in the main to egalitarian values.[41] It explains in part the difficulty that the Communist and Socialist left has had in establishing itself as a viable electoral alternative to the Christian Democrats.

As with the Communist left, so with the extreme right.[42] The policy of state interference in the economy and society since the war has undercut the old, fascist belief in a strong, centralised state that has a duty to intervene to protect the underprivileged and to provide a minimum of public services. The Italian right has been authoritarian and anti-egalitarian, but it has not abandoned its attachment to large-scale corporate industry as an instrument of national economic identity. The result, again in the

words of Calise, 'is that the socialisation of the means of production – if we take this obsolete definition for the modern reality
of state-owned industry – was a programme of the left that the
right turned into reality and the centre was quick to manage'.[43]
Communist ideology, Fascist corporativism and Christian
Democratic pragmatism combined to turn the public sector of
the economy into 'a catch-all mechanism for making the economic, as well as the political, government of the country responsive to a very large part of the electorate'.[44] This is not, of
course, to deny the domestic importance of the 'great fear' of
Communism in Italy; only to contend that the degree of ideological conflict was often overstated.

These outstanding characteristics of the particratic system –
a practice of public patronage by the parties of government
which treats equal citizens unequally but blunts all ideological
conflict about the fundamental role and purpose of the state –
explains and accounts for the long-term, office-holding in-
cumbency of a self-sustaining and self-interested party nomen-
clature which, to almost general acclaim, the coming of a
Second Republic was intended to have swept away. It follows
that the beginnings of an understanding can only emerge with
the help of an appropriate conceptual framework. Using the
idea of particracy is not only 'obligatory';[45] it holds the essential key, in the authors' view, to any reasoned assessment of the
true extent of the Italian revolution.

Whether the effort to reassert a truly democratic legitimacy
succeeds or not is still open to dispute. However, any attempt to
convincingly describe and analyze the recent and continuing
changes in Italian politics is bound to be no more than tentative
and provisional. The newness of any political regime which is
still in the making is always hard to evaluate. All we can do is to
highlight some of the major turning points that deserve close
attention. In particular, we will suggest that the political elections in April 1992 (Chapter 2), March 1994 (Chapter 8), and
April 1996 (Chapter 11), the scandals of corruptions in Milan
(Chapter 4), and the referendum of April 1993 (Chapter 6) are
the key political events of the last eight years. While we will look
for explanations of these key events, exploring their likely causes
and consequences, we are also aware that any valid explanation
inevitably rests on a solid understanding of the variables in the
formula. It follows that each of these chapters will be preceded
by detailed accounts of the respective historical contexts in

which these key events took place, covering the periods from November 1989 to April 1992 (Chapter 1), April to September 1992 (Chapter 3), September 1992 to April 1993 (Chapter 5), April to December 1993 (Chapter 7), March to December 1994 (Chapter 9), and January 1995 to April 1996 (Chapter 10).

Notes

1. For example, U. Eco's 'We are living through our own 14th of July 1789', cited in *The Economist*, 20 February 1993, p.39, and G. Turani's 'Something big is happening which one could term a revolution', quoted by N. Farrell, 'Ministers' heads roll in Italian job bribes scandal', *The Sunday Times*, 21 February 1993. Amongst foreign commentators, Edward Luttwak in 'Screw you', *London Review of Books*, Vol.15, No.16, 1993, has argued that Italy's was an unprecedented revolution in that it was 'carried out by exclusively legal means, and not by blood-thirsty mobs or murderous commissars', p.7.

2. P. Allum, 'Chronicle of a Death Foretold: The First Italian Republic', in *The Italianist* (1993) pp.230–54.

3. Y. Meny, 'Leçons françaises du cas italien', in *Le Monde*, 30 September 1994, p.2.

4. In political science, a revolution always refers to a relatively sudden and radical change in the political order, which may or may not be followed by changes in the social and economic order. See the entry on 'Revolution' in A. Edwards and G. Roberts, *A New Dictionary of Political Analysis* (1991).

5. The most celebrated account is by J. La Palombara, *Democracy, Italian Style* (1987).

6. See L. Bobbio, 'Dalla destra alla destra, una strana alternanza', in P. Ginsborg (ed.) *Stato dell'Italia* (1994). See also E. Scalfari. 'Fascism is not the danger', in *The Independent*, 12 May 1994, p.21.

7. G. Sartori, *Seconda Repubblica? Si, Ma Bene* (1992) p.42.

8. J. La Palombara, op. cit. (1987) p.217.

9. G. Pasquino, 'Unregulated regulators: parties and party government', in P. Lange and M. Regini (eds), *State, Market and Social Regulation – New Perspectives on Italy* (1989) p.34.

10. P. Scoppola, *La Repubblica dei Partiti – profilo storico della democrazia in Italia* (1991).

11. See F. Vitrani, 'L'Italie, un état de "souveraineté limitée"?', in *Le Monde Diplomatique*, December 1990, p.3, and F. Vitrani, 'L'Italie aux mains des clans et des pouvoir occultes', in *Le Monde Diplomatique*, March 1991, p.23. See also S. Guzzini, 'The "long night of the First Republic": years of clientelistic implosion in Italy', (1995).

12. K. Dyson, *Party, State and Bureaucracy in Western Germany* (1977).

13. M. Calise, 'The Italian particracy: beyond president and parliament', in *The Political Science Quarterly*, Special Issue (1994) pp.441–79. See also M. Calise, *Dopo la Partitocrazia* (1994).

14. G. Pasquino, op. cit. (1989) especially pp.29–50.

15. M. Calise, 'The Italian particracy: beyond president and parliament', in *Political Science Quarterly*, Special Issue (1994), p.444.

16. Ibid., p.448.

17. The exception to this rule is R. Putnam's scholarly account of civic culture in the Italian regions in his *Making Democracy Work* (1993).

18. See N. Bobbio, *The Future of Democracy* (1987).

19. As B. Barry in 'Is democracy special?' in his *Democracy, Power and Justice* (1989) points out, 'by a democratic procedure I mean a method of determining the content of laws (and other legally binding decisions) such that the preferences of the citizens have some formal connection with the outcome in which each counts equally', p.25. The point is that a system is democratic if its procedures are seen as being acceptable by the people who are being governed.

20. R. Dahl, *Democracy and its Critics* (1993) p.222.

21. As Brian Barry rightly points out, liberalism is *par excellence* the doctrine of the Enlightenment. It follows that there are three key ideas that define a liberal political culture. First, the belief that inequalities are a social artefact. Second, the belief that every doctrine should be open to critical scrutiny. And third, the belief that no religious dogma can reasonably be held with certainty. See B. Barry, 'How not to defend liberal institutions', *British Journal of Political Science* (1990) p.2.

22. The best known sceptic of the marriage of liberalism and democracy remains Alexis de Tocqueville, whose views strongly influenced John Stuart Mill. For a concise overview of the history of liberalism and democracy, see N. Bobbio, *Liberalism and Democracy* (1990).

23. N. Bobbio, *The Future of Democracy* (1987) pp.25–6.

24. This is the type of liberal democracy advocated by John Stuart Mill. See his essay *On Liberty* [1861] (1972). On the importance of human development in John Stuart Mill's work, see J.M. Robson, *The Improvement of Mankind* (1968).

25. The literature on the feminist critique of the public–private dichotomy is vast. Over the last ten years two of the most influential articles were by C. Pateman, 'Feminist critique of the public/private dichotomy' in her *The Disorder of Women* (1989) and S.M. Okin, 'Gender, the public and the private' in D. Held (ed), *Political Theory Today* (1991), but see also R. Tong *Feminist Thought* (1989), W. Kymlicka, *Contemporary Political Philosophy* (1990) and A. Phillips, 'Must feminists give up on liberal democracy?' in D. Held (ed.), *Prospects for Democracy* (1992).

26. For an account of impartiality, see B. Barry, *Justice as Impartiality* (1995).

27. M. Calise, 'The Italian particracy: beyond president and parliament', in *The Political Science Quarterly*, Special Issue (1994) p.448.

28. See. M. Hollis, *The Philosophy of Social Science* (1995) p.15.

29. See R. Bellamy, *Liberalism and Modern Society* (1992). While Bellamy's historical account of European liberalism is invaluable, we do not share his sceptical views on contemporary liberal philosophy. For an account of how a series of political regimes in Italy (liberal, fascist and then republican) failed due to the chronic absence of political alternation, see M. Salvadori's *Storia D'Italia e Crisi di Regime* (1994).

30. On civic human republicanism, see K. Haakonssen, 'Republicanism', in R. Goodin and P. Pettit (eds), *A Companion to Contemporary Political Philosophy* (1993), and W. Kymlica and W. Norman, 'Return of the citizen: a survey of recent work on citizenship theory', *Ethics* (1994).
31. R. Putnam, *The Beliefs of Politicians* (1973) pp.168–0.
32. Ibid., p.186.
33. The starting point of many recent debates is still G.A. Almond and S. Verba, *The Civic Culture: Political Attitudes and Democracy in Five Nations*, (1963). See for example R. Putnam *Making Democracy Work* (1993).
34. P. Ginsborg, 'Italian political culture in historical perspective', *Modern Italy*, (1995).
35. C. Galli, 'La cultura politica', in S. Vertone (ed.), *La Culture degli Italiani* (1994).
36. See for example the first principle of justice in J. Rawls, *A Theory of Justice* (1971).
37. This is the most popular definition of clientelism, and the one endorsed by F. Spotts and T. Weiser, *Italy: A Difficult Democracy* (1986): 'The constituent organisations and the positions they control – not simply those at the policy making level but tens of thousands down to office clerk and messenger – are parcelled out among the parties by a process that has come to be called *lottizzazione*, "allotment". The party loyalists who are placed in key positions in turn command enormous amounts of patronage. They award contracts for the construction of buildings, highways and factories; they grant bank loans, pensions and promotions; they allocate franchises, financial subsidies and jobs. And they do it strictly on the basis of partisanry. Since the purpose is to establish a patron–client relationship, such political favor is known as clientelism. The ultimate objective of the whole process is the accretion of power–specifically of votes at elections and of influence and funds between them' (p.6).
38. J. Chubb and M. Vannicelli, 'Italy: a web of scandals in a flawed democracy', in A. Markovits and M. Silverstein (eds), *The Politics of Scandal – Power and Process in Liberal democracies* (1988) pp.122–50.
39. The phrase comes from the sociologist Amato Lamberti. See F. Vitrani, 'L'Italie, un état de "souveraineté limitée"?', in *Le Monde Diplomatique*, December 1990, p.23.
40. W. Kymlicka, op. cit. (1990) argues that thinking in terms of right and left ignores a number of important issues (like sexual equality) and key questions (such as historical context).
41. N. Bobbio has recently argued that the Left and Right are distinguished by their political values. See N. Bobbio *Left and Right: The Significance of a Political Distinction* (1996).
42. The extreme right is often referred to as the 'excluded pole'. See P. Ignazi, *Il Polo Escluso* (1989).
43. M. Calise, 'The Italian particracy: beyond president and parliament', in *The Political Science Quarterly*, Special Issue (1994) p.454.
44. M. Calise, 'The Italian particracy: beyond president and parliament', in *The Political Science Quarterly*, Special Issue (1994), p.454.
45. Ibid, p.443.

1 Italy and the Ending of the Cold War: November 1989–April 1992

The general election of April 1992 was a turning point in Italy's transition from the First to the Second Republic. While the results of this election will be analyzed in some detail in the next chapter, before then it is imperative that we become acquainted with some of the incidents of the pre-election phase. Since our analysis starts from 1989, roughly from the fall of the Berlin wall, it is only appropriate that we begin with a brief look at the international context and at Italy's foreign policy. As we shall see, the changing international context had profound repercussions on many aspects of the domestic political scene, from the political parties to the extravagant behaviour of the then President of the Republic Francesco Cossiga. These events, coupled with the suspicion that the Italian state was losing its battle against the mafia, and Italy's deepening economic crisis, were at the centre of political debates in Italy between 1989 and 1992. A grasp of the background to the April 1992 elections goes some of the way towards accounting for its surprising outcome.

INTERNATIONAL CONTEXT AND FOREIGN POLICY

On 29 November 1989, the then Soviet President, Mikhail Gorbachev, began a three-day visit to Italy, the first ever by a Soviet Communist Party general secretary. The primary purpose of the visit, which had been arranged as far back as the Spring of 1989, was to effect a reconciliation between Moscow and the Vatican, opening the way – after more than 70 years of mutual hostility – to full diplomatic ties.[1] Ethnic unrest had broken out in the Baltic states and the Ukraine, and the Soviet President clearly hoped, with legislation soon

be passed allowing for freedom of conscience in the Soviet
Union, that normalising relations with the Pope might do
something to appease religious sentiment at home.[2] A number
of trade agreements for joint ventures in the Soviet Union
were also signed with Italian companies (Italy was the Soviet
Union's third largest currency creditor, after Germany and
Japan), and in a private meeting with Achille Occhetto,[3]
leader of the Italian Communist Party (PCI), Gorbachev indicated his support for Occhetto's attempts to refound the PCI
as a mass, left-of-centre party more closely aligned with
Western European social democracy. But although the visit
helped to enhance Italy's new international standing, its real
importance stemmed from the fact that it fell between two
other events of the greatest magnitude – the fall of the Berlin
Wall separating East and West Berlin, which had occurred just
three weeks before, and the forthcoming summit off the
island of Malta with the American President George Bush
heralding a 'new era' in international relations.

   'The cold war has ended, or is ending', Gorbachev told his
hosts at a state dinner in Rome, 'not because there are victors
and vanquished, but precisely because there are neither'.[4]
There was no triumph of capitalism, he later added, and there
would continue to be two military alliances, even if their ties
were becoming increasingly amicable. As for the possible
unification of the two Germanies, that was a question for the
longer term. His anxieties on this point had already been com-
municated to the Italian foreign minister, Gianni De Michelis,[5]
but De Michelis was said to be adamant – unification was a
matter for the Germans themselves. For the moment, the
Prime Minister Giulio Andreotti[6] remarked, 'we must make
policies, not play at prophets'.[7]

   It was evident, however, that the break-up of Communist rule
in Eastern Europe and the need to forge a new balance of security between East and West was forcing at least a change of tone
in Italian foreign policy. De Michelis, who had only taken up
his post in July, was already – and energetically – looking for
ways to strengthen his country's role as a traditional bridge-
builder with East European states, and in the following months,
as the likelihood of German unification increased, Italy became
an active player in the shaping of the new European order that
was now in the making.[8] De Michelis's *Pentagonale* initiative

(made up of Italy, Austria, Hungary and Yugoslavia and then widened to include Czechoslovakia) brought together a bloc of central European states ostensibly for extra regional coopera- tion but all with a common interest in counterbalancing German economic and political influence. He also proposed giving greater attention to developments in the Mediterranean and the Middle East, which were regarded as further likely sources of future instability. Illegal immigration from North Africa was in particular a growing but thorny political question. The possibility of giving the European Community a greater military dimension, by more closely tying it to Western European Union (WEU) was an additional concern, though it should not, in the Italian view, be brought about at the expense of NATO, which remained the cornerstone of the Western Alliance. There was no doubt, however, that anti-American actions had proved popular with public opinion in the past (viz. Prime Minister Bettino Craxi's[9] refusal to allow Italian air bases to be used for the US bombing of Tripoli in April 1986) and there were many political leaders – even convinced Americanophiles like De Michelis – who were ready to take ad- vantage of the greater freedom from American dictates that the upheaval in Eastern Europe was bringing.

The one area in which De Michelis was most active was in pushing forward the drive towards closer economic and mone- tary union (EMU – and with it a single currency) in the European Community, which he was in a strong position to encourage when Italy took over the half-year presidency of the EC in July 1990. Most member states agreed that the coming into force of the Single Market, and a timetabled commitment to EMU, would have to take precedence over the entry of any new members. The majority vote by the European Council in October 1990 – against British objections – to pledge itself to full monetary union was the most tangible result of these moves, although the lack of a coordinated EC response to the outbreak of the Gulf War, reinforced by the violent break-up of the Yugoslav federation in 1991, also seemed to demon- strate the value of increased political cooperation. De Michelis also pressed for new powers for the European Parliament, able to act in the knowledge of solid parliamentary and public backing in Italy in favour of the 'irreversible' federal goal of a united Europe.

Grounds for scepticism about the Italian position of 'saying yes to more or less everything'[10] agreed by the European Union, derived from its long-standing inability to square its words with its deeds. By the middle of 1990, some 200 EC directives had still to be incorporated into Italian national law, including many relating to the implementation of the internal market, due to be in place by the end of 1992. Efforts to reduce agricultural overproduction within the Common Agricultural Policy met with an Italian claim for special exemption. Measures to enhance competition between EC states by restricting state aid to industry aggravated Italian worries, with Italy having one of the largest state-owned sectors in the Community. Leading private firms, moreover, benefitted from a highly protected home market, even though European legislation required the opening of public contracts to foreign bidders. But most seriously of all, the Italian economy was far from being in the best of shape to meet with the likely terms for the economic and monetary convergence about which it was so enthusiastic, the poor state of the Italian economy presenting – according to the EC economic affairs commissioner – a considerable risk to the entire EMU project. Growth had slowed, while the budget deficit had reached a record level. The economic downturn of 1990 was largely blamed for this declining economic performance, marked by a weakening of exports and poor productivity in the public sector. But there were also institutional deficiencies, owing to the factional nature of policy-making in an unsteady coalition government intent on shoring up parliamentary support and dominated by the sharing-out of posts in industry between the coalition parties, many of whom were averse to the loss of patronage that privatisation would bring.[11] It was part of the Europeanist belief that corrective adjustments carrying a Community label were necessary to bring Italy into line with the rest of Europe; indeed that this was the only way, in the words of De Michelis, to 'overcome our own lack of discipline'.[12] At the same time this carried the considerable danger that the financial markets could take the opportunity to pass judgement on its lack of confidence in the state of the country's finances. Even Italy's budget plan for 1992–4, drawn up with advice from European Commission officials and setting out the government's intention to curb inflation and reduce the deficit, was regarded as

overoptimistic by other finance ministers, with more movement on pensions, public sector costs and privatisation obviously required.[13] For this reason – as one foreign
correspondent noted – the constraining test of Maastricht
threatened to have the same effect on the Italian political
system which the Algerian war had had on the fall of the
Fourth Republic in France.[14]

The building of a new Europe imposed external constraints
on all of the major EC states. But the domestic impact of the
changes bore especially heavily on an Italy whose domestic political scene had been largely shaped by Cold War realities. In
what follows we shall concentrate on the impact of the changing international order on Italy's political parties.

THE DIFFICULTIES OF THE POLITICAL PARTIES

As Italians learned to get used to the idea of a Europe without
the Berlin wall, attention initially and naturally turned to the
PCI, still the largest Communist party in Western Europe, but
a party already in the throes of an agonizing reorientation of
identity. The PCI's national support was continuing to fall
(even from the disappointing level of the 1987 general election) and its strategy of a 'democratic alternative' to the
Christian Democrats was undercut by the strengthening of the
Socialists. Although the PCI had unambiguously broken with
the Soviet model of socialism after the imposition of martial
law in Poland in 1981, relations had been restored with the
new leadership and outlook represented by Gorbachev. The
PCI had, in the meantime, established a good understanding
with the Chinese Communists. After the events in Tiananmen
Square (June 1989) and the rapid disintegration of
Communist regimes in Eastern Europe, these associations
were damaging ones, affecting the PCI as well as the European
left as a whole. External crisis was superimposed on an already
evident internal (electoral, organisational and ideological)
decline.[15] Occhetto had succeeded in relaunching the PCI in
the Spring of 1989, but the speed of the changes in Eastern
Europe overtook and overshadowed what had been achieved.
More drastic action, in the form of a refounded party with a
new name (a move which Occhetto had ruled out earlier in

the year), a new symbol and new statutes, came to be seen by the party's leaders as the only way to escape from the old thinking determined by the logic of bloc politics.[16] 'The collapse of the Berlin Wall has changed the European left', Occhetto announced. 'We must change too'.[17]

Accepted by the PCI Central Committee on 24 November 1989, by 219 votes to 73 (with 34 abstentions), the final decision on the reform proposals went forward to an extraordinary National Congress the following March, with opponents already charging that the party risked losing its moral distinctiveness and endangering its loyalist vote of allegiance. Occhetto, while denying that the collapse in Eastern Europe had prompted him to act, argued that the new developments provided a new opportunity, which the changes in the party itself were designed to exploit. These changes were referred to as *la svolta*, or turning the corner. The two-thirds majority in favour of beginning the creation of a new party was a clear victory for the reforming leadership, but at the expense of a sharp drop in membership[18] and further heavy losses in the regional elections in May 1990. Inauguration of a new party, the Democratic Party of the Left (PDS), sporting the oak tree as its new symbol, took place early in 1991, after which some hard-core Communist members formed the breakaway part Communist Refoundation, thereby once again forcing a split – as on so many occasions in the past – at the very time when a united left was most needed.[19] Even so, there were many senior figures who wondered whether they had gone far enough. The benefit was apparent, however, in the possibility of a grand realignment of the left – the PDS linking up with the Italian Socialist Party (PSI) – in providing the credible alternative to the Christian Democrats (DC) that the PCI, by itself, had never managed to represent.

Although the idea of a PDS/PSI alliance was of some interest to PSI members, it was bluntly rejected by Bettino Craxi, the Socialist leader and former prime minister, at the party's congress in June 1991. After over two decades of almost unbroken involvement in the governing coalition, the PSI still had more to gain than lose from its creative conflict with the Christian Democrats. The PSI vote had slowly but steadily increased, Craxi had hopes of embracing and absorbing the PCI–PDS (as Mitterrand had done to the French Communists), and anyway the Socialists made a speciality of propagandising against Communist politics, even outdoing – as they had in the 1989 European elections – the DC in this respect.

The Communist–non-Communist ideological cleavage had, it was acknowledged, formed a fundamental divide in postwar Italy, from the forced choice between democracy and totalitarianism in the critical election in 1948 through to the struggle to combat 'red terrorism' in the 1970s,[20] and was a key element in the Christian Democrat ascendancy. By occupying leading positions in the economic, financial and social structure, and by establishing Italy as a securely Western and Atlanticist nation, the DC had managed to bar the route to a Communist accession to power. But over time, the party lost the electoral dominance it formerly enjoyed and anti-Communist sentiment amongst voters was, by 1980, 'no longer as solid as it once was'.[21]

New issues and new emancipated social groupings had grown up which went beyond the old left–right division of opinion, symptomatic of a more mobile, demanding and consumerist electorate which many DC politicians were slow to understand or appreciate. For example the very idea of a presidential republic – which earlier constitutional debates had put to one side[22] but which the PSI were now strongly promoting – was, in the DC view, an 'anti-democratic' suggestion that would turn the constitution upside down. 'We don't want to become like Africa or South America', Arnaldo Forlani,[23] the DC party secretary, commented. It was easier for the DC to unite around the defence of the existing social order than to devise a programme of reform, so that blockage, immobility and possibly corruption ensued, leaving 'the party of No' with nothing other than the claim of governability.[24] The reformed PCI–PDS robbed the DC of its principal *raison d'être*. The consequences of a postcommunist left were potentially far-reaching. The cost of the Cold War to Italian democracy was that it was an anomalous democracy 'unlike any other'.[25] Furthermore the arguments used to consolidate republican government after 1945 had far less relevance to the democratising wave of the late 1980s. Italian politicians henceforth had to defend an open and liberal society on its own merits rather than by favourable comparison with the Soviet system. In this sense, the ending of the Cold War would lead to a further loosening of partisan alignment.

The way in which the changing European order was having repercussions on internal politics was dramatically brought home to Italians in the series of controversies that broke out in 1990–91, all of them centring on the personality and past record of the President of the Republic, Francesco Cossiga.[26] It is to Cossiga that we turn our attention next.

PRESIDENT COSSIGA TAKES A PICKAXE TO THE CONSTITUTION

Cossiga, who was elected head of state by parliamentarians in 1985, had been an influential figure in Christian Democrat-led governments in the 1960s and 1970s, and an occasional ally of Aldo Moro, the prime minister-designate kidnapped and murdered by the Red Brigades as he was about to initiate a DC–PCI government in 1978.[27] Cossiga's early tenure of the presidency was unspectacular, save for a speech marking the fortieth anniversary celebrations of the Republic recalling that the purpose of political parties should be to promote the general over the sectional interest, and not to degenerate into 'instruments of mere power'. Indeed, he became renowned for his almost ecclesiastical prudence, to the irritation of the Italian press. In July 1989, however, after the fall of the five-party coalition led by the DC Prime Minister Ciriaco De Mita,[28] and the setting up of a new administration led (for the sixth time) by Andreotti, Cossiga's actions first came in for criticism, raising the issue of the President's obligation – under Article 92 of the 1948 Constitution – to resolve govern-mental crises by nominating a new prime minister.[29] De Mita had endeavoured to operate a strong executive government, built around the immovable centrality of the Christian Democrat party, but even his limited successes in bringing about institutional reform (such as the partial abolition of secret voting in the Italian parliament) had only been achieved after intense arm-twisting of DC MPs and an awkward reliance on the PSI. Local elections in May 1989 saw the PSI outpoll the PCI in some communes for the first time, and when the Socialists subsequently withdrew from the coalition, De Mita had no choice but to resign.

Several weeks of consultation followed, after which Andreotti emerged with a new team of ministers and a new programme, again based on the five-party formula. Cossiga had managed to avoid an early dissolution of parliament and fresh elections; it was less clear whether he had also been able to act as constitutional guarantor, *super partes*, now that the electoral balance of power between the big three – DC, PSI and PDS – was so plainly shifting. From then on Cossiga embarked on a round of public speeches, expositions and outbursts, lashing out at the ills in Italian society, but also provoked by the revival of embarrassing episodes (the bombing of Bologna railway station, and the mysterious Ustica air crash, both in 1980) from his past. When a former CIA agent claimed on the DC-controlled RAI 1 television channel that the CIA had promoted right-wing terrorism in Italy through the P2 masonic lodge, which he said it had financed by as much as $10 million a month in the 1970s, Cossiga called for an investigation and for legal action against the television programme if the claims were unproven.[30] After other interventions in the public debate some began to speculate about Cossiga's sanity. In his defence Cossiga insisted that there was method in his madness – 'I am not crazy, I am playing the fool', in order to capture public attention.[31]

The barely believable discovery, in a flat in Milan, of copies of the handwritten notes made during Aldo Moro's interrogation by his Red Brigade captors, embroiled Cossiga in a full-blown scandal. The Moro transcript, which included passages that had been strangely excised from earlier available drafts, shed light on many obscure events, implicating the Italian intelligence services in terrorist activity, revealing CIA funding of the Christian Democrats and the manufacturers' association, Confindustria, and passing harsh comment on Benigno Zaccagnini (DC party secretary at the time), Andreotti ('a cold, inscrutable manipulator') and Cossiga himself (Cossiga, who was Minister of Internal Affairs during Moro's kidnapping, had for long laboured under the reproach that he did not do enough to obtain Moro's release).[32]

Moro had also referred to a shadowy NATO-organised operation 'to be carried out against enemy forces operating as such on our territory', which might be involved in the destabilising of Italy, but the significance of this remark only became apparent with the shock admission by Andreotti, before the parliamentary commission on terrorism in October 1990, of the existence of a clandestine secret structure codenamed 'Gladio' which had been set up in Italy after the war – and formalised in an agreement with the CIA in 1956 – with the aim of confronting a Warsaw Pact invasion by resistance and sabotage.[33] Andreotti, who had denied such a body existed on two previous occasions, asserted that its activities were purely defensive, and that they had now been frozen. But, as later witnesses who came before the commission revealed, Gladio's covert objectives – in Italy and with similar groups in other NATO countries – had also been to combat internal subversion. The American interest in preventing or pre-empting a Communist takeover in Italy after the war was already well documented. The suggestion that they might also have been instrumental in arranging peacetime bombings with the object of discrediting the PCI was far more sensational, sparking off questions about the constitutional legality of Gladio. De Mita acknowledged that he had been informed of Gladio; Craxi at first denied and then later agreed that he must have known. But the most forthright response came from Cossiga, who, as a junior defence minister, had helped to establish and recruit the Gladio network in the late 1950s. Cossiga argued that it had been a 'great privilege' to be involved, but that it all now belonged to the ghosts of the past and, with 'real socialism' now gone, was best forgotten. Those who took part in Gladio, nevertheless, were 'patriots' doing a job that was 'legitimate, necessary and opportune', and he angrily clashed with the *Consiglio Superiore della Magistratura* (the Supreme Council of the Judiciary, or CSM) when it decided to meet to discuss the case. Observers saw in Cossiga's reaction the anger of the culpable.

Andreotti's motives for coming clean are not certain, although magistrates in Venice had already uncovered many of the details. Andreotti was known to covet the Presidency, and may have wanted to stop Cossiga – who would otherwise step down in 1992 – from going on for a second seven-year term. The move also served to unsettle Craxi, who had his own designs. Whatever the truth, Cossiga was the one who took the matter the most personally, upset at being singled out for something that, as he later explained, everyone had always been informed about. The fact that he was willing to stake his reputation, and the prestige of his office (he was rumoured to be close to resigning) on the Gladio issue had the effect of magnifying yet another political crisis into a near-crisis of the regime. And it showed the degree to which the actions of a foreign ally, combining with key political and military centres of powers inside Italy, had attempted to block any left-wing political alternative, negating the democratic process and – notwithstanding Cossiga's protestations that they were protecting national integrity – severely undermining Italy's claim to sovereign status.

The antagonism between Cossiga and Andreotti spilled over into the new year, and when a new crisis was provoked by the PSI (for the fourth time in a row) declaring in March 1991 that the existing coalition was 'spent' since it had failed to make progress in important policy areas, the President sought to assert his authority by insisting that he would not be content with a routine cabinet reshuffle of the kind which Andreotti had in mind. Major changes were needed if Italy was to be ready for the European internal market, and he claimed the right to bring the parliament to a premature end, even against the wishes of parliament itself. If President and Prime Minister are in conflict, he added, it would be the Prime Minister who would have to go. The struggle divided the Christian Democrat party and disconcerted the other coalition allies, most of whose opinion poll ratings were on the slide. Only the Socialists, pushing for a referendum on the issue of a directly-elected head of state, could be reasonably sure of making any electoral gains. The PDS, for its part, denounced Cossiga's behaviour as a 'constitutional outrage' and led the demands for his resignation. When it transpired that Andreotti still commanded the support of influential factions in the DC, he was asked by Cossiga to bring together a new government, Italy's fiftieth since 1945, which would make reform of the institutions of government (as Cossiga had been demanding) one of its main priorities. At the last moment, the three representatives from the small Republican party pulled out of the governing coalition, after a dispute over their failure to retain the posts and telecommunications portfolio.

A Republican, Oscar Mammí, had drawn up the 1990 media law which gave legal recognition to the media magnate Silvio Berlusconi's[34] control of the three main commercial television channels without (though Mammí had intended this) restricting its monopoly position,[35] and Craxi – a good friend of Berlusconi – was thought to have vetoed a Republican reappointment. The by now four-party coalition survived, with a narrow majority of 15 in the Chamber of Deputies and of only 5 in the Senate. Even so, the impression remained that the coalition parties had been only too ready to look to their own self-interest, convincing Cossiga that they could not be counted on to curb their own power.

His confidence in the popular will was spectacularly confirmed by the outcome of the historic June referendum on limiting the preference vote for elections to the Chamber of Deputies, which had been initiated by cross-party campaigners grouped around the reformist DC deputy Mario Segni[36] and which resulted in an almost unanimous endorsement to cut voter preferences to one single choice for a named candidate,[37] with 95.6 per cent of the 62.5 per cent of the electorate who actually voted supporting the change – the first time a national referendum had gone against the status quo.[38] Segni's gamble in looking to extra-parliamentary opinion, taken in 1990 when the DC and PSI leaderships prevented any amending of electoral rules, paid off.[39] Of the main parties, only the PDS, which was by no means of one view, had given its consistent backing. Craxi even urged a boycott of the referendum, advising people to go to the beach on the Sunday instead. Having been opposed to Segni's campaign, Cossiga chose to turn it to advantage. The people had spoken, he said in a plain-speaking television interview on the night the result was announced. They had expressed their view, without the intermediation of the party leaders. The people, not the parties, should decide. Since the existing parliament and President had ceased to enjoy public approval, Cossiga argued that voters should be given the opportunity to give their opinion about the possibility of progressing to a presidential form of government.[40]

Cossiga's conversion to the cause of change illustrated the strengths and weaknesses of a more interventionist head of state. By appealing to the voting public over the heads of the political class, he became immensely popular, while also making powerful enemies. He was not, he confessed, a national hero and had no financial resources of his own – only the right to speak his mind, and speak it he would. But his commitment to reform remained ambivalent. He was too compromised by his own past and by his desire for self-justification, and his actions could always be interpreted as moves in the game of high politics, from which he might also have hoped to benefit. A self-styled advocate of people power, he was only a late convert to the idea of introducing proposal referenda. Above all, his unpresidential behaviour in 'taking a pickaxe to the constitution' deflected a good deal of criticism away from the two vital policy issues over which the Andreotti governments had been floundering – the public finances, in such a state that the American credit agency Moody's had recently downgraded Italy's credit rating from triple A, and the continuing problem of public order.

The unorthodox behaviour of the President of the Republic, Francesco Cossiga, was not the only threat to the Italian State. Other threats came from the mafia, whose activities were at the centre of all political discussions before 1992, and the deepening economic crisis. We shall look at these two threats in turn.

THE MAFIA THREAT

'Dear Cossiga', the head of the parliamentary anti-mafia commission, Senator Gerardo Chiaromonte wrote to the President in the Summer of 1989; 'the mafia has won'.[41] The modern mafia, the commission had found, functioned like an unofficial, parallel state, with a political, economic and institutional character of its own which now spanned the whole of the peninsula. In 1990, the commission went on to name Milan and its stock exchange as the capital of the recycling of illicit funds, pointing to the mixing of legal and illegal activity and the consequences this could have for the national and the international economy. The trial in Messina in Sicily of 231 alleged mafiosi had collapsed only a few weeks before, driving anti-mafia judges in Palermo to also write to Cossiga complaining of the 'grave situation' they were facing, 'disarmed and isolated', without the means to control the huge flow of dirty money that passed through the city, and forced to work 'within unacceptable constraints which indicate a halting by the state of the fight against organised crime'.[42] Gang killings were widespread. A new courthouse in Naples was destroyed by fire. Mafia interests dominated the market in credit, construction and labour in large parts of the South of Italy, which as was officially recognised were no longer under state rule. Judges, undermanned and overstretched, were hampered by the civil liability of magistrates (introduced by a referendum in 1987) and by the new penal code of 1989 – the first comprehensive revision since 1930 – which strengthened the rights of the accused by placing the burden of proof more clearly on the prosecution. The former DC mayor of Palermo, Leoluca Orlando,[43] who was on the verge of establishing a nationwide anti-mafia movement, added his voice to the protests by calling for the truth about a number of unsolved political killings by the mafia which had, he said, 'disappeared down black holes'.

Cossiga responded by making a public appeal to parliament for emergency measures to counter the increase in criminal activity, but when he summoned members of the judiciary to mark the murder of one of their senior colleagues, he launched instead into a polemical attack on Orlando for behaving like a one-man opponent of the regime. Cossiga also challenged Orlando's counsellor, the Jesuit priest Father Ennio Pintacuda, calling him a 'fanatic' and a 'pseudo-Jacobin'. It emerged subsequently that pressure to silence or move Pintacuda had been put on the religious authorities over several months. Orlando's accusations of a judicial cover-up, Cossiga said, were completely unfounded. But the President's own relations with the Supreme Council of the Judiciary in the wake of the Gladio affair and his reprimand of judges who had expressed reservations about Italian involvement in the Gulf War, had only increased tensions with the higher judiciary and weakened the sense of judicial autonomy.

Over the following months, the position deteriorated. There was a further release of Sicilian mafia bosses on a technicality, including the mafia 'pope', Michele Greco, who were only re-arrested after the cabinet had rushed through a new decree hurriedly closing the loophole. Mafia-related murders intensified. A Sicilian businessman who had become famous for refusing to pay protection money was shot dead. Aid ear-marked for reconstruction after the 1980 earthquake in Naples was shown to have been channelled into a wide range of criminal enterprises. The national turnover of organised crime operations not only in the South but also in Rome and Northern cities was put at some $16 billion a year, as large as the Fiat motor company.[44] Some, considering this estimate on the low side, judged criminal activity to be making up at least 12 per cent of Italy's GNP. The international scale of drug trafficking, arms smuggling and the recycling and reinvesting of untaxed illicit money, was jeopardising the success of the Single Market reforms, offering new opportunities for money laundering, especially in the new unified Germany after 1990. The freeing up of trade and banking meant that illegal busi-ness was now integrated into the formal economy, and far harder to detect. 'The threat from the mafia', it was reported, 'is rapidly replacing Communism as the common enemy in Europe', necessitating greater cross-border cooperation between governments.[45] Although the scale of mafia activity (and pressure from other European capitals, especially from Bonn) forced the interior minister, Vincenzo Scotti, to say that it constituted an 'act of war', it was in fact no longer a purely Italian problem.

Successive parliamentary inquiries had established the con-nections between organised crime, the economy and the exer-cise of political power. The postwar drive to modernise the Italian South, and with it the expansion of special agencies of the party–state, had brought many public functions under mafia influence, the links creating what was called a 'polimafia'[46] of political and criminal business, with which the Christian Democrats, but also the increasingly 'Southernised' Socialists, were implicated. Control of territory made for control of votes, the power to deliver up to half a million captive votes directly, and a further three million indirectly, making the mafia effectively the fourth Italian 'party'. The monopoly of political power deployed by the coalition parties over the economic life of the South dispensed with the need to cultivate a governing consensus, since the stability that comes out of the shared values of elector and elected was replaced by a clientelistic market of rewards and favours in exchange for support – a clientelism that was now a direct product of the rise of the modern interventionist state.[47] It was the eradication of this trade in votes which the 1991 referendum aimed at curbing. Regional assembly elections in Sicily in the week after the referendum revealed a familiar story – the arrest of several local politicians for electoral malpractice (vote rigging) from both the winning Christian Democrats and the Republicans,[48] just as another one-time mayor of Palermo, Vito Ciancimino, was being put on trial for the second time for political corruption and mafia association, and calling as his witness Salvo Lima,[49] the DC Euro-MP and former MP who had been prominent in the unchallengeable machine politics of the DC in Sicily after the war[50] and was widely regarded as the Sicilian 'proconsul' of the current Prime Minister Andreotti. Lima himself was cited 62 times in a parliamentary anti-mafia commission report in 1976.

The other main victor in the Sicilian elections was Orlando, whose new organisation, *La Rete* (the Network), took 7.3 per cent of the vote across Sicily and no less than 25.8 per cent in Palermo itself. Orlando's programme had been designed to translate the new policies of the 'Palermo Spring' to a national stage, but its real distinctiveness lay in its essentially absolutist attitude that the mafia was not just a public order problem. The mafia was so closely entwined with existing party alignments as to comprise a system of power that could only be overthrown once the link between crime and power was broken. If its activities were not stopped soon, Orlando warned, then they would contaminate the whole of the rest of Europe. To his way of thinking, mafia and state – above all in Sicily – were two manifestations of the same disorder. But even his closest collaborators were unsure whether it would be possible to sustain a cross-party with nothing other than 'civic indignation'.[51]

Orlando's criticisms of judicial collusion clashed with the view of senior judges, including Judge Giovanni Falcone, that all that was lacking was the political will to prosecute the fight. Falcone had masterminded the anti-mafia maxi-trials of the mid-1980s (drawing on the confessions of several mafia *pentiti*, or supergrasses), had managed to survive an attempt on his life in 1989, and had only recently taken up the post of Director of

Penal Affairs in the ministry of justice in Rome. He was a constant critic of the new penal code for the way in which it made their task harder, but he had no sympathy with the idea that mafia influence would be halted only with a total change of power relations in society; the political battle with the Christian Democrats must not be confused with the legal battle against the mafia, as the left tended to do.[52] But the attitude of indifference of the state authorities was no less inhibiting. What was needed was an 'unremitting commitment' on the part of government to destroy the feeling of mafia impunity, and he denied suggestions that, by departing for the capital, he had given up the struggle. Italy was not divided into an industrious North and a parasitic South – the message that the swelling *Lega Nord* (Northern League) of Umberto Bossi[53] was doing so much to spread; the reach of the modern mafia united Italy, and spanned the European continent. In so arguing, he favoured the creation of the post of a Procurator General who could collaborate on an intergovernmental basis and follow the trail of criminal enterprise outside of Italian jurisdiction, a post which was, for the time being, being blocked to him.

THE DEEPENING ECONOMIC CRISIS

'Postwar' Europe was brought to an end with the signing of the Charter of Paris in November 1990, which described a Europe 'liberating itself from the legacy of the past'. The old opposition between Capitalism and Communism had given way to a post-ideological universe, hastened by the downfall of Communist states across the Eastern part of Europe and the apparent exhaustion of the socialist project. The 'end of history' presaged a common future of open, market-orientated liberal democracies. Essentially it was the countries of the former Eastern bloc that would, it was believed, be subject to the most radical changes. But this was to underestimate the importance of the transformations that were already underway in the West, to which the end of Communism would add further impetus. Events in the East had a disorientating effect on all of the Western democracies (and not just among left-wing parties and opinion), exposing ruling elites to searching questions about the bases of political authority and economic wellbeing. Popular disenchantment with politics and politicians was only one outward sign of this trend. In Italy, the aftershock was most acutely felt, because of the exceptionally close linkage of external to internal policy,[54] and because of the unusual characteristics of the Italian model of democracy.

The postwar economic advance in prosperity had been guaranteed by Italian membership of the Western Alliance, for which some democratic sacrifices were felt to be justifiable. Once the disintegration of Communism had begun, however, there was a marked shift from military and strategic to economic and social concerns, and a greater willingness to judge government by results. The 'Italy of mysteries' came in for investigation, opening the eyes of many Italians to their own recent history. Although the effects of the fall of the Berlin Wall were apt to be referred to rather indiscriminately, victory in the Cold War and the dissolving of the Soviet bloc 'boomeranged' on the West.[55]

The public debt, though rising throughout the eighties, had soared in 1990, and at 102.9 per cent of Italy's annual GDP was far above the Maastricht requirement of 60 per cent by 1996 – on some estimates, Italy's total public debt accounted for roughly one-third of all European debt (although, because of traditionally high saving, the country was more indebted to itself than to abroad). The budget deficit, fiscally unbalanced by official toleration of widespread tax evasion, stood at 10.5 per cent of GDP, also well in excess of the Maastricht target of 3 per cent. Spending was given a further boost by several pre-election measures, including a last-minute pay rise for the heads of the state holding companies. And although the consequence of joining the *lira* to the narrow band of currencies in the European Monetary System in January 1990 had been to enable the Bank of Italy to pursue a tight counter-inflationary policy, Italy continued to have a consistently higher rate of inflation than other European countries, and higher interest rates accordingly. The automatic indexing of wage increases to inflation had been allowed to wither away, but negotiations with the main trade unions to reform pay bargaining had broken down.[56]

Further pressures were also at work. Externally, with the coming of the Single Market and steps to bring about Economic and Monetary Union in the European Community, which entailed the growing interdependence of European economies and the reduced freedom of action this allowed individual member states to fix exchange rates or control currency transactions. Internally, the challenge to the state from organised crime, which, by enjoying political protection, demonstrated that the actions of government were both corrupt and inefficacious. Italy resembled a medium-sized self-governing nation state of 'limited sovereignty',[57] without the power to take decisions or the ability to enforce them, and with a dominant ruling party whose long-standing grip on political office was being directly contested.[58]

The confused reaction of the political establishment was a reflection of the classic dilemma in which the principal party leaders were placed – whether to embrace reform in order to preserve and strengthen existing institutions, or whether to stand in the way of changes that might in the end prove to be irresistible. Those who spoke the language of stability and responsibility were not encouraged by the findings of public opinion polls showing that most voters had little confidence that the governing parties could find a way out of the country's difficulties. Observers noted a widespread sense of social malaise, triggered by the contradiction of rising materialist aspirations of most individuals and the degradation of collective public institutions, which did not augur well for the future.[59] Against this was a determination by the leading figures to continue to shape public debate and retain control of events, with an eye to short-term profit. Reform had become paradoxical: the more urgent it was, the more difficult (because of the weakening of the governing majority) it was to realise, and yet the incapacity of the system to respond confirmed the necessity of change.[60] Confronted by the pressing problems of the poor state of the economy, law and order and institutional overhaul, the competitive coexistence among the ruling coalition parties came under increasing strain – from new political forces representing a changed and changing electorate – with the drawing to a close of the 1987 parliament and the approaching general election.

THE CAMPAIGN RUN-IN

In February 1992, after many months of high political feuding, President Cossiga exercised his right to dissolve parliament, which was coming to the end of its five-year term, arguing that it had 'exhausted its ability to legislate'. In fixing a general election for the first week of April, he declared that the "magic moment" had arrived to 'refound the republic with a new national pact'.[61] The President's blunt refusal to be the guarantor of an 'embalmed constitution' had not, however, escaped censure. Following the President's attempts to stifle judicial criticism of his part in the Gladio affair, the PDS had already called for Cossiga's impeachment for violating his constitutional role. In reply, Cossiga summoned Massimo D'Alema – Occhetto's deputy – to the *Quirinale* (the official President's residence in Rome), and released details of 'black' funds said to have been forwarded to the PDS by the Soviet Communist party, threatening to open up the secret service files 'one by one'. His relations with the Christian Democrat party were no better. Cossiga was unhappy at having publicly to shoulder the blame for Italy's Cold War activities, and upset that senior Christian Democrats had not come to his defence. When the official party newspaper, *Il Popolo*, rejected another outburst of personal attacks by Cossiga in January, he left the party for good, bitterly telling a friend that they had failed to understand what he had been trying to do. He may, by his erratic demagoguery, have intended to show that the old consociational governing by the government and opposition parties was over. The growing electoral challenge of the *Lega Nord*, which had sensationally outpolled the DC in voting in the traditionally 'white' (Christian Democrat) province of Brescia in November – forming a blocking minority of 14 seats out of 50 on the council – represented more tangible proof of an impending upset. Cossiga's rows with the CSM had also raised new anxieties about political interference in anti-mafia investigations. Paolo Borsellino, the newly-appointed assistant prosecutor in Palermo (and a close collaborator with Judge Falcone) complained that the administration of justice had been 'paralysed' by the new penal code, such that there were no major criminal investigations in progress. Notwithstanding this, drug trafficking and money laundering flourished without restraint across Italy. The planned national post of Superprocurator, Borsellino warned, risked subordinating the work of the judiciary to even greater executive manipulation.

With unofficial campaigning in full swing, however, the outgoing coalition partners were anxious to convey an impression of reassuring stability. The Andreotti government had taken the major, 'irreversible' step of signing up for European monetary union at the Maastricht conference, managing at the same time – through the efforts of the Treasury minister (and former governor of the Bank of Italy), Guido Carli – to secure the concession that the progress made by individual economies in conforming to the criteria and timetable for convergence would be judged by their overall 'dynamic' trend rather than by an 'arithmetical' snapshot in time.[62] The Bank of Italy was granted the freedom to set interest rates independently of the Treasury, but the harsh economic adjustments that the Maastricht commitment implied still needed to be tackled.

Out of the blue, the official start of the campaign on 12 March was interrupted by the shooting in broad daylight outside his villa in Mondello, near Palermo, of Salvo Lima, the Christian Democrat Euro-MP and acknowledged viceroy for Andreotti in Sicily. Lima's mediating role with the mafia (though he was not thought to be a mafioso himself) had been long suspected. The curbing of the personal preference vote in the 1991 referendum – leaving only one *numero uno* candidate per party – had obviously limited the ability of political intermediaries like Lima to deliver votes to recommended candidates, though it also carried with it the danger of increased intimidation.[63] But it was Lima's failure for once, as many speculated, to overturn the sentences in the long-running maxi-trial of four leaders of the mafia 'cupola' before the Supreme Court in January that had probably led to his elimination. Andreotti, attending Lima's funeral in Palermo the next day, was at pains to defend his friend and ally, and issued a mysterious warning about a plot to destabilise Italy. Judge Falcone privately commented that the settling of political accounts had begun.

Andreotti's own advice to electors had been that too many doctors risk killing the patient, while Craxi – promising a renewal of the DC–PSI alliance in government – spoke out against the dangers of a 'Polish-style' divided legislature.[64] Forlani gave it as his opinion that 'we [the DC] deserve to be supported for another hundred years'.[65] But with a constellation of more or less serious fringe parties standing for election, and opinion polls registering a sizeable segment (upwards of 40 per cent) of undecided voters, there was no guarantee that the old governmental formula would survive, or that constitutional reform to the liking of the two main partners-in-government would still be feasible. Rumours in the closing stages of the campaign that the Christian Democrat hierarchy were making overtures to the PDS, of all parties, gave the clearest possible indication that an electoral reversal was not inconceivable.

Notes

1. There was a minor thaw in relations when Khrushchev's son-in-law visited Pope John XXIII in the Spring of 1963.
2. J.B. Urban, 'Gorbachev's state visit to Italy and the Vatican', in F. Sabetti and R. Catanzaro (eds), *Italian Politics: A Review*, Vol.5 (1991) pp.126–37.
3. Achille Occhetto (1936–). Long-standing involvement in the national direction of the PCI. Elected to parliament in 1976. Party leader from 1988 to 1994.
4. J.B. Urban, op.cit (1991) p.131.
5. Gianni De Michelis (1940–). Socialist. Professor of Inorganic Chemistry. MP from 1979 to 1994. Former minister of state participation. Self-proclaimed discotheque fanatic.
6. Giulio Andreotti (1919–). Life Senator. Nicknamed 'The hunchback'. Prime Minister for the seventh time. Protégé of De Gasperi. Helped in drafting the postwar Republican Constitution. First entered government in 1947. Leader of one of the most powerful DC *correnti* (factions). Described by Henry Kissinger as the man who had contributed most to the postwar history of Italy.
7. Quoted in *Le Monde*, 28 November 1989, p.8.
8. C. Seton-Watson, 'Recent Italian Foreign Policy', *Rivista*, (1991) p.2.
9. Bettino Craxi (1934–). Socialist party secretary between 1976 and 1993. Record-breaking ('and the ship sails on') Socialist Prime Minister 1983–7. Architect of the 'long wave' of the PSI's electoral advance. Close friend of Berlusconi. Currently living in Tunisia.
10. Unnamed Italian diplomat, quoted in E. Vulliamy, 'Union will strip window dressing off economy', *The Guardian*, 29 November 1991, p.8.
11. J.I. Walsh, 'International constraints and domestic choices: economic convergence and exchange rate policy in France and Italy', in *Political Studies*, June 1994, pp.246–7.
12. G. De Michelis, 'A nation's game of leapfrog', *The Independent*, 7 August 1990, p.15.
13. 'EC urges Italy to take tough line on economy', *The Financial Times*, 12 November 1991, p.3.
14. M-C Decamps, 'Italie: la "crise de confiance"', *Le Monde*, 3 July 1992, p.18.
15. See M. Calise, 'Remaking the Italian party system', *West European Politics*, Vol.16, October 1993, pp.545–60.
16. M. Bull, 'Whatever happened to Italian communism?', *West European Politics*, Vol.14, October 1991, p.97.

17. Cited in M. Sheridan, 'Italy's communists give up communism', *The Independent*, 15 November 1989, p.1.

18. Official party figures put the total PCI membership at 1 319 905 in 1990 and the PDS membership at 989 708 in 1991. See L. Bardi and L. Morlino, 'Italy: tracing the roots of the great transformation', in R. Katz and P. Mair (eds), *How Parties Organise* (1994), pp.242–77. For a comparison of party membership in Italy's main parties between 1950 and 1990, see D. Hine, *Governing Italy* (1993) p.114.

19. N. Bobbio, 'Divided fathers and split heirs', in *The Guardian Review*, 8 May 1992.

20. Although the Italian Communist Party was extremely critical of any form of Left-wing terrorism in the 70's and 80's, other political parties used the pretext of Left-wing terrorism to discredit the PCI. See G. Galli *Storia del Partito Armato* (1986).

21. G. Sani, 'The political culture of Italy: continuity and change', in G. Almond and S. Verba (eds), *The Civic Culture Revisited* (1980) p.316.

22. D. Hine, in his 'Italy: condemned by its constitution?', in V. Bogdanor (ed.), *Constitutions in Democratic Politics* (1987) pp.206–28, discusses in particular the otherwise highly varied proposals aired during the work of the Bozzi Commission of 1983–5.

23. Arnaldo Forlani (1925–). MP from 1958 to 1994. Prime Minister 1981–2. Elected Christian Democrat party secretary (for the second time) in 1989.

24. For this see R. Leonardi and D. Wertman, *Italian Christian Democracy – the Politics of Dominance* (1989).

25. S. Cassese, quoted in *The Guardian*, 3 April 1992, p.25.

26. Francesco Cossiga (1928–). Lawyer. First elected to parliament in 1958. Former minister of the interior. Twice (briefly) Prime Minister. Nicknamed 'the tired kangaroo'.

27. Aldo Moro (1916–78). Elected to the postwar Constituent Assembly at the age of 29. Prime Minister 1963–8 and 1974–6. Advocate of the controversial policy of opening to the left known as the 'historical compromise'. Killed by the Red Brigades.

28. Ciriaco De Mita (1928–). MP from 1963 to 1994. Minister with responsibility for the *Mezzogiorno* 1976–9. Elected as DC party secretary in 1982 on a platform of party renovation, but met with strong opposition, and was removed in 1988.

29. See G. Pasquino, 'The De Mita government crisis and the powers of the president of the republic: which form of government?', in F. Sabetti and R. Catanzaro (eds), *Italian Politics: A Review*, Vol.5 (1991), pp.40–54.

30. P. Willan, *Puppet Masters – the Political Use of Terrorism in Italy* (1991), pp.77–8.

31. 'Un entretien avec M. Cossiga', *Le Monde*, 13 December 1991, p.5.

32. Special supplement in *L'Espresso*, 4 November 1990.

33. A full account can be found in F. Ferraresi's 'A secret structure codenamed Gladio', in S. Hellman and G. Pasquino (eds), *Italian Politics: A Review*, Vol.7 (1992) pp.29–48.

34. Silvio Berlusconi (1936–). Self-made entrepreneur. Originally building contractor. Creator of Milano Due urban area. Founder and

managing director of the Fininvest media empire and owner of
A.C.Milan. Alleged member of the P2 masonic lodge. Prime Minister
from June to December 1994.

35.   V. Bruno and M. Gambino, *Berlusconi – enquête sur l'homme de tous les pouvoirs* (1994) pp.72–4.

36.   Mario Segni (1939–). Son of the former President of the Republic,
      Antonio Segni (1962–4). Professor of Law. Elected in parliament for
      the DC in 1976. In forming the Comitato per la Riforma Elettorale
      (COREL) with Catholic, lay and some Communist sympathizers, Segni
      had risked expulsion from the DC.

37.   Previously voters had up to four preference votes, depending on the
      size of the constituency, which facilitated the channelling of votes
      towards 'dubious' candidates. Use of the preference vote was known
      to be more prevalent in the South.

38.   Article 75 of the Italian Constitution permits an abrogative referen-
      dum to be held to repeal part or the whole of a law subject to the pro-
      posal in question mustering at least 500 000 signatories in support.
      The proposal is approved providing that a majority of eligible voters
      vote, and that a majority of those voting indicate that they favour the
      change(s) proposed.

39.   For further details see P. McCarthy, 'The Referendum of 9 June', in
      S. Hellman and G. Pasquino (eds), *Italian Politics: A Review*, Vol.7
      (1992) pp.11–28.

40.   As reported in *Il Corriere della Sera*, 11 June 1991, p.1.

41.   *La Repubblica*, 28 July 1989, cited in C. Sterling, *The Mafia* (1990)
      pp.296–7.

42.   E. Vulliamy, 'City puts mafia and politicians on trial', *The Guardian*,
      3 August 1990, p.15.

43.   Leoluca Orlando (1947–). Jesuit education. Young, left-wing Christian
      Democrat who became mayor of Palermo in 1985, initiated a popular
      movement against the mafia, was ousted by the DC and the PSI in
      1989, but returned as mayor in 1990 and 1993 with assorted cross-
      party support.

44.   *The Guardian*, 10 January 1992, p.24.

45.   'EC states combine to combat the mafia', *The Independent*,
      18 September 1992, p.15.

46.   The expression used by G. Pansa, and quoted in F. Vitrani, 'L'Italie
      gangrènée par la criminalité d'état', in *Le Monde Diplomatique*, April
      1992, pp.6–7.

47.   An argument developed by P.F. d'Arcais, in 'Une stabilité politique
      décourageante', in *Esprit*, December 1989, pp.11–24.

48.   D. Gambetta's outstanding *The Sicilian Mafia – the business of private protection* (1993) pp.184–5.

49.   Salvatore Lima (1928–92). Long-serving Mayor of Palermo and secre-
      tary of the Christian Democrat party in Palermo Province. Elected to
      parliament in 1968. Elected to the European Parliament in 1979.
      Killed by the Mafia.

50.   See J. Chubb, *Patronage, Power and Poverty in Southern Italy – A Tale of Two Cities* (1982).

51. Claudio Fava, quoted by P. Tretiack in *La Vie Blindeé* (1992) p.97.
52. Falcone's views on this can be found in chapter six of M. Padovani, *Men of Honour – the Truth About the Mafia* (1992) pp.139–62.
53. Umberto Bossi (1941–). Sometime rock musician, medical student and political activist. Elected to the Senate on an Autonomous Lombardy League ticket in 1987. Formed the *Lega Nord* out of the Lombardy League and various other regional groups in 1991.
54. S. Romano, *Guida alla Politica Estera Italiana* (1993) and C. Merlini, 'Italy and Europe', in J. Story (ed.), *The New Europe – Politics, Government and the Economy Since 1945* (1993) pp.228–44.
55. A. Rizzo, *Big Bang – il cambiamento italiano nel cambiamento mondiale* (1993) p.87.
56. 'Italy', OECD Economic Survey (1992).
57. F. Vitrani, 'L'Italie, un état de "souveraineté limitée"?', in *Le Monde Diplomatique*, December 1990, p.3.
58. P. Ferdinand, 'The party's over – market liberalisation and the challenges for one-party and one-party dominant regimes: the cases of Taiwan and Mexico, Italy and Japan', in *Democratization*, (1994) pp.133–50.
59. See especially the work of G. Calvi, founder of the Eurisko polling institute, in 'Italie: une société sans état?', in *Futuribles*, December 1990, pp.3–16.
60. P. Scoppola, *La Repubblica dei Partiti – profilo storico della democrazia in Italia* (1991) p.400.
61. A. Mitchison, 'Method or Madness?', in *The Independent Magazine*, 29 February 1992, p.20.
62. P. Daniels, 'Italy and the Maastricht Treaty', in S. Hellman and G. Pasquino (eds), *Italian Politics: A Review*, Vol.8 (1993) pp.178–91.
63. Police in mainland Calabria made over 300 raids during the campaign exposing candidates who it was thought had come to an electoral understanding with criminal organisations.
64. The previous October, in the first free elections in Poland since 1936, no less than 29 different parties had won representation in the Polish parliament.
65. Quoted in M. Mafai, 'Tutto cambia, Arnaldono', in *La Repubblica*, 7 April 1993.

2 The General Election of April 1992

In the Introduction, we argued that one of the peculiarities of Italian politics is the lack of a liberal culture. Italy never fully embraced liberal democracy, and the particratic form of government that evolved is the most clear confirmation of this deficiency. Having said that, it cannot be disputed that things have started to change in Italy, indeed the chapters that follow aim to chronicle the substantial changes in Italian politics in the 1990s. In terms of explaining political change in Italy, the 1992 general election was a pivotal event. One could argue that the tremors felt in 1992 were part of the same process that provoked the real political turnover four years later. In what follows the significance of the 1992 election will be analyzed, paying special attention to two key questions. First, was the 1992 general election the equivalent of a referendum against the particratic form of government? Second, did the 1992 election suggest a shift of Italy's political culture towards liberal values?

THE RESULTS

The outgoing four-party (DC, PSI, Italian Social Democratic Party (PSDI) and PLI) coalition managed to narrowly retain a majority of seats in both the Senate (163 out of 315) and the Chamber of Deputies (331 out of 630) but its combined share of the vote fell below the critical 50 per cent mark (48.2 per cent). For the first time in its history, moreover, the Christian Democratic party did not even reach 30 per cent. Both the treasury minister, Guido Carli, and the head of the budget committee in the Senate, Beniamino Andreatta, lost their seats. The Christian Democrat's main coalition partner, the Socialist party, also performed poorly, failing to make any advance on its 1987 position, and indeed bringing to an end an upward trend started in 1976. With the former

Communists divided between the reformed PDS and the fundamentalist Communist Refoundation (winning 16.1 per cent and 5.6 per cent respectively, compared to the 26.6 per cent of the PCI five years before), a great many voters either abstained (more than one-in-eight) or else switched to the newer protest groupings – the Greens, the anti-mafia *La Rete* and, most spectacularly of all, the Northern League, spearheading the attack on particratic rule and pressing for extensive regional autonomy. The Northern League, in particular, in obtaining the election of 25 Senators and 55 Deputies, established itself as the second largest party in the North of the country, picking up support – notably among first-time and younger voters[1] -in former Christian Democratic strongholds, and contributing to a far greater regional variation in voting patterns, accentuating the reliance of the DC and the PSI on votes in the South. Bossi received a record 240 517 preference votes in Socialist Milan-Pavia, humbling Craxi. Altogether 16 different party lists won representation in the new parliament, registering a further and substantial expansion in the votes going to non-traditional political forces.[2] Mobile voters, instead of moving between neighbouring parties, spurned all the established parties *en bloc*. According to the Cattaneo Institute, no less than one-quarter of the electorate changed allegiance, an historic shift in voting behaviour not seen since the watershed Italian election of 1948.[3]

It is our supposition that, in view of the exceptional strength of opposition to particratic rule (the so-called 'front of unease'), the general election of April 1992 was a deliberate rejection by a sizeable proportion of voters and non-voters – the 'anti-party system' vote comprised 31.9 per cent of the total electorate – of existing political rule. They were not just rejecting the governmental coalition, and all that this implied; the electoral mass were collectively spurning the governing elite, which the proportional voting system, by registering the splintering of opinion, faithfully reflected. The magnitude of popular discontent had not, as some formerly alleged, been overstated. It followed that the more volatile the voters and the more unsure the process of government formation, the more the end result could only amount to a 'casual parliamentary majority', representative of the uncertain and shifting state of party politics and the public mood.[4]

Table 2.1   Results of 1992 election (Chamber of Deputies)

Political parties	Votes (%)	Seats
DC (Christian Democracy)	29.7	206
PDS (Party of Democratic Left)	16.1	107
PSI (Socialist Party)	13.6	92
NL (Northern League)	8.7	55
RC (Rifondazione Comunista)	5.6	35
MSI (Italian Social Movement)	5.4	34
PRI (Republican Party)	4.4	27
GL (Green Lists)	3.0	16
PLI (Liberal Party)	2.8	17
PSDI (Social Democratic Party)	2.7	16
LA RETE (The Network)	1.9	12
PANNELLA	1.2	7
Other Leagues	1.2	1
PPST (S. Tyrol People's Party)	0.5	3
Pensioner's Federation	0.4	1
Val d'Aosta local list	0.1	1
Parties not winning seats	2.7	
Total	100.0	630
Turn-out	87.2	

Source: adapted from *Il Corriere della Sera*, 8/IV/1992.

Almost all of the leading newspapers – as well as many politicians – were driven to describe the result of the April 1992 election as, not very originally, a 'political earthquake'.[5] Analogies aid understanding; they express the unfamiliar in ways that correspond to the already known. But they depend for their effect on a clear and unambiguous meaning. Natural world analogies abound in political science, in spite of the difficulties and imprecisions that they evoke.[6] Electoral 'earthquakes' were often spoken of in Italy in the 1970s and 1980s, when the slightest change in party support took on an exaggerated importance. The extent – however – of the electoral change in April 1992, far from justifying the geological tag, exposed its inadequacy. This is not all. An earthquake is an unexpected and unavoidable occurrence, often referred to as an act of nature or God. Political events, by contrast, do not just happen. They come about as a result of human actions, if not intentions, which are susceptible to reasoned explanation. Although there is some dispute about how much of a unpredictable surprise the outcome of the election actually was,[7] this does not, in any case, render that outcome inexplicable. In what follows, we will try to explain the contrasting fortunes of the two major protagonists of the 1992 election results, respectively the DC and the Northern League. The electoral fortunes of these two parties is, we believe, the key to answering the two questions we posed at the outset of this chapter.

THE FIRST CRACKS IN THE DC SHIELD

'Omnipresent and central' as the Christian Democrat party still was,[8] the erosion in its popular support (which was in truth more severe than it at first appeared from the aggregate result[9]) was one of the striking facts about the election, occasioning a good deal of psephological[10] debate. Two types of explanation are possible – one which looks for causes within the party itself, the other which gives greater emphasis to external factors.

An explanation of the first type has been advanced by Gianni Baget Bozzo.[11] Baget Bozzo argued that, in spite of its prolonged centrality in Italian political life, the Christian Democratic party had never been able to generate a distinctive political outlook. He saw the clue to analyzing the DC in the relation of the party to Catholic culture, distinguishing between three main strands: the liberal Catholic (represented by Luigi Sturzo, founder of the *Partito Popolare*, the precursor to the DC, and Alcide De Gasperi); the social Catholic (typified by figures like Amintore Fanfani and Giovanni Gronchi[12]); and the democratic Catholic of Aldo Moro. On the basis of this distinction, Baget Bozzo claims that so long as the DC was controlled by liberal Catholics in the immediate postwar period of De Gasperi's premiership, Catholicism and democracy were reconciled by the new legitimacy of the republican state; the party did not aspire to be a 'total synthesis' of civil society. But with the new direction of Fanfani and

Gronchi in the mid-1950s, the social Catholics gained the upper hand, isolating or excommunicating the liberal Catholic tendency. The politics and policies of the DC began to be driven by compromise and mediation, expressed by a radical but enduring turn towards increasing state intervention in the running of the economy. This intervention went far beyond any kind of social democratic-inspired redistribution of income. The state was instead established as the focus of both entrepreneurial and financial activity.

In one of his finest insights, Baget Bozzo holds that the advent of the social Catholics marked the collapse of the fundamental liberal separation between civil society and the institutions of the state, killing off the liberal ethical engagement and sowing the seeds of political corruption – in the confusion between public and private, power and money became interchangeable. As a consequence, the Christian Democrat party, though it 'guided' society in a way reminiscent of fascist rule, was unable to impart moral leadership or inculcate civic responsibility. Baget Bozzo reproaches the DC for being leaderless, programmeless and directionless, bereft of ideas and ideological vision, and only concerned with managing power. While at one level Baget Bozzo's account is interesting, it falls well short of an adequate explanation. The key problem with Baget Bozzo's analysis is that it fails to explain precisely why the electoral demise of the DC began when it did.

Alternative explanations for Christian Democrat decline take greater account of the many contemporaneous changes from without that were, by and large, beyond the party's control, and that created a generalised context of crisis. A common explanation for the timing of the debacle of the DC points to the ending of the Cold War. The events of 1989 not only eliminated the Communist threat, and coincided with the folding-up of the old PCI, but paradoxically the end of the Cold War undermined the hegemony of the PCI's main rival, the DC. In other words, by winning the ideological war against Communism, the DC found it increasingly difficult to justify its *raison d'être*. In fact, this explanation is more unconvincing than many realize. As we shall see in Chapter 8, in 1994 Berlusconi's fervent anti-communist rhetoric was one of the reasons behind *Forza Italia!*'s electoral success, which goes to show that the end of the Cold War is perhaps a necessary but not sufficient condition to explain the collapse of the DC.

Apart from the ending of the Cold War, the poor state of Italy's social and economic life must also be taken into consideration. Douglas Wertman[13] argues that there are many factors contributing to an explanation for the poor showing of the DC in the 1992 elections, including widely-publicized political corruption and scandals; the failure to initiate much needed reform of the political system; the poor quality of Italy's public services; the inability to deal effectively with organized crime; Italy's accumulated debt and huge budget deficit; and the fear that Italy was falling behind in Europe. All-embracing in scope, and doing full justice to the situational complexity, such an explanatory framework could point to 'the intertwining of diverse factors which provided the foundation for real change'.[14] A comprehensive account of this kind certainly broadened the analysis, and conveyed a sense in which the background origins to the upheaval (see Chapter 1) were so compelling that events could not have turned out other than they did. Nevertheless, it is less clear whether this recounting of proximate causes also provided the necessary depth. It could at best give an indication of suggestive starting-points. All the factors listed by Wertman are hardly a novelty for the Italian electorate. For the last 50 years the DC had been able to survive all sorts of scandals, and Italy's perennial crisis had never damaged the credibility of Italy's major party. In the last analysis it is still not clear why it was in 1992 that these factors became important (indeed decisive) for the electorate, and one is left feeling in want of an explanation for the poor showing of the DC at the 1992 elections.

Wertman does say that the DC, as the epitome of Italy's political establishment, was a major target of the electorate's anti-party protest. New political movements, benefitting from the 'freeing up' of a more 'secularised' electorate, exploited and mobilised growing popular hostility (fanned by President Cossiga) to the *partitocrazia*.[15] Even if one accepts the idea (and it is a vital assertion) of a generalised rebellion against party rule in general and the DC in particular, one is only left with a circular argument, since this does not tell us why it was that voters became dissatisfied with the power of the parties to

begin with. In other words, we may be mistaking the consequence for the cause. If the fall of the DC is intrinsically tied
to a widespread rejection of particracy, then in order to
explain the former, it is necessary to explain (and not only
assert) the latter. The key question thus becomes: what triggered the electorate's rebellion against particracy in general,
and the DC in particular?

One tentative answer[16] is given by Pasquino, who suggests
that the DC suffered most from the maturing of a more dis-
criminating and pluralistic electorate (as shown by the development of new professional, cultural and economic
associations over the previous decade) which had become
more politically aware and had grown tired of being held to
ransom by the political parties. A major process of 'dealign-
ment' was underway, of which the 1992 election was the first
sign, marked by a much greater readiness on the part of a
significant number of voters to voice their discontent with excessive party power. Pasquino believes that it was a pre-election
deal reportedly struck by Craxi (PSI) and Forlani (DC) which
proved to be the final straw:

> What probably disturbed many voters was the arrogance of
> the two major partners: their bluntly declared attempt to
> predetermine the political and institutional future regard-
> less of the outcome of the elections or their own electoral
> performance, as well as the allocation of the two most im-
> portant offices, prime minister and president of the
> Republic, as if they were partisan property.[17]

Pasquino's argument is valuable but tantalising. That there
was a large exodus of votes from the dominant parties in government to other anti-party groups and movements necessarily
implied that the electorate were not satisfied with the parties in
power, so that the level of dissatisfaction in the electorate does
not explain but simply describes, *post facto*, what took place.
Furthermore, it is misleading to single out the increasing level
of dissatisfaction as the root cause of change, since that dissatisfaction must itself have been the result of some other prior (but
unexplained) factor or factors which caused it. Attributing the
alteration in the outlook of voters to the arrogant behaviour of

the power elite (which was hardly a novel phenomenon) offers a psychological explanation for what was on their minds which – because it lacks an empirical purchase – is very hard to corroborate. One might decide that Pasquino's notion rings true. But we have no surefire way of telling.

In what follows, the basic assumptions of an alternative approach to the question 'What triggered the electorate's rebellion against particracy in general, and the DC in particular?' will be considered. This approach aims to give an account of the electorate's choices based on rational (as opposed to moral) grounds, where the assumption is that all individuals to the best of their abilities act on the basis of their beliefs and desires in order to maximise their interests. Thus an individual will undertake a cost-benefit analysis of the consequences of a certain action, that is to say he or she will want to maximise the benefits while at the same time minimising its costs.[18] We begin with particracy. After all, if the decline of the DC is tied with the decline of particracy, then perhaps an explanation of the former can be found in the analysis of the latter. The reader will recall from our analysis of particracy in the Introduction that one of the distinguishing characteristics of particracy is its affinity with an unrestricted spoils system. In fact Mauro Calise not only argues that party patronage is the 'true rationale' of a particratic system, but that the spoils system is functional to the particratic form of government.

Because of the nature of particracy, we want to suggest that the relationship between the electorate and the DC is dependent on the latter's success in resource allocation. To a great extent, in 1992 the DC could still rely on its cultural hegemony, characterised in part by what Parisi–Pasquino[19] referred to as the 'vote of belonging' (*voto di appartenenza*) and the 'vote of exchange' (*voto di scambio*), as opposed to relying on the vote of opinion (*voto di opinione*). The vote of belonging is a socially-embedded expression of class, cultural or territorial identity typical in the agricultural and industrial proletariat. The vote of exchange, which applies especially in the South, refers to votes which are clientistically traded in return for a share of public resources. It is important to emphasize that Parisi–Pasquino give a very narrow definition of the vote of

exchange, claiming that its breeding ground is the urban and
rural lumpenproletariat.[20] Finally the vote of opinion is the expression of a choice based on the programmatic definitions
proposed by the competing parties.

While the 29.7 per cent of the votes secured by the DC
(11.5 million votes for the Chamber of Deputies) in 1992 can
be explained largely in terms of the votes of belonging and
exchange, we must find an explanation for the fact that the
DC lost its grip on the electorate, especially in the North. For
the Chamber of Deputies, in the regions of the North the DC
won 19 per cent of the votes in Emilia Romagna; 21 per cent
in Piedmont, Liguria, and Trentino Alto Adige; 22 per cent in
Tuscany; 24 per cent in Lombardy and Umbria. Compared to
31 per cent in Marches and Latium; 33 per cent in Sardenia;
35 per cent in Puglia; 36 per cent in Calabria; 40 per cent in
Abruzzo; 41 per cent in Campania and Sicily; 44 per cent in
Basilicata; 51 per cent in Molise. Amongst the regions of the
North, the only exception to the rule could be found in
Veneto (31 per cent) and Friuli Venezia-Giulia (28 per cent).
In these two regions, the strong Catholic sub-culture would
indicate that the vote of belonging still applied.[21]

In order to explain the poor showing of the DC in the
North, we want to suggest that perhaps the answer lies in the
rational choice of the electorate in the North to change its
party allegiance. By rational choice, we refer specifically to a
cost/benefit analysis based on the pursuit of maximizing individual egoistic self-interest.[22] It is important to distinguish the
rational vote from what Parisi–Pasquino refer to as the vote of
exchange and the vote of opinion. As Rosa Mulé righly point
out, the vote of exchange is in no way comparable with or
similar to the rational-choice voter using a cost–benefit framework.[23] The conditions which make the vote of exchange possible are defined in terms of urgency rather than choice,
therefore the exchange between the voter and the party
becomes both personalised and immediate. On the other
hand the rational voter is acting upon choices and preferences. Of course, we are not suggesting that the electorate in
the South, where the vote of exchange is predominant, is irra-
tional. The difference between North and South is not one of
rationality but one of choice. In the South, due to the hegemony of the DC, the electorate has a far more restricted

choice. The rational voter should also be distinguished from the vote of opinion. As Parisi and Pasquino point out, the distinctive element of the vote of opinion is the fact that this vote is not based on a direct personal relationship between the elector and the elected. According to the vote of opinion it is impossible to distinguish the individually pursued benefit from conceptions of a collective good, where the collective good can refer to a precise group or class, or more generally attached to the whole system.

It could be argued that in the North, the rational vote is tied up with a party's ability to put the spoils system in motion. It is on this point that the debacle of the DC can be explained. There are two aspects of Italy's social and economic life that seem to suggest that the DC was struggling to make the spoils system yield the desired results, and of course the spoils system is the pillar on which the particratic form of government stands.

First of all, the economic conditions of the country (as mentioned in Chapter 1) were exacerbated to such an extent that the country was now on the verge of a catastrophic crisis, brought about by an overloaded burden of new spending projects aimed at shoring up political support. Andreotti, aided and abetted by his ministers (in the view of one critic), had favoured all kinds of clients and lobbies, without regard for prior limits on expenditure, all the while concealing the hazardous state of the economy.[24]

Secondly, the DC was no longer the sole administrator of the spoils system. In the Socialist Party of Craxi they had a competitor. The competition between the DC and the PSI for a larger share of the market of corruption, needed by both parties to satisfy their respective electorates, had a number of inauspicious effects. The price of kickbacks increased at a time when many small businesses, because of the adverse economic climate, were struggling to keep afloat, with the result that many were forced out of the market of corruption.[25] It would appear that as of 1992, playing the game of corruption was no longer paying the expected dividends, thereby removing one of the principal reasons for voting for the DC and maintaining the *status quo.*

Once finds a partial confirmation of the above analysis in the fact that the Northern League, the true winners of the 1992 elections in the North, attracted many votes from the self-employed, especially from the independent middle class and working class, who no longer had anything to gain from supporting the DC. It is not a coincidence that a large part of the Northern League electorate consists of former DC voters. It is to the electoral success of the Northern League that we want to turn to next.

THE GREAT LEAP FORWARD

The success of the Northern League in the elections of April 1992 represents the crowning achievement of a political movement less than ten years old. At the general elections of 1983 the League failed to secure any seats, winning only 13 000 votes in Lombardy. In the general elections of 1987 the League secured 2.9 per cent of the votes in the regions of the North, electing one senator (Bossi himself) and one representative to the Chamber of Deputies (Giuseppe Leoni). In the regional elections of 1990 the League won 10.2 per cent of the votes in the regions of the North, and in the general elections of 1992, the League elected 80 MPs (25 senators and 55 representatives) and 2 MEP, with 17.3 per cent of the vote in the regions of the North. In percentage terms, after 1992 the Northern League was fourth in electoral popularity, after the DC, PDS and PSI.

The great leap forward of the Northern League was the subject of intense journalistic interest, clouded somewhat by an academic distaste for what was seen as the Northern League's frustrated racism.[26] On one point there was general agreement: the Christian Democrat loss was the Northern League's gain, the Christian Democrats 'lost most votes where the *Lega* did best', and that the two were 'directly bound up together'.[27] What has still to be established is the exact nature of the Northern League's electoral appeal. Evidently it was multifaceted, and – Renato Mannheimer insists – not explicable in terms of simple or specific attributes.[28] Broadly speaking, the Northern League was (i) a sub-national political movement, (ii) populist in character and (iii) sustained by a large proportion of protest voters exhibiting a wide range of attitudes and orientations. Each aspect requires fuller elaboration.

The Northern League's share of the vote was unquestionably regional, since it won 17.3 per cent of the validated vote in the North, but only 1.5 per cent and 0.2 per cent in Central Italy and in the South. The promotion of Lombard folklore and dialect had been a key element in Bossi's early strategy,[29] and although this was liable to spill over into anti-immigrant sentiments, the motive force behind the movement was its ultimate aim of a 'Republic of the North', which gave it a distinctive ideological objective on an issue which the mainstream parties had ignored. The point is driven home by Stefano Allievi,[30] who, in examining the way the movement defined itself by studying back numbers of the *Lombardia Autonomista* newspaper (set up in 1982), finds that it was ethnic self-identity which tied together and justified the ideas of liberation and autonomy in a hybrid form of ethno-regionalism first sketched out by the *Liga Veneta*. This regional character made it especially difficult, if not wrong-headed, to categorise the Northern League in left-right terms.

Bossi's populist approach stemmed from his unconventional public image, exemplified by his use of crude, earthy language – 'The League has a hard-on'[31] – and shabby appearance.[32] Far from assuming that Bossi's public image was naive and unintentional, it is important to see this as a calculated political move. Bossi went to great lengths to present himself as one of the populace, proud to show all the defects of the average person. His uncomplicated, demotic style meant that he could be understood by everyone, marking him out from the professional politicians, whose convoluted speech and manners often betrayed an elitist unconcern. Bossi's movement soon became identified with the voice of the masses at a time when the electorate was showing signs of annoyance with mainstream political parties. Shrewd exploitation of hot issues – run-down public services, Northern taxes going to subsidise the corrupt South, the antipathy of small businessmen to Italy's industrial barons – heightened the disgust of what he called 'Roman rule'. Because the Northern League spurned the traditional media, moreover, this only added to their appeal as an adversarial movement 'uncontaminated' by power,[33] enabling them to convert their official illegitimacy into a new, popular legitimacy.[34]

The rise of the Northern League was, finally, commonly identified with a protest vote, even though the basis of that protest was modified by the evolution of the various Leagues (which were only unified by Bossi in 1991). The *Liga Veneta* began as a movement in the smaller towns and among less educated artisans, bound together by a sense of shared territory on the geographical periphery, and emphasising the protection and safeguarding of the local cultural and linguistic heritage. The Lombardy League, by contrast, grew up in industrialised, urban areas where the more materialist message of common socioeconomic interests was employed to win over new, usually politically inexperienced recruits sympathetic to criticisms of the centralised state. It is not surprising to find the Northern League portrayed as leading a crusade against fiscal extravagance, attracting the votes of those who felt over-taxed.[35]

But this would be to miss the full extent of its profound impact. The Northern League's challenge was essentially subcultural, combining an ethnic, localist outlook and a neo-liberal, entrepreneurial programme. Drawing on electoral survey data, Cento Bull arrives at the conclusion that the Northern League had been so successful at replacing the Christian Democrats in so many industrial districts of Lombardy in the April 1992 election precisely because it had been able to put itself forward as 'the new political voice' for small businesses, popularising a shared system of moral values as well as of economic interests, at a moment when that subculture – loyal to the DC during the period of postwar expansion – was 'facing the risk of decline'.[36] This explains, to her, the relative failure of the Northern League to make similar inroads into the PDS-held 'red' region of Emilia-Romagna, where the local administration was more active in fostering economic development. It also explained, though it did no more than partly substantiate, Bossi's notorious claim (to be made in June 1993) that the Northern League was the new Christian Democrat party. Whether the Northern League was a secondary symptom of national upheaval or, in fact, the major catalyst of change was beside the point, for it was both.[37]

The great merit of Cento Bull's analysis is that it examined the evidence on the ground, attempting to evaluate the political behaviour of certain classes of voters in a living and dynamic electoral environment. The Northern Lega, as Diamanti has also shown, was an agent of change, but it was acted upon as much as it acted. Cento Bull does not claim to have found the analytical master key to the Northern League's success. Nor is she relying on the idea of some kind of all-embracing, ineluctable process of political upheaval, in which the collapse of the Christian Democrat vote was preordained. Instead her argument rests on observable – and testable – hypotheses about structural changes in voting in particular places at a particular time and for (purportedly) particular reasons. This approach actually 'explains' the popular revulsion against the parties in power in general, and the DC more specifically, in a way that the earthquake headlines in the days after the election never could. At the same time it does not pretend to ascertain how permanent this switching of allegiances was likely to be.

At this point, we need to ask ourselves if the votes cast for the Northern League represent an effort to reconceptualise Italian democracy on liberal values. We believe that the answer to this question is negative. The revealing fact that a large part of the Northern League's electorate consists of former DC voters, and that Bossi himself was not afraid to portray the Northern League as the new Christian Democrat party, can be interpreted to suggest a less than radical transformation in Italian politics.

The two dominant and most successful parties since the war, the Christian Democrats and the Italian Communist Party, were both grounded on a political culture which failed to distinguish between the state and civil society, or in other words between the public and the private sphere. It is important to realize that Bossi's political movements have followed the same non-liberal democratic tradition as the DC and the PCI, although arguably more successfully than any of its adversaries. Bossi's political movements were not identified with the political philosophy of liberal democracy; it appears that Bossi's Lombardy League first, and the Northern League subsequently, instead appealed to a 'communitarian' sense of democracy,[38] not very different from the tradition of civic Republican humanism briefly discussed in the introduction.

One of the core assumptions of a communitarian political culture is that all political values must be articulated within the contingencies of particular cultures, or as the result of common practices defined by the community. Needless to say, this also applies to the concept of democracy, in fact by democracy communitarians understand decisions that embody the will of the citizenry, as opposed to the liberal ideals of universal and trans-historical conceptions of what is right. It appears that Bossi's explosive mix of federalism[39] and populism endorses the same communitarian conception of democracy. This analysis finds confirmation in Paul Piccone's analysis, who suggested that the Northern League enshrines a participatory rather than a representative notion of democracy.[40] Once again, it is not accidental that the Northern League is the only major political party in Italy where the leader is confirmed by a show of hands at the party congress, subject to the principle of revoke. The lack of a liberal political culture in Bossi's political movement suggests that there are important similarities between Bossi's Northern League and the other political parties in Italy, therefore re-dimensioning zealous proclamations of 'revolution', 'earthquakes' and democratic self-renewal that have accompanied recent changes in Italy's political landscape.

The fact that Bossi's Northern League was the most clear winner of the 1992 election reinforces the point we made in the introduction that the political culture of liberal democracy has never fully taken root in Italy. With the substantial increase in the votes going to non-traditional political forces, the Italian electorate registered its discomfort with traditional political parties, although not with the political culture they represented. By rewarding the efforts of the Northern League, the electorate is opting for a party which is even less liberal in its conception of democracy than the traditional parties. Another way of expressing this point is by saying that the electorate punished the traditional parties for failing to deliver the goods which characterised the particratic spoils system. Contrary to the orthodox interpretation, we believe that the elections of April 1992 were not about change. The results of these elections can be interpreted to reflect a vote for more of the same: more direct democracy, and therefore (arguably) more particracy and more spoils system.

THE FAILURE OF THE LEFT

In searching for answers to our two questions, the focus of our analysis has been directed towards only two aspects of the 1992 elections: the fall of the DC, and the rise of the Northern League. Of course we are not suggesting that these were the only relevant aspects of the election results.[41] This chapter on the 1992 elections would not be complete without an assessment of the major loser of this electoral turn: the left.

The PDS did rather poorly in the 1992 election. In 1987 the PCI obtained 26.6 per cent of the votes, yet by 1992 the PDS could only secure 16.1 per cent. While the poor electoral showing of the PDS at the 1992 elections cannot be disputed, there is much debate about the issue of responsibility: to what extent was the PDS responsible for its electoral failure? This question welcomes two types of responses – one sympathetic, the other more critical.

The sympathetic response clears the PDS from any blame. After all, the 1992 elections were the first elections since the party changed its name, if not its structure and political culture, from the PCI to the PDS.[42] This important change undertaken by the major party of the left was supposed to bring in long-term benefits, even if it was to be expected that in the short-term the period of adjustment was going to be difficult. Thus by April 1992 the PDS was still struggling to come to terms with its new identity. Furthermore it had to contend with opposition from the left of the breakaway party Communist Refoundation (in its first election in 1992, Communist Refoundation won 5.6 per cent of the votes in the Chamber of Deputies, equivalent to 35 seats, and 6.5 per cent in the senate). In the last analysis, it could be argued that given the changes that were sweeping through Italy, in 1992 the PDS did as well as one could expect.

The more critical response, while acknowledging the reality of changes both within and outside the PDS, points to a number of key issues that were handled poorly by the PDS, which indicate that it could have done better in the 1992 elections. As Patrick McCarthy[43] convincingly argues, the PDS's disappointing electoral performance in 1992 is to be explained by the slow and incomplete transformation from the old PCI. According to McCarthy, although the PDS wanted to present itself to the electorate as a modern reformist party, the necessary organisational changes were too slow to materialise, and the PDS was unsuccessful in shaking off some of the characteristic traits of the old PCI.

For any new political party trying to break into the electoral market, its genesis is a delicate but crucial phase. What the PDS needed most was a strong leader able to make a swift and clean break with the past. Unfortunately, in Occhetto it had a weak leader who reflected a weak party, which retained a form of organisation that stems from democratic centralism. The fact that the *svolta*, or turnaround, from the PCI to the PDS took 15 months and two party congresses was a costly mistake, especially when we consider that at the end of the painful process Occhetto was not even elected secretary of the party he had founded. As we shall see in Chapter 8, Occhetto's weak leadership was also a key reason why the PDS lost the next general election in 1994.[44]

A second similar trait between the old PCI and the new PDS was the presence of strong factions within the party. As McCarthy points out, the factions within the party were not operating inside a shared project, instead they were pulling in opposite directions, which contributed to the difficulties of the transformation from the PCI and the PDS, as well as to the erratic electoral campaign in the referendums of 1991 and the general elections of 1992. The strong factions and internal divisions reflected a lack of cohesion in the party.[45]

Finally, the PCI had so much trouble becoming a reformist party because of its diffuse culture of opposition. As McCarthy explains, 'again and again in the Occhetto years we see, alongside his bid to turn the PCI into a party of government, the re-emergence of the PCI as a party of utopian opposition'.[46] There is no doubt that the ambiguous identity of the PDS created major difficulties in defining its electoral programme.[47] Yet we would argue that it was not so much the fact that the PDS was trying to be both a party of government and a party of opposition that was the problem. After all, what else should a party in opposition do during an election campaign. The real problem was that the PDS did not do this well. The PDS (like the PCI before it) was never convincing in its role as the main opposition party, and therefore even less convincing as a party of government. The short lived experience of the shadow government in 1989 is a clear indication of the inadequacy of the major party of the left to present an attractive alternative to the parties in government.[48]

The evidence seems to be conclusive: the PDS must take some responsibility for its poor electoral showing in 1992. Having said that, its responsibility is only partial, in fact even if the PDS did not make the mistakes listed above, there is no certainty that that would have been sufficient to win the election. The failures of the PDS must be seen in light of the two questions we raised in this chapter on particracy and liberal culture. To the extent that the vote for the Northern League was not necessarily a vote against particracy, the PDS would not have attracted many more votes, whatever it did. The death of the PCI and the genesis of the PDS represents, in part, an attempt to break away from the old-fashioned communist political culture. It was an attempt to move towards liberal positions.[49] Yet the 1992 election results did not register a switch towards a more liberal political culture, hence by 1992 victory for the left was always going to be premature.

CONCLUSION

In this chapter, we have posed the questions whether the surprising results of the 1992 general elections can be construed as (a) a vote against particracy, and (b) a switch towards a more liberal political culture. Contrary to the overstatements that have accompanied recent changes in Italian affairs, we believe one should be cautious about endorsing positive responses. On the question of particracy, while it can be argued that the decline in support for the major parties, particularly the DC, was indeed a protest vote, at the same time the notion of rational voting suggests that in fact we are not necessarily looking at a normative protest against particracy, but a vote which may be driven by self-interest. On the latter question of a change towards a more liberal political culture, the evidence concerning the electorate of the Northern League suggests that in terms of the way the electorate conceptualises democracy, a vote for Bossi was in fact a vote for more of the same, or in other words not a vote for a more liberal culture.

58 *Italy since 1989*

Notes

1. Support for the Lega was noticeably higher in the election to the Chamber of Deputies – where the voting age is 18 – than for the Senate, where the suffrage is only open to those of or over 25.
2. R. Mannheimer, 'The electorate of the Lega Nord' in G. Pasquino and P. McCarthy (eds) *The End of Postwar Politics in Italy. The Landmark 1992 Elections* (1993).
3. Information supplied in a post-election analysis in *La Repubblica*, 8 April 1992, p.11.
4. Adapted from G. Sjoblom, 'Political change and political accountability: a propositional inventory of causes and effects', in H. Daalder and P. Mair (eds), *Western European Party Systems – Continuity and Change* (1983) pp.395–7.
5. *Il Corriere Della Sera*, 'L'Italia Protesta, Elezioni Terremoto'; *La Stampa*, 'Elezioni, Un Terremoto'; *Avanti!*, 'Un Terremoto Politico'; Enzo Carra, the Christian Democrat spokesman, was quoted as calling it 'an earthquake for the whole government'. Only *La Repubblica*, significantly, claimed that the Christian Democrat wall had collapsed.
6. M. Landau, 'On the uses of metaphor in political analysis' in *Social Research*, (1961); B. Barry, 'On Analogy' in *Political Studies* (1975).
7. R. Mannheimer, op. cit. (1993) p.85.
8. G. Sani, 'DC comunque', *Panorama*, 12 April 1992, p.53.
9. M. Donovan, 'A party system in transformation: the April 1992 Italian election', *West European Politics* (1992), p.175.
10. The study of voting and elections.
11. Gianni Baget Bozzo, *Cattolici e Democristiani* (1994).
12. G. Gronchi (1887–1978). President of the Republic from 1955 to 1962. A. Fanfani (1908–). DC party secretary from 1954–9 and 1973–5. Prime Minister six times, beginning in 1954.
13. D. Wertman 'The Christian Democrats: A Party in Crisis', in G. Pasquino and P. McCarthy (eds), *The End of Post-war Politics in Italy: The Landmark 1992 Elections* (1993).
14. M. Bull and J. Newell, 'Italian politics and the 1992 elections: from "stable instability" to stability and change', in *Parliamentary Affairs* (1993) pp.203–27.
15. M. Donovan, op. cit. (1992) p.173.
16. There is a vast and growing literature on electoral behaviour in Italy, and we cannot do justice to all the theories and approaches that have been put forward. For an excellent overview of studies on electoral behaviour in Italy, see R. Mulé, 'Electoral behaviour in Italy', *European Journal of Political Research* (1993).
17. Introduction in G. Pasquino and P. McCarthy (eds), op. cit. (1993) p.6.
18. For a basic introduction to rational choice theory, see J. Elster, *Nuts and Bolts for the Social Sciences* (1989) and M. Hollis, *Reason in Action* (1996), Part 1.
19. A. Parisi and G. Pasquino, 'Changes in Italian electoral behaviour: the relationships between parties and voters', in *West European Politics* (1979) pp.6–30.

20. Parisi–Pasquino qualify this claim by explaining that the exchange vote is diffused among small farmers and the rural petty bourgeoisie, as well as among that portion of urbanised petty bourgeoisie which, culturally and structurally, maintain some tie with its social and geographic background. This background referred to here is the South.

21. The statistics on electoral results for the Chamber of Deputies by regions can be found in G. Pasquino and P. McCarthy (eds), op. cit. (1993) pp.178–80.

22. See L. Lewin, *Self-Interest and Public Interest in Western Politics* (1991) pp.45–8.

23. R. Mulé, 'Electoral behaviour in Italy', (1993) op. cit., p.419n6.

24. M. Caciagli, 'Italie 1993: vers la seconde république?', in *La Revue Française de Science Politique* (1993) p.232.

25. This analysis will be expanded on in Chapter 4.

26. Works by D. Vimercati, *I Lombardi alla Nuova Crociata* (1990), G. Savelli, *Che Cosa Vuole la Lega* (1992), S. Scarpino, *Tutti a Casa, Terroni* (1992) and M. Ottomani, *Brigate Rozze: A Sud e a Nord del Senatore Bossi* (1992) are descriptive and rhetorical and so of little scientific interest, apart from amusing biographical details about Bossi. The best book-length studies are by R. Mannheimer (ed.), *La Lega Lombarda* (1991) and I. Diamanti, *La Lega: Geografia, Storia e Sociologia di un Nuovo Soggetto Politico* (1993). The Italian journal *Polis* (August 1992) devoted an issue to the phenomenon of the Leagues. All the above works are in Italian, but the reader can find a brief English review of some of them in T. Gallagher 'Regional nationalism and party system change: Italy's Northern League', *West European Politics* (1993).

27. M. Bull and J. Newell, op. cit. (1993) p.216. Confirmation that a large part of the Northern League electorate consists of former DC voters comes from P. Natale 'Lega Lombarda e insediamento territoriale', in R. Mannheimer (ed.), *La Lega Lombarda* (1991) and L. Ricolfi 'Politica senza fede', in *Il Mulino* (1993).

28. R. Mannheimer, op. cit. (1993).

29. Umberto Bossi, the leader of the Northern League, made his political debut as the founding member of smaller group, the Lombardy League. In the 1980's Bossi's Lombardy League was not the first of the only political movement to appeal to the sub-national political culture of its electorate. Apart from the well-established Sudtiroler Volkspartei in the German-speaking Tyrol, there was also the Liga Veneta targeting the electorate in Veneto and the Sardinian Action Party targeting the electorate in Sardinia.

30. S. Allievi, *Le Parole della Lega* (1992).

31. See R. Iacopini and S. Bianchi, *La Lega ce l'ha Crudo!* (1994) on the Northern League's idiosyncratic form of political communication.

32. Bossi always wears a tie on an open collar, and suits which look as if they have been borrowed for the occasion.

33. A point made by P. Allum, 'The Liga Veneta', *ASMI Newsletter*, (1993), p.16.

34. M. Lazar, 'Italie: pour comprendre la Ligue' (reviewing Diamanti's book) in *La Revue Francaise de Science Politique* (1993) p.1026.

35. Savelli pays particular attention to the Northern Leagues's campaign against fiscal injustice.
36. A. Cento Bull, 'The Politics of Industrial Districts in Lombardy: Replacing Christian Democracy with the Northern League', in *The Italianist* (1993) pp.209–29.
37. E. Mingione, 'Italy: the resurgence of regionalism', in *International Affairs* (1993) pp.305–18.
38. By 'communitarian' here we refer to the political philosophy of communitarianism. In contemporary debates communitarianism shaped its identity in terms of a critique of liberal political theory. See S. Mulhall, and A. Swift *Liberals and Communitarians* (1992) and S.Avineri and A. de-Shalit (eds), *Communitarianism and Individualism* (1992).
39. Bossi has openly embraced federalism as its prime political objective. For many years Bossi's right hand man was the constitutional theorist Gianfranco Miglio, arguably Italy's most outspoken advocate of federalism. See G. Miglio, *Verso una Nuova Costituzione* (1983); *Per una Costituzione per i Prossimi Trent'Anni* (1990); *Come Cambiare: Le Mie Riforme* (1992). For English-speaking readers, see G. Miglio's 'Towards a Federal Italy', *Telos* (1991–2). Miglio's views on the constitution are criticised in our Conclusion.
40. P. Piccone 'Federal Populism in Italy', *Telos,* No.90, Winter 1991–92, saw the rise of the Lombardy League as part of the world-wide phenomenon of the crisis of the nation-state and national unity. With the end of the Cold War and bipolarism, almost every nation-state was beset by major internal problems of national unity. Thus the League is associated with the emergence of 'a plethora of autonomous movements in search of concrete alternatives to the central state' (p.6).
41. One issue we failed to consider, which is admittedly very important, is the fact that these were the first elections after the referendum of 9 June 1991 which abolished multiple preference vote. Thus in the 1992 election, the electorate was allowed only one preference to be expressed on the ballot paper. See S. Parker, 'Electoral reform and political change in Italy, 1991–1994', in S. Gundle and S. Parker (eds) *The New Italian Republic* (1996) pp.41–2. See also G. Pasquino (ed.), *Votare un Solo Candidato: Le Conseguenze Politiche della Preferenza Unica* (1993).
42. This process, which took 15 months, is well documented by P. Ignazi, *Dal PCI al PDS* (1992). See also M. Bull, 'The unremarkable death of the Italian Communist Party', in F. Sabetti and R. Catanzaro (eds), *Italian Politics: A Review* (1991); M. Bull, 'Whatever happened to Italian communism? explaining the dissolution of the largest communist party in the west', *West European Politics* (1991); M. Donovan, 'Party strategy and centre domination in Italy', in P. Mair and G. Smith (eds), *Understanding Party System Change in Western Europe* (1990).
43. P. McCarthy, 'The Italian communists divide – and do not conquer', in G. Pasquino and P. McCarthy (eds) op. cit. (1993).
44. See P. Ginsborg, 'La sinistra, la crisi, la sconfitta', in P. Ginsborg (ed.) *Stato dell'Italia* (1994).

45. M. Bull, 'The PDS, the Progressive Alliance and the crisis', in *Modern Italy*, Vol.1, No.1, Autumn 1995.
46. P. McCarthy, op. cit. (1993) p.41.
47. See G. Pasquino, 'Programmatic Renewal, and Much More: From the PCI to the PDS', *West European Politics* (1993).
48. On the PDS's attempt to create a shadow government, see M. Carducci, 'Un nuovo modello di organizzazione dell'opposizione parlamentare: "il governo ombra del PCI"', *Politica del Diritto* (1990).
49. See G. Berlinguer, *I Duplicanti Politici in Italia* (1991).

3 The Storm Breaks (April–September 1992)

THE AFTERMATH OF THE 1992 ELECTION

The general election of 5–6 April 1992 – effectively the first post-Cold War Italian election[1] – did little, at first sight, to help clarify and resolve Italy's mounting political and economic difficulties. Voters had been turning against sitting governments in other parts of Western Europe, frustrated by the growing dislocation consequent upon German unification and the momentum towards European integration.[2] But in Italy the protest was ostensibly anti-systemic. Not only was the outgoing *quadripartito* coalition denied any kind of convincing electoral re-endorsement; *all* of the main parties (except for the small Liberals and the Republicans) had suffered a significant fall in support, the dispersal of votes to a number of other reform parties and movements creating an outcome of – even by Italian standards – unprecedented fragmentation.[3] Although it was a moot point as to which of the coalition partners had been dealt the greatest setback, the result left the country without an immediately recognisable government or opposition, destroying one governmental alliance without seeming to offer any obvious replacement. It was, as many observers were led to believe, ironically recalling the campaign warnings of Craxi, Forlani and others, a vote for chaos.

The fact that the supremacy of the old parties had been given such a severe jolt was not, however, unwelcome to the advocates of institutional and electoral change, most of whom belonged to Mario Segni's cross-party reforming pact, who could claim the verdict as a system-busting blow to entrenched party rule.[4] Reformers could now put a powerful case for arguing that 'the Italy of the parties' had long since ceased to correspond to the real politics of the country. In this sense, the apparent confusion of the vote was a necessary prelude to a modernising of the Presidency, parliament and eventually

62

the political parties themselves. The 1992 election marked an important further stage in the campaign set in motion by the referendum of June 1991 on single preference voting.

Pulling in the opposite direction to the advocates of institutional reform, and despite the fact that the results of the elections upset all pre-electoral calculations, there were many DC and Socialist notables who were hoping that the four-party arrangement might still be revived in its old form. President Cossiga, speaking while on an official visit to the United States, moved to quash this idea, making it clear that in his view the old governmental alliance could not carry on regardless. On his return, he then issued a warning to party leaders that unless there was a speedy recomposition and broadening of the government, he might be prepared to step down within a matter of days, making way for a more 'robust' successor who would be able to wield the threat of new elections. Notwithstanding Cossiga's ultimatum, inter- and intra-party divisions remained a considerable obstacle to progress. Few of the old guard DC factions seemed sufficiently shaken to go over to the reformist side led by De Mita, the Republican Party was still withholding its support for Andreotti, and Craxi, though pressured by some colleagues wanting to create a broader left, was unwilling to weaken the PSI's indispensability by opening the door to the PDS in government. His talks with Occhetto, whose own position was by no means secure, soon reached an impasse. When the new legislature convened on 23 April, Andreotti had resigned but was staying on at the head of a caretaker administration. The eventual election of Luigi Scalfaro[5] and Giovanni Spadolini[6] as the new speakers of the Senate and the Chamber, both enjoying a broad consensus, did not, however, suggest that the popular will had made itself felt, since neither had pro-reform credentials. Scalfaro, indeed, was known as a strong defender of the existing rights of parliament, and it was Cossiga's anger at this belated choice, along with his suspicions that the PSI were no longer supporting him, which seem to have brought about his abrupt resignation. In a tearful farewell broadcast, he made a final assault on the powers that had governed Italy over the previous 45 years, and especially his old colleagues in the Christian Democrat party who had not yet understood that everything had changed. 'They are behaving as if the elections had never happened', he subsequently told an interviewer. 'I know how it's going to end: people will stone them in the streets'.[7] By robbing Italy of its head of state, Cossiga's resignation threw the political world into turmoil.

MANI PULITE

It was in the midst of this dangerous period of drift that the Socialist party, already troubled by growing internal arguments, was dealt a further heavy blow with the widening out of a judicial investigation into political corruption in the party's (and Craxi's) stronghold of Milan.[8] A middle-ranking party functionary, Mario Chiesa, had been arrested on 17 February while in the act of receiving a £3000 bribe in his capacity as president of Milan's largest state-run old people's home, the Pio Albergo Trivulzio. The bribe-maker, Luca Magni, who ran a cleaning company, had gone to the Carabinieri after tiring of having to pay out in order to win contracts, and had agreed to cooperate in setting Chiesa up. Held in preventative detention in San Vittore jail, Chiesa at first refused to talk. Craxi – on the election stump – had fended off questioning by disowning Chiesa, calling him a rogue who had deceitfully infiltrated the PSI. Chiesa's wife, who was divorcing him in the courts, had made much of the discrepancy between his private wealth and his public declarations. After a while, however, Chiesa began to speak freely to the investigating magistrate, Antonio Di Pietro, exposing a systematic network of pay offs and kickbacks in the awarding of public contracts in Milan stretching back to 1979 and persisting right up until the general election campaign. Although the flow of funds was intended – in apparent contravention of the law on the financing of political parties[9] – to finance the PSI's organisational and votecommanding apparatus, much of it also appeared to be going into the pockets of the party cashiers themselves (Chiesa turned out to have almost £3 million in foreign bank accounts or invested in property in Italy).

Eight Milanese businessmen brought in for questioning confirmed and expanded on what Chiesa had said, describing a highly structured distribution of bribes and commissions to each of the main parties – including the PCI/PDS – in pre-agreed proportion to their local electoral strength, taking in whole areas of public administration and the health services, housing construction, the Milan metro and the new Milanese airport.[10] What had come to light was a web of 'generalised connivance and complicity',[11] implicating politicians, administrators, entrepreneurs and contractors in the corrupt and abusive manipulation of local markets which – as the witnesses despairingly made plain – had been pushed to breaking point. Without exception, they complained that the parties had become money-eating machines and that politics was costing them too much. On 3 May, the prosecutors in the Milanese *Mani pulite* ('clean hands') operation sent notification to parliament asking for the lifting of immunity from prosecution of two former mayors of Milan, Carlo Tognoli and Craxi's brother-in-law Paolo Pillitteri, both of whom now sat as PSI MPs. Both had been cited by Chiesa. Pillitteri, it also emerged, was said to have been implicated in mafia money-laundering in Milan in the 'Duomo Connection' police operation in 1991. Craxi lashed out at the *Mani pulite* inquiry, alleging that he was the victim of sabotage, while despatching his deputy, Giulio Amato, to Milan with the task of purging the local party and containing the damage.[12] Although other arrests soon followed, causing the resignation of the entire Milan city council and the regional Lombardy council, as well as the detaining of the DC national treasurer, Severino Citaristi, it was the Socialist party that was the most harmed, undermining Craxi's continuing bid for high office.

THE ELECTION OF THE NEW PRESIDENT

The President of the Republic is elected by parliament in a joint sitting of the Chamber of Deputies and Senate. Presidential elections take place by secret ballot, and initially a two-third majority of the assembly is required. If this is unsuccessful, after the third ballot an absolute majority (50% + 1) becomes sufficient.

When voting by the grand electors of parliament for a new President got underway on 13 May, the situation was fraught with uncertainty. Holding only a paper majority in Parliament, the combined forces of the DC–PSI–PSDI–PLI were in practice weakened still further by the activities of dissident 'snipers' within the ranks of the Christian Democrats,[13] many of them embroiled in the faction-fighting between De Mita and Andreotti, by the veto power of Segni's pact supporters (who were prepared to thwart anyone unsympathetic to electoral reform) and by the unpredictable manoeuvring of the Northern League. Before voting had even begun, MPs traded blows and insults after some MSI deputies had taunted the DC benches with the cry of 'thieves'. In the first three rounds, when any successful aspirant would have needed the backing of at least two-thirds of the total vote, no serious candidates were put forward. Thereafter, with only the hurdle of a simple majority to clear, Forlani allowed his name to go forward, only to fall – in the best of three separate attempts – 29 votes short after which he again tendered his resignation as party secretary. Andreotti's own intentions were still unclear. A succession of further rounds followed, but in each of them the hopefuls were knocked to the ground in what *La Repubblica* compared to a disorganised pigeon shoot. By the fifteenth ballot, once it had become clear that his own chances were slim, Craxi withdrew from the fight, leaving the contest in a state of parliamentary deadlock. Wracked by internecine disagreements, the power brokers of the old order were evidently no longer able to agree upon or impose a candidate of their own choosing, in a clear indication that the initiative was starting to slip from their grasp.

It took the shocking murder of Giovanni Falcone on 23 May, the anti-mafia judge, along with his wife and three bodyguards – blown up by a mafia bomb on the road leading from Palermo airport into town – to spur parliament into action. Falcone's movements were normally a matter of the strictest secrecy, so that his killing pointed to a high-level informer, implying that no one was invulnerable. Falcone's appointment as the national anti-mafia prosecutor was imminent. By filling the power vacuum left by the politicians, it served as a powerful reminder that the mafia was still a force that any new administration would have to contend with. Intriguingly, Falcone turned out to have been working closely with Di Pietro, paying 'continuous attention' (in Di Pietro's words[14]) to the *Mani pulite* investigation, especially in relation to several non-lira Swiss bank accounts suspected of being used for money laundering by mafia and political clients. A request to inspect the accounts had been handed to the Swiss Ticino Banking Association only the week before, but had been turned down because of Swiss banking regulations. As one of Falcone's colleagues observed, it was no coincidence that Falcone was killed at the moment the Milan inquiry moved its focus of attention to Switzerland.

At his funeral in Palermo two days later, thousands gathered in and around the church, in a unique display of public sentiment. Bed sheets displaying anti-mafia slogans were draped defiantly from the balconies of apartment blocks. Prominent politicians like Spadolini, Scotti and Martelli[15] (the minister of justice in the Andreotti government) were loudly heckled and booed, and in a moving appeal, one of the wives of the dead bodyguards broke down in despair at the endless spilling of blood. Whether or not out of a greater sense of urgency, an agreement on a compromise presidential candidate satisfying to all the main parties was now forthcoming, the choice falling between the respected and untainted speakers of the two Chambers, Scalfaro and Spadolini. Scalfaro's election by 672 votes[16] reflected the breadth of his support from the government parties as well as the PDS, with only the Lega Nord, the MSI, the Republicans and Communist Refoundation opposing him. The circumstances in which he became head of state did mean, however, that – being a traditional Catholic of the right and yet somewhat of an outsider – he was less beholden to any one faction or alliance than any of his immediate predecessors. In this regard, the remarks he made in his inaugural speech in upholding the constitution, endorsing the popular wish for reform, calling for urgent action on the country's finances and in denouncing the evil association of politics with business carried more than usual conviction.

But just as early consultations by the new President on the formation of a new government were getting underway, the *Mani pulite* inquiry took a decisive turn. A senior Milanese socialist, Silvano Larini, who fled the country before he could be arrested on 9 June, was found to be holding £5 million of funds in a secret bank account in Switzerland, and Amato, while denying that the money belonged to the Socialist party,

outspokenly criticised the 'robbers' and opportunists who had
risen in the party only to further their own careers. Just days
later, documents were lodged with parliament listing deputies
that magistrates wanted to begin proceedings against and containing testimony by Chiesa for the first time directly implicating Craxi in a violation of the law on the financing of political
parties, claiming that he (Chiesa) had been asked by Craxi in
1990 to fund the campaign of his son Bobo Craxi who was
running for a council seat in Milan, in return for which Chiesa
would be reconfirmed as the director of the old people's
home.[17] Craxi issued a prompt denial, calling the statements
'as false as Judas', but the damage had been done, weakening
his support in the PSI (sections of which were increasingly critical of the party's tactics over the previous 18 months), his
public popularity and – most of all – his chances of being
nominated as the next Prime Minister. 'Tognoli and Pillitteri
are [Craxi's] men, backed by him, appointed by him, wanted
by him, promoted by him', wrote the editor of *La Repubblica*;
'with Tognoli and Pillitteri, politically if not judicially, we get
to Bettino Craxi'.[18] On 17 June, in an admission of defeat after
refusing to back down, Craxi ceased to press his claims on the
prime ministership, forwarding to the President the names of
three Socialists who enjoyed the confidence of the party –
Amato, De Michelis and Martelli. With Craxi's withdrawal, the
last remaining member of the presiding triumvirate of
Craxi–Andreotti–Forlani, known as CAF, which dominated
Italian politics in the 1980s, had departed from the scene.

AMATO AT THE HELM

Entrusted by the President with the task of constructing a new
government, it fell to Amato to – as he told reporters – 'sail
the boat through the tempest'. Amato's personal qualities
made him a credible reforming figure. A Craxi loyalist, he nevertheless was known to favour institutional and electoral
change, had formed close ties with leaders of the main trade
union federations, and was respected in business circles for his
economic competence. Just as importantly, Amato was acceptable to the large majority of Christian Democrat MPs who –
split six or seven ways – had still to agree on a successor to

Forlani as DC secretary. Bold schemes, such as the fusing of the Treasury, Budget and Finance portfolios into a single super-ministry, were even spoken of. But in spite of attempts to broaden the parliamentary base of support beyond the four former coalition parties, Amato proved unable to entice either the Republicans or the PDS into the 'area of government'. Forlani's insistence that any Christian Democrats taking up a cabinet post should at the same time give up their parliamentary seat (as a way of giving greater stability to the Council of Ministers) seemed likely to further deprive the government of members of weight or standing. Amato's final sharing-out of appointments, shorn of many ministerial and under-secretarial positions, reflected an uneasy compromise between continuity and the will for change. Many figures of seniority were excluded. But although the new coalition was held to be open to the constructive support of opposition parties, it was ultimately dependent for its slender majorities in both the Chamber of Deputies and the Senate on forces that were falling increasingly under the shadow of scandal, were threatened by further electoral losses (as was shown by the DC and PSI returns from the local government elections in early June) and were certain to be hostile to any measures jeopardising their own party and political survival. For these reasons, Amato was not thought by many to be anything more than a 'stop gap' Prime Minister.

Yet there was also an important sense in which Amato's weakness was also his strength. None of the coalition partners would want to do anything that might provoke a second election. By dint of being the President's own choice, Amato had more of a free hand to choose his colleagues and settle on a programme. Scalfaro – it was generally thought – had indicated that the new administration would retain his support so long as there was no viable governing alternative. These personal guarantees from the highest office turned out to be more than enough in helping Amato to outline his policy priorities of economic, electoral and moral reform to parliament and to clear the initial hurdle of parliamentary votes of confidence – by 173 to 140 votes in the Senate and 330 to 280 in the Chamber.

The time taken before the forming of new governments was an accustomed feature of Italian politics, but in the economic circumstances of mid-1992 the three month hiatus seemed like a grave dereliction. Control of public finances had been allowed to slip throughout 1991, exacerbated by a pre-election spending surge. The protected public sector of the economy had become more and more out of step with the trend towards increased competition in international markets. Before and after the campaign, capital had drained out of the country, along with a sharp worsening in the balance of payments. With the national debt, the budget deficit and inflation all climbing, EC finance ministers had already issued a third warning, arguing that without 'strong measures' to curtail public expenditure Italy would end up failing to meet the convergence criteria agreed to at Maastricht, with disastrous repercussions for the rest of the Community. In his annual report at the beginning of June, the Governor of the Bank of Italy, Carlo Azeglio Ciampi, had set out the formidable array of monetary, industrial, fiscal and spending problems that had accumulated and that they were coming under growing pressure from Brussels to tackle.

Therefore from its earliest days in office the Amato government came up against the full force of the country's exposed economic position. The speed with which Amato acted took most commentators by surprise. The Treasury, headed by a nonpolitical (though DC sympathetic) technician, the banker and academic Piero Barucci, was given enhanced authority, and its staff reinforced by enlisting outside experts. Franco Reviglio, the budget minister, was an economics professor, but had been in charge of ENI, the state energy and chemicals conglomeration, in the eighties. Only Giovanni Goria, at Finance, was a practising politician. The three of them formed the economic team given the job of applying the eleventh-hour 'shock therapy' – Reviglio's phrase – that was now to take effect. The *lira* had been under speculative attack in the foreign exchange markets for several weeks, with investors anticipating that the new government might decide to devalue, and was trading close to its EMS floor of 765 to the Deutschmark. Central bank intervention had already seriously depleted the reserves. By raising the discount rate, a signal was sent to traders that the policy of a strong *lira* would be maintained, even though, locked into a debt trap, each percentage point rise added £700 million to the budget deficit for 1992 (debt interest payments accounted for almost all of the budget deficit), itself originally set at L128 000b but already threatening to wildly overshoot. The strong *lira* was regarded as an important test of the Italian government's European commitment, all the more so following the narrow 'No' vote against the Maastricht treaty in the Danish referendum of 2 June.

Amato also moved quickly to explain the government's intention to start from 'year zero' in restructuring the five main state holding companies National Petroleum Company (ENI), Southern Manufacturing Industry (EFIM), State Electricity Company (ENEL), Institute for Industrial Reconstruction (IRI) and National Insurance Agency (INA) into two larger action societies with a view to preparing them for eventual privatisation, freeing their management so far as possible from political patronage and also raising much-needed revenue – a proposal which Amato was said to have introduced at the last minute in a late evening cabinet meeting. As to an incomes policy, the tripartite negotiations between the trade unions, employers and the government – which had been broken off – were started up again. Although the *scala mobile*, automatically linking wage rises to the rate of inflation, had already been frozen, wages continued to outpace the increase in the cost of living; a renewed effort was made to persuade representatives of the General Confederation of Italian Labour (CGIL) (close to the PDS), the Italian Confederation of Workers' Union (CISL) (Christian Democrat) and the Union of Italian Labour (UIL) (Socialist) to moderate their demands. Finally, after a marathon eight-hour session on 10 July, the Council of Ministers adopted an emergency package of across-the-board spending cuts and one-off tax increases for the remainder of the financial year, formulated to reduce the budget deficit by L30 000b, equivalent to 2 per cent of GDP. Though harsh, the mini-budget was meant to be equitable, the cabinet having abandoned income tax increases about which the unions had been especially unhappy. Asking Italians to 'put one hand on their hearts and one in their wallets', Amato described the combined proposals as the first step to take Italy away from the edge of the abyss, and they were sent in the form of a decree to the Chamber of Deputies with the Prime Minister making it plain that if they met with opposition he would treat it as an issue of confidence.

Such a bold assertion of the main lines of government policy was in marked contrast with the policy-making of past administrations. Amato was prepared to take risks, but only because of his keen sense of the practicable and the possible. He was set on reforming the system he was so familiar with from within, aware of the kind of changes which had to be effected by someone on the inside. To this extent his readiness to 'change the rules'[19] was not just economic and financial, bringing calm and buying time, but also essentially political, striking at the corporatist, inflationist, social compact of special interests which had flourished in the expansionary 1980s. Preoccupied in the short-term in finding the means to cope urgently with the legacy of neglect, his longer-term goal was to have done with the whole way of governing.

The Chamber of Deputies had already voted to lift the parliamentary immunity of the five MPs – among them Tognoli and Pillitteri – who were under investigation. In a parallel investigation, the scandal of *Tangentopoli* (bribe city) had also reached the Veneto, implicating the former foreign minister, De Michelis, as well as other suspects in Florence and Rome. But on 17 July, the Milanese police detained Salvatore Ligresti, the Sicilian-born property tycoon who had been behind many of the construction projects in Milan in the eighties and was reputedly one of Italy's five wealthiest men. Questioned by Di Pietro, with a copy of Dostoevsky's 'Crime and Punishment' lying on the desk in front of him, Ligresti admitted to having paid almost 1bn Lire (£500 000) in bribes to secure contracts for the Milanese metro and transport systems. Ligresti was the most prominent figure so far to be drawn into the judicial inquiry; but because of his role as the 'everywhere man' spanning the worlds of politics, business and the stock exchange, it now became clear that investigators were probing at or near to the top, sparing no one, not even the so-called 'untouchables',[20] and shares in Ligresti's various companies all fell.

On the very same day, in a sudden announcement, the entire board of EFIM resigned. EFIM controlled many loss-making businesses in the fields of defence and transportation, and was heavily in debt, mainly to foreign banks – its helicopter subsidiary, Agusta, alone owed L2000b. Shortly afterwards, the reason for the board's action came to light. EFIM was to be wound up and would no longer honour its L8500b

(£3.87b) debts, in any case not until all its assets were sold off. Not only was this a hard knock for investors who had thought that EFIM operated with state guarantees. It also put paid to the plan to merge the remaining state entities into two super holdings to be made ready for divesting, owing to the refusal of the banks to underwrite bonds in the new conglomerates. Once again, the final decision to close EFIM was sprung on the cabinet, after strong representations from party leaders. Faced by this considerable reverse, the industry minister, Guarino (who was by no means an enthusiastic privatiser), offered to resign too. Amato, explaining that he was trying to act in the interests of the companies and not the party factions, insisted that the privatisation programme of the government remained unaffected.

Then, on the following Sunday, the mafia intervened for a second time, killing Judge Paolo Borsellino and his five escorts by detonating a remote-control bomb as he arrived outside his mother's flat in Palermo. Borsellino had been Falcone's closest associate and was widely tipped as the next in line for the post of Superprocurator of the newly created judicial investigating body, the DNA. In recent weeks, according to the German police, Borsellino had been in Mannheim questioning a suspect about the infiltration of organised crime in Germany; he was also believed to be on the trail of certain Italian magistrates thought to have colluded with the mafia. The Pope denounced the murder as an 'insult to Italy', while the founder and leader of *La Rete*, Leoluca Orlando – who was only able to safely visit Borsellino's widow in the dead of night – claimed that the country was turning into a 'banana republic'. A number of judges in Palermo resigned in disgust at their lack of police protection, and a wave of protest demonstrations broke out. At the public burial of Borsellino's bodyguards, Scalfaro and Amato were rowdily jostled. Borsellino's widow rejected a state funeral, convinced, as Father Pintacuda put it, that some of those in authority had lost all credibility. Amato openly admitted that 'the state is not innocent'.

Steps to speed up the coming into operation of the new DIA – the anti-mafia investigative directorate – and the DNA (charged with the coordination of law enforcement) had been taken at the end of June by the justice minister, Claudio Martelli. A statement by the lawyer representing Salvatore

'Toto' Riina, the alleged mafia 'boss of bosses', that his client, who had been sought for more than 20 years, had been able to move freely about Sicily and even get married, further inflamed public opinion.[21] In response to this latest development, and to President Scalfaro's declaration that democracy had to prove itself stronger than violence and criminality, Italy embarked on the most imposing mobilisation of force since Mussolini's campaign in the 1930s, despatching 7000 troops to Sicily, transferring many imprisoned mafia bosses to the island-prison of Pianosa, and introducing – in record time – an arsenal of new anti-mafia laws giving police greater investigating powers (for example, the power to search without a warrant) and increased protection for witnesses, as well as tightening the law on electoral malpractice. Magistrates like the procurator, Piero Giammanco, whom Falcone and Borsellino distrusted, were transferred by the CSM.

Such a concatenation of events – at such a critical juncture – strained the resilience of the Italian polity to its limits, in what had become an apocalyptic crisis to end all crises. The corruption scandal, beginning in Milan but extending to other cities and regions, was revealing how far the party system had degenerated. Economic dynamism, which in the past had always made up for the weaknesses of the state, had been imperilled by the poor public finances. Mafia activity exposed the impotence of the public authorities. Together they amounted to a triple challenge, in part justifying Amato's statement in a televised address that 'everything is conspiring against us'.

As suggested in Chapter 1, Italy was clearly caught up in the cross-pressures created by the post-1989 fragmentation of the ideological clash of East and West and the quickening drive towards closer European economic integration, both of which were having an impact on Italian peculiarities: the colonising of the state by the monopoly parties, the heavily statist economy most at risk with the liberalisation of EC trade, and the unofficial connivance of politics and crime. For many, the Amato government was deserving of support precisely because it represented 'the last and best hope' of bringing about the drastic corrective measures that alone would restore governmental legitimacy. The sceptical doubted whether either the time or the resolve existed to do what was necessary, in view of how deep-seated the problems were. This was not just Italian misfortune. It was an indictment of Italy's governing classes, calling into question whether Italy could survive as a modern, unified, industrial nation at all.[22]

By turning crisis into opportunity, Amato was able to pull off some early – and striking – successes. The Chamber of Deputies agreed to grant emergency status to the July budget proposals, and although over 2000 amendments were put forward, largely by the Lega Nord and Communist Refoundation, along with considerable opposition from sections of the Christian Democrat party to the privatisation plans, the economic ministers made it plain that they would quit if the budget did not pass intact. Barucci's disclosure, on 27 July, that the budget deficit for the first five months of 1992 had already climbed to L83 000b – way above the projected figure – and that the budget plan for 1993 would be correspondingly more severe, contributed to the mood of urgency. By treating it as an issue of confidence, the government also threatened its own dissidents with expulsion, and the budget passed the Chamber by 318 votes to 246 – a larger than expected margin because of the abstention of Communist Refoundation MPs. With Senate approval by the even more comfortable margin of 157 votes to 89, the legislation had gone through from start-to-finish in only one month. The news prompted an immediate strengthening of the *lira* (from 761 to 755.9 to the Dm), and met with only muted trade union protests.

Just as impressively, on 31 July, the Prime Minister brought off what had hitherto seemed unthinkable – a binding agreement with the unions and employers for the complete abolition of the *scala mobile*, and with it the annual round of collective bargaining.[23] There would be no wage increase for 1992 and only a modest rise for 1993. Amato, it appeared, made a direct appeal to the head of the Socialist trade union CGIL, Bruno Trentin, to put the national interest before union or party considerations, leaving him – as Trentin observed – 'with no choice', a position which others condemned as a form of political blackmail. The next day Trentin stepped down in the midst of fierce criticism from his own members, who complained that they had not been consulted, but with praise from Luigi Abete, the president of *Confindustria*, for his act of great responsibility. The Bank of Italy followed up by lowering the discount rate.

A further boost came with the announcement that the boardroom management of each of the main state-owned holding companies was to be restructured, cutting the number of political appointees and leaving only a 'political' chairman, an 'insider' chief executive and a senior civil servant with a privatisation brief, the intention being to create a new Italian national industry, eventually facilitating the selling off of profitable parts to the private sector.

All in all, and in spite of the rushed brinkmanship and tactical backtracking, Amato could point to important evidence of progress on the key economic front, promising social peace, the restoration of industrial competitiveness and a respite from the turbulence of the foreign exchange markets. The budget for 1993 would have to be even more restrictive, and the fate of the government still hung in the balance, but ministers departed for the summer holiday break heartened by how much, in only three months, they had actually been able to achieve.

THE COLLAPSING LIRA

The failure of the Italian economy to approach anywhere near to the convergence criteria laid down in the Maastricht treaty was the fundamental reason why economic reform was so pressing. In the normal course of things, the measures taken might have been enough to bring a temporary reprieve. But in late August and early September, with opinion polls indicating that the result of the French referendum on the treaty (set for 20 September) might be closer than hitherto anticipated, every passing day intensified the speculative strains on the exchange rate mechanism of the EMS, and with it the whole project of monetary union. The *lira*, the weakest currency in the ERM (that is the most overvalued in relation to the Deutschmark, which was anyway attractive because of very high German interest rates) was a natural target, especially now that exchange controls no longer existed. The Italian government hoped to provide a boost by ratifying the treaty, or at least having it passed by the Senate, in advance of the French vote, and the foreign minister, Emilio Colombo, explicitly tied approval of the treaty to the further austerity measures envisaged for 1993. The nearer the day of the vote, however, the more intense the pressure became, and in a race against the clock the government was forced to resort to a series of desperate expedients.

On the 4 September the Bank of Italy raised the discount rate by 1.75 per cent to a record 15 per cent, much to the anguish of business and labour, and the government asked for EMS (European Monetary System) credit facilities. The following day, at a meeting of EC finance ministers, Barucci asked for 'positive help', but the possibility of concerted action by the monetary authorities to bring about a general realignment of EMS currencies was not discussed. On 8 September the State Audit Office warned of the imminent danger of bankruptcy in the national accounts. After a heated cabinet meeting on the 9th,[24] and in the boldest stroke of all, the Prime Minister called in parliament for extraordinary emergency economic powers for a three year period, including the right to halt previously agreed government spending, alter taxes, or speed up investment, enabling the government to rapidly push through changes without the need for parliamentary debate. He accompanied this request with the announcement that the first two privatisations of state – the Credito Italiano commercial bank and Nuovo Pignone engineering group – were being prepared, a move apparently demanded by the Bank of Italy as the price for the discount rate rise. Even this had little discernible effect, as the Italian and German central banks continued to intervene heavily to prop up the existing value of the *lira*. On 10 September the *lira* was trading below its permitted ERM (Exchange Rate Mechanism) floor of 765 to the Deutschmark (DM). Despite further strong intervention and repeated denials of devaluation, it could not be raised above its trading floor, and on 13 September it was effectively devalued by 7 per cent in relation to all the other ERM currencies.

Although Amato presented this as a technical adjustment occasioned by a cut in German interest rates, he had been disappointed by the reluctance of other countries (notably the British) to make a simultaneous move. Nevertheless he emphasised how much more severe the rescue plan for 1993 would now have to be. The markets were unconvinced, with many traders judging that the *lira* was still overvalued, and they continued to sell; when the large investment companies also piled in in what was seen as a 'one-way bet', the *lira* soon fell below its new central band. Cabinet splits (the labour, health and public works' ministers were all opposed to the spending cuts) sparked off a rumour that the government might be on the verge of resigning. When Amato repeated his call for emergency powers in parliament, many branded the idea as unconstitutional. The markets took it as a further sign of weakness. There was also a fresh fear that the unions, troubled by devaluation leading to rising prices, might go back on their agreement to scrap the *scala mobile*. The special decrees on limiting spending in the four main areas of pensions, health, local government and public administration eventually passed in the Senate, helped by the distracting controversy over the granting of emergency powers, but even this was too late to halt the market hysteria that had broken out.

On 17 September, the government finally gave way, deciding to 'abstain temporarily' from intervening in the foreign exchange markets, thereby allowing the *lira* to float outside the narrow band of the ERM. It was an object demonstration of the power of the financial markets – in admittedly exceptional circumstances – to overturn government policy. By the end of September, when the lira had still not re-entered the ERM, it had depreciated by about 8.5 per cent. All told, the unsuccessful defence of the currency cost the Bank of Italy no less than L30 000b (£13.8b) in reserves, along with further short-term obligations of L27 300b to the Bundesbank and the Belgian central bank.[25] The fragility of the Italian economy had, to be sure, left it open to speculative attack. But the lack of concerted EC action also meant that, without rapid domestic steps (of the kind which parliament was unwilling to grant), the sheer volume of currency transactions – dwarfing the combined reserves of the central banks – was enough to sink any single country, economically sound or not.[26]

Promising draconian measures to reduce the budget deficit, Amato reconvened the Council of Ministers for two long and arduous meetings, after which the main outline proposals for the 1993 budget were made public. Working on the basis of revised forecasts, the new austerity plan envisaged holding the deficit to L150 000b (10.5 per cent of GDP) for the following financial year, with real reductions in 1994 and 1995. As a first step, an extra L93 000b (some £42b) was to be raised, by a combination of spending cuts and tax raising schemes. Total government spending would be capped at its 1992 level, with a freeze in the pay of all 3.6 million public sector workers. New income, corporate and property taxes were introduced, including a minimum tax for small businesses and a luxury tax. All of this was in addition to the already contentious economies in free health care and the lifting of the pensionable age foreshadowed in the second 1992 budget. A further L7000b was to come from privatised asset sales. Newspapers were quick to calculate the cost of the package to the average family as an extra L1m (£400) a year, headlining the proposals as a clear assault on the social state. But what was equally remarkable was its innovative approach in dealing with the structural reform of state finance. The new taxes were to be permanent, instead of one-off, and the savings in spending were designed to be cumulative, year-on-year.

There was an instant outcry from those whose interests were most directly affected. Rank-and-file trade unionists, still angry with Trentin for having signed away the *scala mobile* (he had consented not to resign after all) pelted him with eggs, tomatoes and bolts at an outdoor demonstration in Florence, and the main union leaders, anxious not to alienate their members, set in motion several regional strikes and stoppages, culminating in a one-day general strike planned for the start of October. The manufacturer's federation *Confindustria*, alarmed by the outbreak of union antagonism, nevertheless felt that the budget package did not go far enough. The self-employed protested at the imposition of centrally determined tax brackets irrespective of tax returns. And Bossi, seizing on the unrest, called for a fiscal strike and a boycotting of the state bonds. Lobbying by the governing parties sought, as was the custom with the budgetary process in the past, to make every exception the rule. The main thrust of the Amato plan remained unaltered, however, consistent with the Prime Minister's warning (bolstered by support from the President) that the government would resign *en masse* if it was substantially modified. It was a high risk strategy, relying heavily on votes of confidence, reshuffles and the final authority of the

President to make up for the failings of the old parties and the erosion of popular consent.[27] Lacking a mandate, the Amato government attracted unpopularity because of the onset of economic hard times.

CONCLUSION

Apart from the economic difficulties, the turmoil of the six months between April and September 1992 can also be attributed to the successes in the investigations on corruption by the pool of Milanese magistrates. In order to appreciate the magnitude of the impact of the investigations into corruption, let it suffice for the moment to consider the trial of Sergio Cusani. The question of corruption will be dealt in greater detail in the next chapter.

Never before has a trial captured the interest of the Italian public as with the trial of Cusani, which in terms of the interest it generated can easily be compared to that of O.J. Simpson in the US. Cusani acted as the intermediate link between his boss Raul Gardini, the tycoon of Italy's chemical empire, and the Italian political class. Gardini, who committed suicide on 23 July 1993, paid the highest kickback ever known in Italy, valued at approximately L153b (£60m), to all major political parties (although the lion's share of the kickback went to the PSI and DC) in order to buy their support for a government decree that would have secured him a tax-break worth approximately L1000b (£400m).

The trial of Cusani did not simply involve Sergio Cusani himself, arguably one of the smaller fishes in the pond of corruption. Because of its extravagant value, Gardini's bribe has been referred to as 'the mother of all kickbacks'. Hence it was not only Cusani that was on trial, but Italy's entire political elite, and as the trial of Cusani came to its concluding climax on 28 April 1994, it was not only Cusani that was found guilty,[28] but Italy's entire political class. With the trial of Cusani the careers of some of Italy's best known politicians came to an abrupt end, from Craxi, Martelli and De Michelis (all PSI), to prominent Christian Democrats such as Andreotti, Forlani and Pomicino. Furthermore the trial did not spare politicians of smaller parties, from La Malfa (PRI) to Altissimo (PLI). Even opposition leaders were involved, from Bossi (Northern

League) to Occhetto and D'Alema (both PDS). For this reason, it has been rightly said that the trial of Cusani will be remembered as the act symbolising the end of the First Republic and the beginning of the Second.[29]

Notes

1. G. Pasquino and P. McCarthy (eds), *The End of Post-War Politics in Italy – The Landmark 1992 Elections* (1993).
2. Extremist parties made large gains in *Land* elections in Germany; support for the ruling Socialist party had fallen by more than ten percentage points in regional elections in France; in Britain, opinion polls (misleadingly) showed the Conservative government trailing the opposition Labour party during the general election campaign.
3. 'Italians urged to embrace reform of electoral system', in *The Financial Times*, 10 April 1992, p.2.
4. 152 of the incoming Senators and Deputies were signatories of the referendum pact.
5. Oscar Luigi Scalfaro (1918–). Magistrate. Member of the Constituent Assembly in 1946. Former interior minister. Devout Catholic.
6. Giovanni Spadolini (1925–94). Journalist and editor. Republican Prime Minister in two successive governments in 1981–82. Former president of the Senate. Noted historian and political diarist.
7. Cited by P. Willan in 'Cossiga blames malaise on too many doctors', *The Sunday Telegraph*, 3 May 1992, p.18.
8. The question of corruption will be dealt with more extensively in Chapter 4.
9. The 1974 law on 'the state contribution to the financing of political parties' – which was subsequently re-endorsed by referendum in 1978 – introduced a state subsidy to all the political parties in relation to their votes at the previous election. The subsidy was intended to cover both a party's election expenses and its general organisational costs. Scandals in 1981 led to the doubling of the subsidy. The advent of public financing did not, however, close off (as had been hoped) the supply of hidden or 'black' funds from questionable sources, not least because of the effect the new law had in concentrating the control of finance with the central party executives. See G.F. Ciaurro, 'Public financing of parties in Italy', in H.E. Alexander (ed.), *Comparative Political Finance in the 1980s* (1989) pp.153–69.
10. One instant account of the affair was *Tangentomani – storie, affari e tutti i documenti sui barbari che hanno saccheggiato Milano*, by A. Carlucci (1992).
11. D. della Porta, 'Milan: immoral capital', in S. Hellman and G. Pasquino (eds), *Italian Politics: A Review*, Vol.8 (1993).
12. Giuliano Amato (1938–). Professor of Constitutional Law. Criticised Craxi's 'caesarism' in 1979. Socialist Deputy and Craxiite lieutenant since 1983. Former treasury minister (1987–9), vice-president of the Council of Ministers, and Prime Minister 1992–3. Currently the President of the Anti-trust Commission.

13. The secret vote had been retained in voting for a new President of the Republic as well as for the Presidents of the Chamber of Deputies and the Senate. A 'sniper' is someone who votes against his party.

14. E. Vulliamy, 'The man who got too close', *The Guardian*, 26 May 1992, p.8.

15. Claudio Martelli (1943–). Philosophy lecturer. MP for the PSI from 1979 to 1994. Also outgoing deputy Prime Minister. Craxi's number two. Heavily implicated in investigations on corruption, was forced to abandon politics in 1993. In September 1993 was studying for a M.Sc. in political theory at the London School of Economics.

16. Giorgio Napolitano, from the PDS, replaced Scalfaro as president of the chamber of deputies.

17. Chiesa's own account was published in a special dossier in *L'Espresso*, 28 June 1992, pp.12–22.

18. Cited in C. Richards, 'Milan scandal hurts Craxi leadership hopes', *The Independent*, 4 May 1992, p.11.

19. G. Amato, in a *Financial Times* interview, 16 July 1992, p.18.

20. See the interview with Borrelli in 'Non esistono intoccabili', in *L'Espresso*, 10 May 1992.

21. Salvatore Riina (1930–). Served a six-year term in prison at the age of 15 for killing another youth. Became right-hand man of Corleone clan boss, Luciano Liggio, before taking over in 1974. Unleashed ruthless mafia war leaving 1000 victims dead in the space of three years.

22. S. Romano, 'L'unité italienne en question', *Le Monde*, 6 October 1992, p.10.

23. See R. Locke 'Eppure si tocca: the abolition of the scala mobile', in C. Mershon and G. Pasquino (eds), *Italian Politics: A Review*, Vol.9 (1995).

24. For the background to this episode, see M. Valentini, 'Carta bianca per una resa annunciata', in *L'Espresso*, 20 September 1992, pp.10–15.

25. *The Financial Times*, 31 October 1992, p.2.

26. P. Daniels, 'Italy and the Maastricht treaty', in S. Hellman and G. Pasquino (eds), *Italian Politics: A Review*, Vol.8 (1993) pp.178–91; and A. Busch, 'The crisis in the EMS', in *Government and Opposition* (1994) especially pp.89–90.

27. A. Criscitiello, 'Majority summits: decision-making inside the cabinet and out – Italy 1970–1990', in *West European Politics* (1993) p.592.

28. Cusani was sentenced to eight years in jail for false accounting, for violating the law on public financing of political parties and for illicit appropriation of funds.

29. For a full account of Cusani's trial, see A. Pamparana, *Il Processo Cusani* (1994).

4 Corruption: A Rational Analysis

From the moment that the first results of the *Mani pulite* inquiry by the pool of Milanese magistrates came to light in the spring and summer of 1992, the issue of corruption became the preoccupying concern of parliamentary, press and public debate.[1] Even for a country in which corrupt behaviour was the unflattering norm rather than the exception,[2] the initial exposures of *Tangentopoli* had the capacity to shock. The uncovering of widespread illegality, in Italy but also at the same time in many other Western countries, contributed to an already growing academic recognition of the importance of corruption in the functioning and malfunctioning of contemporary modern democracy.[3]

Explaining why the *Tangentopoli* scandal first broke in Italy raises a number of conceptual complications. In the first place, it is not always possible to be clear about what exactly is meant by corruption.[4] Corrupt activity can take different forms (bribery, misappropriation, nepotism, fraud) in different circumstances (in both the public and private spheres). Because standards of conduct are, in part, culturally determined, what may be considered to be wrongdoing in one country may not be legally regarded as such in another. The very term carries value-laden connotations, encouraging some to adopt a variety of non-judgemental alternatives, for example 'slackening', the 'soft state', problems of 'moral hazard'. But secondly, there has been a tendency – encouraged by journalistic sensationalism – to treat each outbreak of corruption as unique to itself, imparting no lessons other than that of the unchangeability of national character or human frailty. The particularity of cases of corruption frustrates the search for a universally applicable general theory of political corruption.

That said, a typology of Italian scandals, confirming the high level of corruptibility of Italian politics in the late 1980s, pointed to several recurring characteristics. Scandals were not

83

isolated instances of petty swindling but interconnected and integral to the management of power. They were all, for this reason, political in nature, and yet in almost every instance the chief perpetrators went unpunished.[5] The striking, and puzzling, fact about the *Mani pulite* investigations is of course that the pool of magistrates made such rapid and dramatic progress, when a string of earlier, equally spectacular high-level scandals (the Lockheed affair; the masonic lodge P-2; the murder of Roberto Calvi; to mention only a few) had all come to nothing. Why, in comparison with these earlier episodes, did the evidence of corruption spread, in the words of Francesco Saverio Borrelli, 'like an oil stain', as more and more people were prepared to speak about what they knew.[6]

When looking at the problem of corruption in Italy, we are not dealing with the ordinary manifestation of corrupt behaviour, when a public servant deviates from the normal duties of his or her public role with the sole intention of making a personal gain.[7] Some of those caught up in *Tangentopoli* were found to be spectacularly wealthy. Instead, and notwithstanding the existing law on the financing of party politics,[8] the principal beneficiaries of corruption were the political parties as a whole. They were the main agencies of bribery and corruption, driven by inflated organisational demands and by the need, especially for the governing parties which were in competition with each other, to meet the cost of elections.

The old Italian party system (famously characterised in the argument between Sartori, Galli and Farneti[9]) had been criticised for its tendency towards ideological fragmentation and extremism, while the new focus of interest was its domination by *affarismo*. As Hine rightly remarks, the resource-hungry parties in Italy were formidable political machines, serviced through rigged contracts, illicit payments, loans, transfers, or contributions in kind from public sector bodies.[10] In Milan, once known as the moral capital of Italy, virtually all decisions taken by party-nominated public officials were dictated by a pervasive market for corrupt exchange, with perverse consequences: while state laws and regulations were constantly violated with impunity, entrepreneurs who refused to respect the illicit rules and conventions of the market of corruption were *de facto* excluded from the tendering of public contracts, so ending their business careers early. In other political systems, such as Germany (where state aid goes to the parties) and Japan (where it does not) the main parties, and the factions within them, draw heavily on often undisclosed company donations, in return for tax concessions or other advantages.[11] But it was the systematic and all-encompassing nature of the role of Italian parties, through which most public business was necessarily transacted and manipulated, which made the revelations of *Tangentopoli* so exceptional and which merits special examination.

TANGENTOPOLI EXPOSED

Di Pietro had already gained an understanding of Milanese politics and society from earlier investigations in the late 1980s, when he had built up a database of suspicious contacts relating to the channelling of slush money to the political parties in the Lombardy region.[12] Working in conjunction with other highly qualified members of the pool, like Gherardo Colombo who uncovered the P-2 story in 1981, and relying on his computer skills, Di Pietro was able to make sense of a wealth of information (Chiesa's contact book contained 7000 names) which would have been beyond the power of any one person to amass or master.

The arrest of Chiesa, described in some detail in Chapter 3, was not therefore a chance happening, but the outcome of long and meticulous preparation, involving extensive phone tapping and the surveillance of bank accounts.[13] What few people could have predicted is that the investigation would snowball, so that, as Neppi Modona had it, 'not only those who were formally notified of being investigated both recognised their own responsibility and exposed others, but dozens of potential offenders, *especially entrepreneurs*, turned themselves in spontaneously in order to confess the payment of kickbacks'.[14]

Neppi Modona adds that the main cause of the 'geometrical' increase in the investigation lay most probably in this willingness of the accused to testify. One of the Milanese prosecutors compared it to the Iraqi army at the end of Operation Desert Storm, with 'many coming to us with their hands up before we even chase after them'.[15] There is little doubt that without the help of spontaneous confessions the existence of the market of corruption could not have been substantiated.[16]

Not surprisingly, this chain of events has been the subject of several studies, and both major and minor cases of corruption have been thoroughly documented.[17] There have, however, been only a few explanatory accounts of the nature and development of corruption, the best of which came out just as the *Mani pulite* inquiry was making headway.[18] Clearly, any overview must deal convincingly with two interrelated aspects – the timing of the breakthrough, and the subsequent wave of voluntary confessions. If corruption had been commonplace for many years, one needs to show why the scandal publicly erupted when it did. And if the key feature of the investigation was that for the first time the individuals under investigation decided to cooperate with the authorities, then one must be able to justify the motives of the accused. Since the second question has such a close bearing on the first one, this might open the way to a comprehensive explanation of *Tangentopoli*.

In what follows, we will consider four possible explanations for the uncovering of corruption in Milan, evaluating how well they measure up to the touchstones of timing and motivation: political explanation; moral/cultural explanation; legal explanation; economic explanation. Although it is reasonable to expect that all four explanations hold some validity and that there will be areas of overlap, we have – for the purposes of exposition – treated each of them as free-standing ideal types, as if they were the only possible explanation. It will be evident that these rival 'ways of seeing' differ not only about matters of fact and about the interpretation to be put on the facts, but also on grounds of ultimate values.

POLITICAL EXPLANATIONS

Although there is no agreement about the reason why the system of corrupted politics came about in the first place, those who give most coverage to the political background to *Tangentopoli* put forward a range of arguments designed to show that it was the upheavals associated with the post Cold War era, and above all the unlocking of party divisions, that provoked the great change.

Christian Democrat apologists tended to maintain that the DC had had to model itself on the guiding, hegemonic PCI of the early postwar period, mainly in self-defence. Edward Luttwak, in true Cold War spirit, blamed the spread of corruption on the 'sinister challenge' of the Communist threat, which had originally led the Christian Democrats 'to develop the methods of covert funding which were to be emulated by almost all the parties, the PCI itself included'.[19] Sidoti advanced a similar view, arguing that the lack of alternation allowed corrupt, economically interventionist practices to flourish:

> The acceptance of corruption was a consequence of the impossibility of any form of renewal: Italians tolerated misgovernment as long as the alternative was a party linked to the Soviet Union. Once the Soviet Union and the PCI no longer existed there were no more reasons for maintaining the parties' corrupt grip on the decision process.[20]

According to Sidoti, *Confindustria* (the Italian Employer's Federation) played a central part in the system of corruption, Northern industrialists especially having reached the conclusion at the beginning of the 1990s that the extravagant public spending of the political class was an obstacle to economic advance and European integration, 'while history and events', in the words of the head of the manufacturers' federation *Confindustria,* 'pass us by'. The magistrates were in a position to launch a powerful attack on the politicians because they could count on the support of the business community.

This line of argument leaves much to be desired. There is a distinct want of hard evidence – Sidoti's justified stress on the role of Confindustria is purely speculative, neglecting the micro-motives of the true protagonists of the affair – which is made up for, in Luttwak's case, by a grotesquely exaggerated and outdated phobia of Communism that risks obfuscating any analytical understanding. And there is a questionable historical basis to many of their key assertions. It is certainly true that, without the possibility of any alternation of power, the main political deterrent to corrupt behaviour (loss of office) had been eliminated. But one of the peculiarities of the Italian phenomenon of party power, or particracy, was the unofficial

collusion – rather than ideological antipathy – of the governing parties and the principal opposition party, and the sharing
out of the political spoils that this created. The existence of
this pattern of organised politics was what gave protest groups
like Bossi's Northern League their chance. More consideration of other long-run themes, such as the oligopolistic nature
of Italian capitalism, typified by the extensive infiltration of
the state in the running of the economy, would also have
added greater depth. Not to mention the historical link
between corruption and clientelism, which was a feature of
Italy's state and nation-building path to modernity.[21]

The more immediate problem of post-electoral deadlock in
April and May 1992 has been cited (by Waters, and also
McCarthy[22]) as one of the most pressing 'political' factors. The
blow to the credibility of the established parties meant that
they were powerless to impede or divert the course of the
Milanese investigation. Di Pietro later admitted to having held
up his work while the election campaign was going on; thereafter it took on a momentum of its own. It has been suggested
that that was the real reason why Cossiga stood down so
promptly – because he had been unable to forestall Craxi's co-
involvement.[23] President Scalfaro's call in his inaugural speech
for greater morality in public life was an important declaration
that the inquiry should be allowed to proceed unhindered.

The political explanations – even though they do not tally –
are strong on providing the background context to the unfolding of events. There is no doubt that the fall of the Berlin
Wall, the transformation of the PCI into the PDS and the
advent of the Northern League contributed to the eventual
undoing of the old ruling parties. Having said that, it is important to remember that history is in the detail, and this line
is promising but, at best, partial and incomplete. One cannot
claim to self-evidently explain just by describing. To imply a
causal relationship (and one that is not noticeably illuminat-
ing about timing or the motivation of the main actors) does
not help to indicate the direction of causation. 'Was corruption a cause of the crisis', Calise asks somewhat despairingly,
'or was it the weakening of the political system that made
exposure of corruption possible? At the present time, one can
only say that political corruption made the ongoing crisis
more readily visible.'[24]

CULTURAL/MORAL EXPLANATIONS

An alternative approach has been to concentrate on the political culture of corruption in Italy and the impact of changing moral attitudes. There are two separate strands to this explanation. One of them is predominantly cultural, as suggested by Hine,[25] acknowledging the structural incentives to corruption,[26] but going on to speak of the climate of moral relativism in Italian politics, and the low prestige of the state and its laws. Often this is attributed to the strength of the two dominant Catholic and marxist subcultures which traditionally compel an equal (if not higher) moral allegiance. Donovan even talks of a close correlation between the Catholic culture and a predisposition to corrupt politics.[27] A number of other active social influences are also said to have encouraged this undermining of the legitimacy of the liberal state, evident in the persistence of a strong sense of local community (often hand-in-hand with antagonism towards centralised government), networks of organised crime, and the activities of secret elite organisations like P-2.

A related, more normative strand inclines towards the idea that there was a growing moral revolt against corruption, sparked off by the fact that the level of corruption had crossed an unspecified threshold of public tolerance. Neppi Modona looks for an explanation in what he calls 'a radical change in the attitudes and mentality of the collective consciousness',[28] which had a liberating effect on the inquiries of the magistrates. Pizzorno[29] contends that the answer lies in 'the moral costs of corruption', in which the weighing up of the moral cost to each individual reflects his or her ethical socialisation and education. Finally, while specifically rejecting the suggestion that the revolt was confined to a revolt by those who paid the bribes, della Porta[30] contends that the entire political system underwent a crisis of legitimation. Clientelism, maladministration, organised crime and political corruption were all intertwined in a tangle of vicious circles, widening out from top to bottom and from one public institution to another, and with bad politics driving out good. *Tangentopoli* provoked a shift away from these vicious circles to a new, virtuous circle.

Explanations based around the catch-all variable of culture are undeniably interesting and useful in tackling the 'big' problems; where they fall down is in their shaky empirical grip.[31] By appealing to the shortcomings of Italian political culture, Hine and others may be able to indicate why corruption was more than likely to take root and develop, and why indeed it may have become functional to the survival of the system. They are very inventive, but less persuasive, at coming up with plausible reasons why the mechanisms of organised illegality should suddenly reach breaking-point. If we are to believe that Italians are driven to act by a metaphysical entity called culture which makes them accept bribes in Milan and join the mafia in Sicily, then how do we explain that at a certain point in time a sizeable number of entrepreneurs decided *en masse* to testify against themselves by denouncing everything in their past? 'The cultural stuff', as Ernest Gellner calls it, cannot be used both ways.[32]

Equally, the moral accounts of *Tangentopoli* all hinge on the underlying belief that there has been either a change in moral attitudes or a change in moral evaluation, yet they all fail to explain in precise enough terms the character of these changes. It follows that the moral case commits the logical fallacy of *petitio principii*, better known as begging the question: it assumes as a premise for an argument the very conclusion that it is intended to establish. The change in moral attitudes is not proven, it is simply presumed. The even larger question of connecting changes in cultural behaviour to institutional structures is omitted altogether.[33]

LEGAL EXPLANATIONS

An explanation of the phenomenon of *Tangentopoli* rests on the ability to answer a number of key questions, such as what was *Tangentopoli*? How could *Tangentopoli* happen? Why did *Tangentopoli* happen when it did? David Nelken[34] tries to answer these question in terms of a legal explanation. According to Nelken, *Tangentopoli* could happen because of the existing form of judicial organisation in Italy, which made it difficult to block the judges' investigations. Furthermore in Italy there is a lack of formal political control over the judges. As to why *Tangentopoli* happened when it did, Nelken points to the important fact that the system of corruption was inherently fragile, in particular the bonds of loyalty between corrupt politicians and corrupt businessmen were not strong enough to make businessmen pay bribes in the face of decreasing returns from their investments and growing international competition.

The legal explanation, as presented by Nelken, must be taken seriously. Acknowledging the changes in the legal framework must no doubt be part of any explanations of the success of the magistrates in their fight to uncover corruption in Milan. Having said that, there is an important difference between suggesting that these changes in the legal framework were *necessary* for the success of the judges in their investigations on corruption, and showing that these changes were in fact *sufficient* to bring down the market of corruption. On this latter question, the judges are still out.

In order to strengthen the legal explanation, and bridge the gap between a necessary and a sufficient condition, most commentators have paid generous tribute to the enterprising heroics of the *Mani pulite* magistrates in bringing corruption to light. This judicially-angled viewpoint begins with the pivotal and momentous changes contained in the new code of criminal procedure that came into effect in 1989, and the opportunities that this afforded. The new code replaced the Rocco Code (Codice Rocco) introduced by the Fascist regime in 1931. The most significant modification was the substitution of an Anglo-American 'accusatorial' for the Napoleonic 'inquisitorial' approach, squarely placing the responsibility for judicial inquiries with the public prosecutor, with the judge now an impartial spectator during the cross-examination of witnesses conducted by the prosecution and defence lawyers.[35]

By giving new investigative powers to the public prosecutor, enabling the setting up of groups of magistrates who could coordinate their activities in particularly complex and sensitive cases, and permitting more discreet preliminary work in the first six months of an inquiry, the new code was instrumental in the unearthing of *Tangentopoli*. Moreover, in a paradoxical way, changes which had been brought in to curb judicial excesses (such as the milder *avviso di garanzia*, merely advising someone that they were under formal investigation, and a tightening of the rules allowing for preventative detention,

except in cases of criminal association) had made it easier
rather than harder to secure arrests.[36] Suspects who cooper-
ated enjoyed the full benefits of more lenient treatment, one
of the weapons found to have been so effective in the fight
against terrorism. In addition to this, the gravity of the crime
of aggravated concussion (that is extortion), as distinct from
corruption, where the two parties to an offence conspire together, was enough to prevent the inquiry from being transferred – and sidelined – elsewhere, as had happened on so
many previous occasions.

Although members of the Milan pool were insistent that
judges should be oblivious to the climate of public opinion,
the leaking of stories to sympathetic journalists also helped to
fuel public indignation, reviving the accusation that magistrates had turned into politically-inspired protagonists who
were no longer able to separate their official duties from their
own partisan opinions. The surprising success of the *Mani
pulite* inquiry, in this sense, emphatically confirmed the constitutionally guarded independence of the judiciary from other
institutions in the state, and its very real ability to check and
offset political power.[37]

The skill of the magistrates in employing 'objectionable'
methods was obviously a key factor. All the actors participating
in the market for corruption hold considerable bargaining
power, based on their access to threatening information. It
follows that after the first corrupt player is arrested, he or she
finds him or herself in a real-life prisoner's dilemma.
Magistrates created the conditions which gave those under investigation a strong incentive to confess, by reproducing the
incentive structure of rewards for those who cooperate when
they are unsure whether others, also arrested, will refuse to
collaborate or break their silence. It could be argued that this
was the crucial trigger.

Such a view is not unassailable. Every competent investigative magistrate is supposed to recreate the prisoner's
dilemma in order to extract a confession from the accused, so
that there is no reason to think the *Mani pulite* team were
doing anything novel. They had all been active for a number
of years, without hitherto being able to break through
the wall of silent collusion or *omertá'*. Moreover, as Neppi
Modona remarks, it would have been very difficult for any

entrepreneurs frozen out of the market to supply conclusive proof of wrong-doing in the allocation of contracts.

It is no disrespect to the magistrates to suggest that they progressed by luck as much as by skill. The analytical distinction between luck and skill is admirably expressed in his analysis of power by Barry:

> There are two ways of getting outcomes that you want. One is to bring them about yourself by exercising power. The other is to have them occur (often as a result of the exercise of power by others) without exercising any power yourself. Someone who is commonly in a position to obtain wanted outcomes by exercising power is powerful; someone who commonly obtains wanted outcomes without exercising any power is lucky.[38]

It is not necessary to explore the complexity of the relationship between luck and power in any great detail. The point is that desired outcomes can be the result of either power, or luck, or a mixture of the two. In terms of our interests in this chapter, we can say that the collapse of the market for corruption is explicable in terms of the skill of the magistrates (power), to fortuitous circumstances (luck), or to an explanation which combines elements of both. It is our view that the *Mani pulite* magistrates were at least as lucky as they were powerful.

What does it mean for the magistrates to be lucky? The answer to this question is that it was the magistrates' good fortune to be pursuing their inquiries at the very moment when the market for corruption was already on the point of disintegrating. In other words, the causes of the success of the Milanese magistrates were in part, but only in part, exogenous to the system of corrupt politics. Their efforts are a necessary part of any explanation about when and why the time was ripe. They created the conditions in which witnesses were willing to talk. But their success was also owing to some endogenous changes in the crucial mechanisms of the market of corruption itself, and in particular, to a change for the worst in the structure of the entrepreneurs' pay-off. The expansion of the market of corruption was such that by late 1991 it had reached an unsustainable equilibrium point.

An equilibrium is a state in which people's plans are consistent with each other.[39] The notion that the equilibrium point in the market of corruption could no longer be sustained means that many entrepreneurs, who for many years took advantage of the system of corruption, for the first time found themselves in a losing position. We feel that this is a possible and promising explanation for the curious and unprecedented phenomenon of the *Mani pulite* investigation, namely the fact that the accused were willing to testify to their culpability, so much so that large numbers of them spontaneously went to the authorities to confess their involvement in illicit transactions. This hypothesis would indicate that the market was undermined by the same actors who operated within it. In order to substantiate this claim, it will be necessary to make a closer examination of some crucial mechanisms of the market of corruption.

AN ECONOMIC EXPLANATION[40]

The following economic explanation attempts to explain the nature of the market for corruption on the basis of an equilibrium model of corrupt exchange. Applied to Italian conditions, and in particular the case of Milan, the model clearly demonstrates the pivotal role of political parties in fostering corruption.

Let us start from a simple hypothetical situation, that of a public official who oversees a tender for a public contract (*gara di appalto*) and a number of firms who wish to obtain such a public contract.[41] Let us also assume that the official wishes to *sell* the tender to one of those firms for the price of a kickback. To the extent that the expected costs of entering into the corrupt transaction (hereafter CT) are less than the expected gains, the firm will be willing to secure the tender by paying for the kickback.

Even assuming that there is a potentially corrupt official (hereafter CO) and a potentially corrupt entrepreneur, and that both would gain from the CT, a communication problem ensues: how are they going to tell each other of their willingness to enter into such exchange? The realm in which they operate is illegal and therefore they cannot openly advertise their intentions. Moreover, their actions are stigmatised by social norms. They have to be careful not to give away their intentions, yet they do not want to be secretive to the extent of ending up with no interaction.

A solution to the conundrum is to send a *signal* which will be understood *only* by those who are willing to enter into the corrupt transaction. The signal is a device to ascertain the disposition to enter into the CT, without testing it in the open. A signal is supposed to reveal a disposition without incurring the costs of probing. Such costs, in an illegal realm, are evident. Mistakes can be severely punished by authorities. The signal is the trigger that sets the wheels of corruption in motion.[42] In Italy, political parties provided the solution to the communication problem.[43] Political parties would provide *social invisibility* for contacts as well as a safe place where the public official could address his 'demand for corruption' to the entrepreneur.

The signal of party affiliation was the crucial resource in the first stages of the corruption market in Italy. A crucial by-product of using such a form of signalling should be analysed. The party has property rights over the signal, monitoring membership and utilisation of its label. When faced with a CO from its own ranks, the party has two choices: either to throw the CO out, or to claim part of the income that will accrue to the actors involved in the CT. In case the party follows the latter course of action, it will scrutinise the performance of the CO as a collector of illicit funds. To the extent that the performance is considered to be positive, COs will receive party support throughout their career. Careers are important for CO because the more they rise up the career ladder, the greater their opportunities for raising illegal funds. Such a vicious circle will bring the party to grant its label only to the most obedient and efficient COs.

This will in turn increase the party's income. These newly acquired financial resources coming from the illegal market may be invested in further augmenting the number of loyal party members it can place in crucial public offices. This has been the case in Italy, in the form of what has come to be called *lottizzazione*, or 'allotment', whereby all aspects of the public sphere, from senior jobs in state-owned banks to the political control of RAI, the state broadcasting organisation, are parcelled out among the parties.[44]

Permeability of state institutions to party influence is the crucial factor for understanding the nature of Italian corruption. It is also crucial for accounting for the diffusion of corruption *Italian style*. The more the political parties control state institutions and influence their decisions, the greater will be the role of the parties. Holding the opportunities for corruption constant, corruption will infiltrate a given social system depending on its institutional framework. The weaker the institutions of state are in comparison with parties and lobbies, the greater the chances are that corruption will spread.

So far we have tried to explain how the market of corruption is born and why it grows. What needs to be explained now is the fact that the market of corruption was intrinsically frail, which goes a long way towards explaining its self-destruction. The key to the analysis that follows is the following point: corruption spreads as long as the population converges to a new equilibrium point which yields a superior pay-off. When this equilibrium point fails to materialise, the market collapses.

A process of learning enables the 'honest' population – which was once blind to signals – to realize that a certain correlation holds between signals and success in the tender, hence more members will try to recognise and respond to the signal. This model holds for Italy, where dishonesty proved to be a more efficient strategy for a number of reasons. Bribes were only *apparently* paid by the entrepreneur, whereas in fact the collectivity paid for it. The cost of the public work would rise enormously during the process of production (*in corso d'opera*). Thus the entrepreneur was able to discharge the kickback paid to the party on the state finances, by claiming that costs had increased in the meantime. On the other hand the state bodies would deliver as long as the entrepreneur had duly paid the kickback. As a result the kickbacks were in effect paid by all tax payers – who saw their taxes rise – and by public service users – who experienced inefficiencies and delays. Ricolfi vividly makes the point:

> All too often one forgets that the *kill* was made by the entrepreneurs rather than the politicians. While the latter only retained a percentage on the value of the production orders between 1 and 10 per cent, the former either were selling their products at prices well above the market rate or allowed to claim higher production costs.[45]

Ricolfi adds that the price for the contracts awarded after 1993 (when presumably no kickbacks were paid) was roughly *half* than in the past. This means that before 1993 it was *double* the market price. Who was pocketing the difference? The entrepreneur, of course, who paid back to the parties only a small fraction. The deal was very tempting: 'I get 10 and pay [to the parties] 1'. It was an offer nobody could refuse.[46]

The more corruption spreads, the less the need for the *invisibility* offered by the party. Gradually, the need for invisibility becomes superfluous, because it is common knowledge among all those taking part in the tender that an illegal, alternative system is operating. As bargaining becomes explicit and openly carried out in the public officials' office, party affiliation will no longer be a *secret* signal among a few corrupted entrepreneurs and COs in a generally honest society. Instead, entrepreneurs will openly pay parties by paying the single CO. The CO will in turn split these illegal incomes with the party.

A major increase in the level of corruption increases the number of people who collect kickbacks.[47] There are two aspects of this phenomenon worth considering. First, it is important to emphasise that contrary to the basic laws of economics, an increase in supply of COs does not bring about a reduction in the price of the kickback. In other words, the cost of each kickback will not be reduced under a more extensive level of corruption, as one would expect. The opposite is, in fact, the case. The cost of each kickback will not decrease because there is no competition among the suppliers. The market for bribes is characterised by the fact that a public official has a monopoly over the resources he controls. There are no substitutes for his services. The citizen or the entrepreneur cannot 'shop around' until they find somebody offering a competitive price for the service. He is forced to always buy from the same supplier. The increase in the number of COs does not increase the supply of people who offer the same service. A CO in a competitive market for bribes would be a price taker. On the contrary, the monopolist CO sets the price.[48]

Secondly, the expansion in the number of people who collect kickbacks will produce an enforcement and a coordination problem within each party. Given that the party ceases to act as the provider of invisibility, how is it going to make sure that the corrupt officials will not bypass the party and pocket the kickback? The more corruption spreads, the greater will be the CO's independence from the party structure. He-or-she may still split the illegal incomes with the party, but at this point the money may be used as resources in the internal party-faction struggles, rather than simply to enrich the party coffers. For example there is conclusive evidence to suggest that this was a realistic concern for the Socialist party.[49] The leader of the PSI, Bettino Craxi, was terrified that kickbacks would end up in the wrong pockets. Craxi himself has made this point absolutely clear in a revealing book, *Il Caso C.* (The C. Affair), where he explains how different groups and centres of power within the PSI were increasingly able to escape the checks set up by the party's central headquarters to monitor both their means of providing self-financing and the political line being taken on key issues.[50]

In order to ensure that local party officials would not bypass the centre, a process of centralisation in the collection of kickbacks took place. This process took two forms. Major firms were invited to pay their kickback directly to the national headquarters of certain political parties.[51] Alternatively, the process of centralisation was enforced by tightening the control within the party structure between the centre and periphery. These changes are well documented for the PSI under Craxi. A number of people, loyal to Craxi, were assigned the role of collecting kickbacks and had to report directly to the Chief. In the last years of Craxi's reign, he made a rather successful effort to increase the chances that the money paid to the party would in fact reach the party's coffers, rather than being lost in the pockets of party officials around the country. In order to do so, entrepreneurs were asked to pay a lump sum each year to the party. Such a sum would allow them to enter into tenders, rather than pay a kickback on each contract they obtained.[52]

So far we have described some mechanisms that made it possible to reach an equilibrium where corruption was pervasive. What remains to be explained is how and why at a certain point the entrepreneurial pay-offs of staying in the market of corruption changed. It was asserted before that the reason why people involved in exchanges of corruption testified cannot be explained simply in terms of the methods used by the Milan magistrates in the conduct of their investigations. In what follows, the basic assumptions of an alternative explanation will be provided, grounded on the general frailty of the market of corruption, focusing on the nature of the good which was used to pay the kickback and on the implications for the entrepreneurs in terms of their financial resources.

The evolution of the market amounted to a specialisation process. Transaction mechanisms evolved so that actors could obtain (or steal) the greatest amount of resources in the most efficient way. The specialisation process produced an 'optimal' adaptation to the environment. On the other hand, however, individual actors became more vulnerable to sudden outside shocks, such as delays in state payments of contracts. The bribe was efficiently collected but the delivery of state funds to overcome the cost of bribing became increasingly slow. An increase in specialisation amounts to a reduction of flexibility as far as environment changes are concerned. It was the lack of flexibility that brought an end to the market of corruption.

Who will be the first victims of the reduced flexibility of the system? The nature of the product sold by the enterprise will affect its ability to endure the costs of corruption. For example, a company selling infrastructure will be in a different position from one selling information. A company operating in the media sector, such as Berlusconi's Fininvest, sells a good that is demanded and highly priced by the political class as well. This enables the company to pay for the kickback *in kind*, by charging reduced prices for political advertising, inviting politicians to talk-shows, or giving preferential treatment in 'serious' news programmes. The ability to pay for a kickback *in kind* rather than in monetary form has the added advantage that it does not weigh negatively on the finances of the company.

After all, a television channel must still produce television programmes. In financial terms, the decision to give greater prominence to a certain politician rather than another has a marginal cost equal to (almost) zero. Having the opportunity to pay kickbacks in kind has also the virtue of not incurring penal risks, as Ricolfi rightly points out. By paying in kind, actual money transactions are reduced and so is the risk of being investigated by magistrates. This should explain why Berlusconi's Fininvest empire has so far escaped investigations into the granting of air-waves rights. A widespread belief among Italians is that the faithful support given by Berlusconi to Craxi's PSI was paid back by Craxi's government through a number of favourable government decrees, such as the Legge Mammí.[53] It was no accident that Berlusconi's subsequent troubles were with the *Guardia di Finanza* (Italy's special tax-inspectorate police force), since the latter could not be paid in kind (that is with granting TV time) but only in cash (see Chapter 9).

On the contrary, a seller of goods such as hospital needles or cleaning services cannot pay in kind; the kickback has to be paid in cash. This increases the financial risks to the entrepreneur, who becomes exposed to the schedule of payment by the public authorities of the public contract. In fact it is only after the public contract is fully paid that the entrepreneur will be in a position to recover the previous investment made in the form of a kickback. The schedule of payment for public contracts *vis-à-vis* liquidity becomes crucial. The private entrepreneur has to advance large sums of money. The less he or she can count on a sound liquidity situation, the more exposed they are towards the banking system. For the entrepreneur, the fact that the payment of his work by the public authorities is not delayed becomes of crucial importance. Unfortunately for the Italian entrepreneurs involved in the market of corruption, that was not the case in Italy, where the public administration is often in the red.

The increasing slowness of the state to pay for public works hit the smallest and most vulnerable companies more severely than larger companies. Not all companies were able to sustain paying for the increasing cost of kickbacks, when there was a delay in the payment for the work already accomplished. The companies that had a sound financial base, hence facing fewer problems of liquidity, were in a better position to weather the storm while the payments were being delayed. The same does not apply for those firms who are constantly struggling, and who are overstretched by accepting a kickback of 7 per cent or even 10 per cent.

These entrepreneurs who would have been marginal to the system would have started to lose out considerably. The system was becoming increasingly predatory, rather than 'fair'. It should then not come as a surprise that the first defectors were in fact liquidity-stricken small businesses, such as that of Luca Magni, the man who incriminated Mario Chiesa in the first major corruption scandal of the *Mani pulite* investigations (see Chapter 3). These were companies that could not successfully *exit* from the local market, hence the market of corruption, and compete internationally. They were highly dependent on public contracts and, at the same time, were not in a position to pay the kickback in kind. It is here that the frailty of the market of corruption is most apparent, which may explain why its internal contradictions eventually undermined the extensive, pervasive and deep-rooted system of corruption.

A further question worth mentioning is why confessions occurred first and foremost in Milan rather than in other parts of Italy, such as Sicily or Campania, where corruption was just as widespread. The point cannot be discussed at length, but is related to the presence of organised crime. In the *mezzogiorno*, organised crime led by the mafia and the camorra has actively participated in organising the market of corruption.[54] In these contexts, organised crime would supply a crucial resource that was not so readily available in the North: credible violent threat to people (politicians and entrepreneurs alike) who wanted to defect from the system. In Palermo alone, 34 entrepreneurs and 78 shopkeepers were assassinated by the mafia between 1978 and 1987.[55]

CONCLUSION

In this chapter we have looked at the dominant explanations of the phenomenon of corruption in Italy, from its origins to its collapse in 1992. We found the political and cultural/moral explanations wanting, while the legal explanation is important but incomplete. In particular, we have questioned the widely held belief that the success of the *Mani pulite* investigation can be attributed exclusively to the skills of the Milanese magistrates. Instead we have argued that the success of the investigations into corruption in Milan was, at least in part, a question of luck.

In order to substantiate our analysis, we suggested that an adequate framework for understanding the success of the *Mani pulite* investigation ought to start from an analysis of the internal logic of the market of corruption. In particular, the spectacular success of the investigations may have something to do with the fragility of the market of corruption itself. The more the market of corruption grew, the more fragile it became, until eventually the equilibrium point could no longer be secured. As a result, the pay-offs of many individuals changed for the worse. It was this change in pay-offs that induced many individuals to exit the market of corruption altogether; in these circumstances, exiting took the form of spontaneous confessions to the investigating magistrates.

While such a narrow, parsimonious, 'economising' analysis of the collapse of the market of corruption does not concentrate so much on the role of the magistrates, we do not mean to suggest that these two forms of explanation are mutually exclusive. The point is not to deny that the magistrates played an important role in what is undoubtedly one of the most striking episodes in Italy's recent history. Rather, the argument has been that the pool of magistrates were fortunate to be conducting their investigations at a time when their efforts coincided with the changing pay-offs of the individuals they were investigating. It was 'rational' for entrepreneurs to engage in corrupt activity in a party-mediated market, until such time as it ceased to be 'rational', irrespective of any appreciation of the public interest or the common good. This conclusion may be a disillusioning one for democrats – but it aptly accounts for the way in which the political parties behaved and what they had become.

Notes

1. By *Mani pulite* we refer to the investigative magistrates (*sostituti procuratori della Repubblica*) of the Milanese pool, which included G. D'Ambrosio (coordinator), G. Colombo, P. Davigo, P.Ielo and A. Di Pietro. Their immediate superior was S. Borrelli (*procuratore della Repubblica*). *Tangentopoli* (*tangente* – bribe) was the expression coined about Milan to describe the substance of those investigations.
2. J. Chubb and M. Vannicelli, 'Italy: a web of scandals in a flawed democracy', in A.S. Markovits and M. Silverstein (eds), *The Politics of Scandal – Power and Process in Liberal Democracies* (1988), p.138.
3. See especially H.W. Kilz and J. Preuss, *Flick – Die Gekaufte Republik* (1984); K.D. Ewing, *Money, Politics and Law* (1992). See also the journal *Corruption and Reform*.
4. For an account of the difficulties associated with defining corruption, see A. Gardiner, 'Defining corruption' in *Corruption and Reform* (1992).

5.   J. Chubb and M. Vannicelli, op. cit. (1987). For an historical account
     of corruption in Italy, see J.-C. Waquet, 'Some considerations on cor-
     ruption, politics and society in 16th and 17th century Italy', in
     W. Little and E. Posada-Carbo (eds), *Political Corruption in Europe and
     Latin America* (1996); for more recent events, S. Turone, *Politica Ladra:
     storia della corruzione in Italia, 1861–1992* (1992).
6.   Comment cited by C. Richards, 'Milan scandal moves closer to Italy's
     leaders', in *The Independent*, 13 June 1992, p.11.
7.   For a definition of corruption along these lines, see J.S. Nye
     'Corruption and Political Development: A Cost-Benefit Analysis', in
     A.J. Heidenheimer *et al.* (eds), *Political Corruption: A Handbook* (1989).
8.   See Chapter 3, endnote 8.
9.   Summarised by P. Furlong 'Government stability and electoral
     systems: the Italian example', in *Parliamentary Affairs*, January 1991,
     pp.50–9.
10. D. Hine, 'Party, personality and the law: the political culture of corrup-
     tion in Italy', in P.N. Jones (ed.) *Party, Parliament and Personality*, (1995).
11. A. Glees, 'The Flick affair: a hint of corruption in the Bonn Republic',
     in *Corruption and Reform*, Vol. 2, 1987, pp.111–16.
12. The date of 1988 has been supplied by Di Pietro himself in
     E. Nascimbeni and A. Pamparana *Le Mani Pulite* (1992), p.16.
13. *Il Corriere della Sera*, 1 June 1992, p.13.
14. G. Neppi Modona, 'Tangenti e Mani pulite: dopo le indagni i
     processi', in P. Ginsborg (ed.), *Stato dell'Italia* (1994), pp.527–8,
     emphasis added.
15. Quoted in F. Sidoti, 'The Italian political class', in *Government and
     Opposition*, Summer 1993, p.346.
16. Even the payment of a bribe into a Swiss bank account can be verified
     only after the accused has provided magistrates with the name of the
     bank and the account number. See P. Davigo, 'I limiti del controllo
     penale sulla corruzione e i necessari rimedi preventivi', in D'Alberti
     and R. Finocchi (eds), *Corruzione e Sistema Istituzionale* (1994).
17. M. Andreoli, *Andavamo in Piazza Duomo* (1993); A. Pamparana, *Il
     Processo Cusani* (1994). There are also a number of publications
     valuable for reproducing extracts from court files, as in A. Carlucci,
     Tangentomani (1992); 'Tangentopoli, le carte che scottano', supple-
     ment to *Panorama*, February 1993; and 'Di Pietro, le sue inchieste',
     supplement to *Avvenimenti*, No.48.
18. D. della Porta, *Lo Scambio Occulto* (1992), especially the important
     introduction by A. Pizzorno.
19. E. Luttwak, 'Screw you', in *London Review of Books*, Vol.15 (1993), p.6.
     Luttwak goes on to claim that 'it all began very purposefully in the
     Fifties, when money was needed not for yachts and filial Ferraris but
     to resist the unique power of Italy's Communist party', p.6.
20. F. Sidoti, op. cit. (1993), p.349.
21. For a detailed overview of these longer-range factors, see
     M. Donovan's 'Corruption in Italy: A Dominant Reality', Working
     Paper, The Centre for Mediterranean Studies, University of Bristol.
22. S. Waters, 'Tangentopoli and the emergence of a new political order
     in Italy', in *West European Politics*, January 1994, pp.169–82;

P. McCarthy, 'Inching towards a new regime', in G. Pasquino and P. McCarthy (eds), *The End of Post-War Politics in Italy – The Landmark 1992 Elections* (1993) p.163.

23. E. Veltri, *Da Craxi a Craxi* (1993), p.244.

24. M. Calise, 'Remaking the Italian party system: how Lijphart got it wrong by saying it right', in *Western European Politics*, Vol.16 (1993) p.556.

25. D. Hine, op. cit. (1995).

26. Such as the configuration of the party system, the operation – until it was restricted in 1991 – of the preference vote, and the ineffectiveness of mechanisms of checking and control.

27. According to Donovan, op. cit. (working paper), the Catholic church held the view that the creation of an impersonal state based on the rule of law, and the corresponding political obligation which arises from this, is essentially an unachievable fantasy. It follows that 'such convictions created, and maintained, a situation in which political corruption was frequently not even perceived to be corrupt. Helping one's friends, not being stupid (*fesso*), ie. honest, over the payment of taxes or the observation of regulations, was common sense. A particularly Catholic common sense'.

28. G. Neppi-Modona, op. cit. (1994) p. 527

29. A. Pizzorno 'La corruzione nel sistema politico', introduction to D. della Porta, op. cit. (1992).

30. D. della Porta and A. Vannucci, 'Politics, the mafia and the market for corrupt exchange', in C. Mershon and G. Pasquino (eds), *Italian Politics – Ending the First Republic* (1995).

31. For a critique of sociological explanations based on the idea of culture, see B. Barry, *Sociologists, Economists and Democracy* (1970) p.180.

32. We are grateful to Federico Varese for this insight.

33. D. Laitin, 'The civic culture at thirty', in *The American Political Science Review* (1995) pp.168–73.

34. D. Nelken, 'A legal revolution? The judges and *Tangentopoli*', in S. Gundle and S. Parker (eds), *The New Italian Republic* (1996).

35. The reader is referred to M. Volcansek, 'Decision-making Italian style: the new code of criminal procedure', in *West European Politics*, Vol.13 (1990), and G. Colombo 'The new code of criminal procedure', in F. Sabetti and R. Catanzaro (eds), *Italian Politics: A Review*, Vol. 6 (1991) for fuller detail.

36. The new *avviso di garanzia* had replaced the old *comunicazione giudiziaria*, which was felt to have carried too great an implication of guilt. Preventative detention was only allowed on the decision of a judge not directly involved in a case, and only where it was thought that a suspect might interfere with evidence or take flight.

37. The institutional and political set-up of the Italian judiciary, and the impact of judicial actions on the Italian political system, is described in C. Guarnieri, *Magistratura e Politica* (1993).

38. B. Barry, 'Is it better to be powerful or lucky?', in *Democracy, Power and Justice: Essays in Political Theory* (1989).

39. In the words of Elster, 'an equilibrium point is a set of individual strategies each of which is optimal against the other': J. Elster, *Ulysses*

and the Sirens (1984) p.118. See also his *Nuts and Bolts for the Social Sciences* (1989).

40. We are grateful to Federico Varese for his help on this part of the chapter.

41. *Mani pulite* was mainly about entrepreneurs and public officials, though some lines of investigation were conducted into more trivial issues, such as the illegal issuing of driving licenses. We are limiting our discussion to the former category.

42. Path-breaking work in the economics of signalling was by A.M. Spence, *Market Signalling* (1974). Recently, more sophisticated work on signalling for inscrutable commodities can be found in D. Gambetta's 'Inscrutable markets' in *Rationality and Society*, July 1994.

43. For a brief account of the advantages associated with using party affiliation as a signal, see V. Bufacchi 'The success of "mani pulite": luck or skill?', in R. Leonardi and R. Nanetti (eds), *Italy: Politics and Policy* (1996). The role of political parties in the market of corruption is also discussed by D. della Porta 'Political parties and corruption: reflections on the Italian case', in *Modern Italy*, Vol.1, No.1, 1995.

44. In the case of RAI, what this meant was that the main television channel (RAI 1) was controlled by the Christian Democrats, the second channel (RAI 2) by the Socialists and the third, smaller channel (RAI 3) by the then Communists. The three channels had their own news programme, where the different political orientations were clear.

45. L. Ricolfi, *L'Ultimo Parlamento* (1993) pp.136–7.

46. Ibid. (1993), pp.136–7.

47. See J.C. Andvig and K.O. Moene, 'How corruption may corrupt', in *The Journal of Economic Behaviour and Organisation*, Vol.13, 1990, pp.63–76.

48. The moral costs for each agent on both the demand and the supply side will decrease as the incidence of corruption increases. As corruption becomes more widespread, there is no more shame in addressing the morally ambivalent issue of corruption, hence there is no longer any need to justify ideologically the 'demand' for corruption. The entrepreneur that did not accept the system of corruption could opt for the *exit* option. *Exit* implies either closing down the business altogether, or operating in markets outside the reach of COs (such as the international market for the same products, or by changing the sector of specialisation, moving as far as possible from sectors where public officials can ask for bribes). However, this option is not open to everybody: only very efficient firms could compete in the international markets, and to change sector implies investing a lot of capital in changing the process of production.

49. While in this chapter we will concentrate on the PSI as our case study, the same analysis probably applies to the Christian Democrats as well as to the other major parties involved in corrupt transactions.

50. B. Craxi, *Il Caso C.* (1994) pp.27, 38.

51.   This was admitted by Vincenzo Lodigiani, a prominent building constructor, during his trial. See 'Di Pietro: le sue inchieste', in *Avvenimenti*, No. 48, 1994, p.53.

52.   L. Ricolfi, op. cit. (1993) p.136.

53.   Although Berlusconi's Fininvest controlled 45 per cent of the market and 85 per cent of commercial television, thanks to the Mammí law passed in 1990 this was not judged to be an infringement of the anti-monopoly legislation. This law was challenged by a number of small televsion operators, and it was only at the beginning of December 1994 that the Constitutional Court ruled Berlusconi's Fininvest media empire unconstitutional.

54.   See See D. Gambetta's *The Sicilian Mafia* (1993) pp.214–20. The same point is made by D. della Porta and A. Vannucci, 'Politics, the mafia and the market for corrupt exchange', in C. Mershon and G. Pasquino (eds), *Italian Politics – Ending the First Republic* (1995) pp.165–85.

55.   U. Santino and G. La Fiura, *L'Impresa Mafiosa* (1990), p.400, quoted by D. della Porta and A. Vannucci, op. cit. (1995) p.182.

5 The Close of an Era (September 1992–April 1993)

The political events between 1989 and 1992 are a clear indication that particracy in Italy was being seriously challenged. The events which took place in the eight months from September to April 1993 confirm this trend. The traditional political parties were fighting for their life, while new political forces gained momentum. As the investigations on corruption in the North and the mafia in the South produced spectacular results, the political careers of established political figures like Bettino Craxi and Giulio Andreotti came to an abrupt end. More than any other event, the undignified departure of Craxi and Andreotti from the political scene signalled the end of an era. In a desperate attempt to come out of the ongoing political crisis, a popular referendum was mandated in April 1993 which, amongst other things, pushed for changes in the electoral system.

POLITICAL PARTIES ON THE ROPES

Voting patterns in the April 1992 general election had pointed to a collapse of popular confidence in the traditional governing parties. The scandals of corruption that followed all but destroyed the operational bases of the Italian party system. The parliamentary elites were unwilling or unprepared to embark on reform, even though the problems of the debt and the deficit could obviously be traced back to the coalitions of the late 1980s. Machine politics, instead of articulating and mobilising opinion, had evolved into the corrupt disbursement of public resources by, on one estimate, up to 130 000 party bureaucrats. The failure of the institutions of the Italian state was also widely regarded as a failure of the system of parties with which they were so closely identified.[1]

107

The Socialist party, the most seriously affected by the *Mani pulite* inquiry, was thrown into turmoil.[2] Craxi had attacked the professional probity of Di Pietro in August, complaining again of a plot and demanding a counter-inquiry, but the factional strains inside the party increased rather than diminished. Craxi's deputy, Claudio Martelli, compounded criticisms that the PSI had grown too close to the DC by his impatience to form an alliance with the PDS. Finally, on 30 October, he led the calls for Craxi to step down, and for a special party conference to be urgently convened. Craxi, still with sizeable support, would not be budged. Prime Minister Amato observed a diplomatic silence. While the leaders argued, the hard-up national and local organisation of the party began to disintegrate.[3]

The difficulties of the PDS were no less constraining. Marginalised by the fall in its core support, the party was also in danger of being outflanked by the more militant attitude of Communist Refoundation, which was finding favour among union activists. The PDS leader Achille Occhetto had it in mind to outline certain terms for the entry of the PDS into government that included a commitment to modifying the budget, but this strategy was unpopular with those on the left of the party, as well as with those moderates anxious to waste no time in building bridges with a purged and revitalised PSI. The lack of a clear lead left the party dangerously exposed to further inroads by the Northern League.

None of this could compare, however, with the electoral crumbling of the Christian Democrat party, struggling to recapture its organisational cohesion and sense of purpose. The Communist party enemy had disappeared, the dogma of Catholic unity had long been on the wane, but the DC had yet to adjust to the new threat posed by groups like the Northern League and, further South, an improving MSI. The election of a new general secretary, the respected Mino Martinazzoli,[4] and a new party president, Rosa Russo Jervolino, were indicative of an intention to renew the party's structure, aims and image, and even possibly change its name. Even so, it was unclear how much latitude Martinazzoli would be granted by party elders, or whether he could succeed in heading off the reforming surge of Mario Segni, who had already broken ranks by launching a popular reform movement for an 'honest Italy' that would – in competing with the Northern League – bring new people into politics and was making his continued membership of the DC dependent on how far it was ready to change. The essential problem for the new leadership was that, try as it might (and the past of Martinazzoli and the new president, Jervolino, were unimpeachably clean) their efforts to purify the DC were continually overtaken by succeeding scandals and arrests of national and now also local representatives. Indeed the toppling of incriminated town councils was only just beginning.

BOSSI GOES FROM STRENGTH TO STRENGTH

While the traditional parties disintegrated, new citizen-based protest movements were gaining ground. Of all the anti-system phenomena, the Northern League had, by the Autumn of 1992, done most in consolidating its hold on the minds of voters, prospering by its unique ability to draw support away from all other rivals, but not confined – like *La Rete* or the Greens – to a single-issue platform. Surveys pointed to the growing popularity of the Northern League among the young. In one poll taken in Milan,[5] more than 30 per cent of those in the under-24 age group declared their support. In an attempt to broaden the Northern League's geographical appeal, however, Bossi was contemplating the idea of replacing the aspiration for full autonomy with the less divisive-sounding (though equally nebulous) project of a federal Italy. Their persisting attack on the inefficiencies of the central state enabled the Northern League to pose as a rallying-point for all 'honest' Italians opposed to the immorality of the powerful.[6] 'We are the poison in the veins of the old parties', Bossi repeatedly boasted.

Local elections in Mantua in late September and in Varese and Monza in mid-December showed just how vulnerable the bedrock support of the governing coalition had become. In Mantua, coinciding with protests against the government's austerity package, the Northern League took almost 34 per cent of the vote, an increase of 12 per cent since the election in April and a near-trebling in support since 1990. The Christian Democrats – falling to 14 per cent – and the PSI to

7.2 per cent – lost practically half of their old electors. The PDS, down by three percentage points to 17.8 per cent, survived relatively unscathed. For the first time, the Northern League had inflicted a humiliating defeat on the DC in one of its own 'white' electoral heartlands, goading the latter into refusing to cooperate in forming a new council. The populist reach of the Northern League was undeniable; the implications of the anti-political mood for Italy's democratic future were far more disturbing.

THE FALL OF CRAXI

In the last week of January, the *Mani pulite* investigation achieved a decisive advance. More senior Socialist politicians were rounded up, including Giovanni Manzi, the former PSI provincial secretary and head of Milan airport, who had been in hiding in the Caribbean. Fresh *avvisi di garanzia* (formal notifications of investigation) were sent out to Craxi. Finally, there was a search and seizure of documents from the Rome headquarters of the PSI, causing Craxi to say that everyone active in politics was being 'criminalised' by the judiciary.

Amato, Italy's socialist prime minister, refused to attend a crisis meeting of the party's executive, insisting that the PSI's predicament must not be allowed to jeopardise the government's survival. A threat by Craxi to pull the party out of the coalition was at first floated and then denied. Then, on 7 February, Di Pietro travelled to Ventimiglia on the French border to take into custody the architect and party fixer, Silvano Larini, wanted for questioning since June 1992.

Larini spent four days being grilled by Di Pietro, revealing his role as the unofficial treasurer of the PSI and admitting that a celebrated secret bank account (codenamed 'Protezione') with the Union des Banques Suisses in Lugano was held in his name and was used for depositing party funds since 1970. It was into this account that $7m had been paid by the Banco Ambrosiano in 1981 shortly before the bank collapsed and its president, Roberto Calvi, was found dead in London. Larini said that he had personally taken approximately between 7000m and 8000m *lire* (£3.5m) in bribes to Craxi's own office in the four years from 1987 to 1991 as part of a regular and extensive transfer of payments made by prominent industrialists in order to secure business for their companies.[7] On 10 February Craxi and Martelli received notices of investigation for complicity in the bankruptcy of the Banco Ambrosiano. The next day Martelli – the first serving cabinet minister to be drawn into the 'clean hands' inquiry – resigned as justice minister and gave up his membership of the Socialist party, stating that he wanted the chance to clear his name. Finally, on 12 February, after 16 years of uncontested leadership and no fewer than six separate judicial investigations pending, Bettino Craxi paid the highest price and announced to the PSI national congress in Rome that he was giving up as leader.

THE WEEK OF FIRE

The resignation of Craxi as leader of the PSI was only the beginning. In the 'week of fire' which the Milanese magistrates had promised would follow, there were two further cabinet casualties. Giovanni Goria, the finance minister and ex-prime minister, was the victim of renewed stories about his involvement in bribe-taking in the building of a hospital in Asti. Similarly the health minister, Francesco De Lorenzo, of the Liberal Party, already accused of vote buying in his home base of Naples, stood down for 'personal reasons' after the arrest of his father on corruption charges. More cautionary warrants were also served on Gianni de Michelis, ensnared in the illegal diversion of overseas aid during his time as foreign minister, who only eluded an irate Venetian crowd by leaping onto a gondola. These were in addition to the resignation of five under-secretaries, the arrests of the head of the Socialist group in the Chamber of Deputies and of the former press spokesman of Arnaldo Forlani, and an *avviso di garanzia* sent to Raul Gardini,[8] one of Italy's leading industrialists, in connection with the short-lived Enimont joint venture of 1989-90.[9]

De Lorenzo's departure was particularly awkward, since Amato's failure to speak up in his defence provoked the 17 Liberal Deputies to consider pulling out of the government (which had a paper majority of 16) – a threat which eventually came to nothing. 'Italy needs a government, it has a government, and this government will continue', Amato told the Senate, 'it can't be governed by a vacuum'.[10] But, unable to broaden the composition of the coalition, he carried through a mini-reshuffle during the weekend of 20–21 February, bringing in three new, party-affiliated technocrats.

The prime minister was criticised by party leaders for the lack of consultation over the changes, with Martinazzoli refusing to recognise Baratta's new post, but Amato was adamant that he had had to act swiftly before the markets reopened, indicating how insecure his administration still was. Irked by the reaction to the reshuffle, Amato decided to call for a fresh vote of confidence in the Chamber, arguing that having to operate in a state of permanent uncertainty was damaging to jobs, to the *lira* (which by that stage had lost 30 per cent of its value relative to the Deutschmark) and to the community. The early signs were that discontented elements in the Christian Democrat and Socialist parties would not fall into line, unhappy that Amato had established too great a degree of independence from party control. Even before the vote was held, there were still more shocks: the detaining of two senior Fiat executives on charges of corruption; the resignation of the Republican party leader, Giorgio La Malfa; the placing under house arrest of Giampiero Pesenti (president of the *Italmobiliere* construction company); and the suicide of Sergio Castellari, a senior official in the Ministry of State Participation who was due to be questioned about his knowledge of the Enimont affair. Notwithstanding the adverse circumstances, Amato persevered in his path, and in what he described as 'the most dramatic and difficult days of the Republic', he gave a stout defence of the need to create the privatisation portfolio, and by the surprisingly wide margin of 310 votes to 265 (with 3 abstentions) the confidence motion was passed.

RIINA'S CAPTURE

It was not just the gathering momentum behind the *Mani pulite* and similar inquiries on corruption, taking in by October 70 MPs and involving an estimated L4000b in bribes and kickbacks, that damaged the traditional parties. There was also, in the last quarter of 1992, an extension of judicial probing into new areas, a change of direction that also indicated a momentous change in the character of what exactly was being investigated. The issue no longer centred only or mainly on the relatively narrow question of the illicit funding of the political parties. The wider pattern of politics and business was being opened up to scrutiny, symbolised by the arrest of Florio Fiorini, the former financial director of ENI, and by the questioning of the former chief executive of the Ferruzzi–Montedison conglomerate, Giuseppe Garofano, about the payment of what he called a large 'personal gift' he had made to a senior DC official in Lombardy for the party's election war chest. More damagingly still, a breakthrough was being made in the far more delicate realm of politico-mafia collusion, and of long-suspected links between the political and the criminal fraternity which hitherto had remained obscure. Those accused of filling their own or their party's pockets had, apologists could claim, acted irregularly but hardly immorally. The newer line of investigation was, by contrast, laying bare the exercise of power itself.

This latest turn of events came about as a direct result of the security clampdown against criminal activity initiated in the wake of the murders of Falcone and Borsellino, and of a new determination on the part of the authorities to centralise and coordinate the anti-mafia war. In mid-September, the three Cuntrera brothers, whom Falcone had identified as the organisers of a major drug smuggling and money laundering syndicate, were detained on their arrival at Rome airport after being deported from Venezuela. Furthermore at the end of the month, 'Operation Green Ice' (launched in conjunction with the US Drug Enforcement Agency) climaxed with the breaking up of mafia links with important Colombian drug cartels, and the capture of senior members of the Corleone gang. Substantial rewards were also offered for information about the most wanted mafia bosses. Much of this progress was owing to the large number of *pentiti* (supergrasses) – 52 in a matter of months – who had decided to turn state's evidence and implicate others, their conversion encouraged by the fierce internecine mafia war led by Riina that was in progress.[11]

What was also new, however, was their readiness to talk about the mafia's political involvement, especially over recent matters. The first fruits of this were made public in a report by the magistrate looking into the murder of Salvo Lima, which – on the basis of evidence from four *pentiti* – accused mafia chiefs of ordering Lima's assassination after he had failed to fix the outcome of the main maxi-trial of *mafiosi* convicted in January 1992. Lima was not himself a 'man of honour', one of the witnesses asserted, but was very close to the *Cosa Nostra* and acted as their intermediary with Giulio Andreotti. The claim that there was a direct chain linking the *Cosa Nostra*, Lima, and Andreotti was supported in a newspaper interview in *The New York Times* by Tommaso Buscetta (who played a key role in the maxi-trials of the 1980s and was now held under protection in the United States). Although Andreotti had already denied that there was any substance to the claims in advance, they were grave enough for the parliamentary anti-mafia commission to open a fuller inquiry, and this despite the opposition on the committee of many DC members.

When Buscetta appeared in person before the commission on 16 November, he added fuel to the flames by suggesting that it was the mafia that used politicians and not the other way around. Additionally, Buscetta revealed that some judges had also collaborated in fixing mafia trials, and that – without mentioning any names – a high-level plan had been devised to assassinate General Carlo Alberto Dalla Chiesa as early as *in 1979* (Dalla Chiesa was assassinated in 1982), when he was still pursuing the Moro case and long before he was sent to Sicily to combat the mafia, Buscetta cryptically adding because the General was 'inconvenient for the state and inconvenient for a particular politician'. Lima would have been killed on the orders of senior mafia figures so as to 'denigrate' Giulio Andreotti by depriving him of votes and prestige. Ignazio Salvo (shot dead in September 1992) was eliminated for the same reason. According to Buscetta, the mafia was in its death throes; now was the time to strike.

Mafia testimony had a further effect with 'Operation Leopard', carried out later in the same week, which landed over 200 suspects, including local politicians, officials and business-men, on charges of bribery, extortion and electoral corruption.

Licio Gelli, the former Grand Master of the subversive P-2 masonic lodge, was finally ordered to stand trial, while a variety of Calabrian 'Ndrangheta-related activities were being investigated by Judge Agostino Cordova. In a first 'political' case of its kind, the prosecution began of several politicians and *mafiosi* said to have conspired to murder, in 1989, the one-time DC MP and head of the state railways, Lodovico Ligato.

The anti-mafia drive was crowned by the startling capture on 15 January of the mafia don 'Totó' Riina, who had been on the run since 1969 and had already been condemned in his absence to life imprisonment, as well as being implicated in the murders of Falcone and Borsellino. Police arrested one Baldassare Di Maggio – who turned out to have been Riina's former driver – on a minor charge in Turin, and he had volunteered information about Riina's precise whereabouts, including a list of his mafia associates. Riina was picked up at a traffic checkpoint on the outskirts of Palermo during the morning rush hour. He had false identification papers on him but was unarmed and made no attempt to escape. After his arrest, he was flown by helicopter to the high security Rebibia prison in Rome for questioning. The location of his home – on a secure private estate – was allegedly discovered a few days later. According to press reports, Riina told magistrates that he was just a simple book-keeper employed in a shipyard, denying point blank – as he did later on in his first court appearance – that he had ever heard of the mafia. But it also transpired that Riina had in fact been under close surveillance by a special team of *carabinieri* for five months (since shortly after Falcone's death), following his every movement and filming his meetings with as many as 200 *eccelenti*, among them 'a politician at the highest level',[12] and that he had a been active during that time in a Sicilian masonic lodge. Publication of these details did nothing to quell speculation that Riina may have decided to give himself up, or that his capture had been suspiciously easy.

What the arrest of Riina did do was to throw open the whole issue of political connivance with organised criminal activity, a central theme of the anti-mafia commission report which appeared in April.[13] The report, trusting to the veracity of the mafia supergrasses, spoke of the climate of 'cohabitation' between the mafia, the governing class and the institutions of government which had grown up after the war and which had created and sustained the political, economic and social conditions favourable to mafia interests. Such collusion, involving elements of the police and the carabinieri, the courts and the communal, regional and national assemblies was not just at the lower levels, but went to the very top, establishing 'a logic of pure convenience' which enabled lawbreakers to act with impunity. The party of the relative majority – the DC – and its political allies had agreed a 'non-aggression pact' (in the phrase of the head of the commission, Luciano Violante)[14] with organised crime. There were, as a consequence, two distinct and sovereign powers – with the mafia a parallel power to that of the state – which had compromised the openness and integrity of modern Italy. Italy's limited external sovereignty, as a frontier democracy in the Cold War, was conjoined to its internally compromised postwar political settlement.

The point was that these power relations were in the process of changing. New objective circumstances, such as the fall of Communism, the uncovering of *Tangentopoli* and a new mood of popular revulsion at mafia killings, were helping in the moves to reconstruct the political system now taking place. As leading mafia commentators pointed out, the first-ever official report into the mafia and politics was a document of the first importance.

For all these reasons, the arrest of Riina can be regarded as a critical watershed. The newly coordinated anti-mafia campaign (with the full assistance of the American FBI) meant that any progress made was no longer only down to the courage of individual judges, even though there were still complaints to be heard about the continuing obstructiveness of the Justice Ministry, and a widespread feeling that the old political notables were not behind this campaign. Revelations of the political dimension of mafia crime finally put paid to the misconception that it was somehow only a matter of public order, with no wider significance. Buscetta's theorem of a highly structured, highly organised system of mafia enterprise gained broader acceptance. The political cover of the 'polimafia' was being stripped away by public outrage and a new political will.

THE FALL OF ANDREOTTI

The 'explosion' of *Tangentopoli* came late to the South,[15] but it now struck with devastating effect. In an atmosphere of increasing alarm, with assaults on the integrity of the President (Borrelli had to deny that Scalfaro was caught up in any past corrupt behaviour) and loose talk of a *coup d'état*, the Christian Democrat power base in Southern Italy began falling to judicial examination. Much was due to the voluntary collaboration of two key witnesses – the Camorra turncoat, Pasquale Galasso, who revealed the existence of a Neapolitan 'business committee' of politicians and mafia, and the first political *pentito*, the MP Alfredo Vito, popularly known as 'Mr 100 000 votes' but now apparently full of remorse.[16]

'Gentlemen', Vito told judges, 'you have before you the collector of kickbacks for the DC in Naples'. Claiming that bribery was present 'in every corner of society', he called on other colleagues to follow his example. Pursuing more than fifteen separate lines of inquiry[17] and carrying out hundreds of arrests, cautionary warrants were sent to a number of prominent politicians (among them Antonio Gava, Paolo Cirino Pomicino, Vincenzo Meo and Raffaele Mastrantuono)[18] associated with the local power structure and suspected of involvement in a dovetailing history of political patronage and criminal enterprise. The judges explained that in each case of bribery, embezzlement and intimidation, they had also found a link with organised crime, in what many businessmen had referred to as a 'pact of mutual solidarity' between the political class and the *Camorra*.

Having 'invaded' the institutions and paralysed their working, the same political groups had presented themselves as the only ones capable of solving the individual or social problems for which they were originally responsible, such that voting in Campania did not signify consensus so much as recognition of the right to rule.[19] The relationship between those allied to Gava and the recently arrested *Camorra* boss Carmine Alfieri was not, however, one of equality – 'it is not I who invites the politicians', Alfieri was supposed to have once said, 'it is they who invite themselves at election time ... I don't guarantee anything to anyone'.[20]

The scandal of scandals broke on 27 March, when Giulio Andreotti, life Senator, seven times prime minister and the personification of the old regime, announced to the press that he was under investigation for 'mafia-type association' and for acting in Rome as the political reference of the Sicilian *Cosa Nostra*. Based on the cross-confirming interrogations of various *pentiti* – one of whom said that Andreotti was known affectionately as *lo zio* (uncle) in mafia circles[21] – the evidence had been collected over a nine-month period and assembled by magistrates in Palermo in a 243-page deposition to the Senate, signed by Judge Gian Carlo Caselli,[22] asking for permission to proceed.

Andreotti was quick to denounce the 'absurd' hearsay, suggesting that it was part of an orchestrated mafia plot in revenge for all the anti-mafia legislation he had introduced in his time, and he vowed that he would fight the lifting of his immunity from prosecution. Mario Segni, along with his closest DC supporters, promptly left the Christian Democrat party, finally convinced that the attempt to purify it was hopeless. The prime minister, disorientated by losing Reviglio on 30 March (the sixth minister to resign in as many weeks), drew comparisons with the defeated and disillusioned atmosphere of 8 September 1943 – the date of the signing of the armistice – and he put the government at the President's disposal.

With the date of a popular referendum looming (18–19 April),[23] Scalfaro turned his efforts to constructing a stronger parliamentary majority to see the country through the next three weeks until the referenda, while reiterating that the magistracy must be allowed to follow up its inquiries in complete freedom. The only promise he could secure was one from the PDS that it was prepared to join a post-referenda coalition of national emergency. A further notice of investigation against Andreotti and the DC secretariat Arnaldo Forlani, for illegal party financing arrived from Milan on 5 April. Although the latter alluded to a judicial conspiracy to undermine the party, there was a limit as to how far they could prudently press their complaints.

The impact of this latest development, heightened by the convening of hearings into the evidence against Andreotti by a Senate committee, almost entirely overshadowed the final days of campaigning for the referenda. When the full text of the submission by the Palermo magistrates was published in a booklet by *Panorama* magazine, it sold out in hours. Most of the testimony confirmed the details that had already been circulating, pertaining to Andreotti's relations with Salvo Lima, the Salvo cousins and the 'manoeuvrable' Appeal Court judge, Corrado Carnevale. Furthermore the text referred to Andreotti's interest in the murders of a journalist, Mino Pecorelli, in 1979, and of General Dalla Chiesa in 1982, both of whom were thought to know too much about the circumstances surrounding the failure to obtain the release of Aldo Moro from the Red Brigades.

But new material was also added at a late stage, based on fresh depositions by Buscetta and another supergrass in the United States, Marino Mannoia, directly involving Andreotti in three 'summit' meetings with senior mafia figures said to concern political killings and trial-adjusting. After one meeting, Mannoia recalled being told that Stefano Bontade (a Mafia godfather) had warned Andreotti that 'in Sicily it is we who give the orders, and if you don't want Christian Democracy to disappear altogether do as we say, otherwise we will take away all your votes in Sicily, as well as in Reggio Calabria and all of the South. That will only leave you the North, and there they all vote Communist ...'[24] Andreotti's ties to the mafia, the documents concluded, were of a 'multiform' and 'non-episodic' kind, aimed at organising and regulating the economy of western Sicily and 'conditioning' the judicial process in the service of his political allies, providing disturbing evidence (together with the information gleaned from other inquiries) of the conscious participation of representatives of the post-war Italian state in 'grand criminality'.[25]

In his defence, Andreotti made much of the lack of hard proof, questioning the motives of the supergrasses and pointing out that he never travelled anywhere without tight police protection, never having been in Sicily except for official engagements. By freely distributing copies of the allegations to the press, the magistrates were accused of an 'intent to persecute'. But as experts pointed out, surveillance and telephone tapping were not enough; the main evidence against the mafia could only come from *mafiosi*. Andreotti's weak point was not his enemies but his former friends.[26]

A 'POLITICAL SOLUTION' TO *TANGENTOPOLI,* AND ITS DEFEAT

The fact of widespread corruption had never been in doubt; the sheer extent of *Tangentopoli* – taking in over 30 other 'bribe cities' apart from Milan – was beyond the belief of even well-informed *aficionados.* More than 1000 politicians and business figures were, by March 1993, under investigation. Tens of thousands of party bureaucrats were implicated. The parliamentary immunity against prosecution of 75 Deputies and Senators had been lifted. Large swathes of public administration and private industry had functioned in a distorted market of entry fees, commissions, inflated costs and reduced competition. Depending on how the calculation was arrived at, the parties had been extorting anything from L3.4b to L5b a year[27] in illicit funds, equivalent to one-tenth of Italy's state deficit, with an unknown amount going towards private aggrandisement.

'We are not confronted with isolated instances of corruption: the entire system was like that, from Milan to Sicily', said one of those who had confessed, the Christian Democrat Roberto Mongini; '… it was the Italian way of doing things.'[28] The more the judicial whirlwind proceeded, so, in scenes reminiscent from 'Z' (the 1960s film of Costa Gavras), the more the investigations multiplied, blurring any distinction between an 'honest' and a 'dishonest' Italy. Gherardo Colombo, one of the milanese magistrates, even suggested that the investigations on corruption in Milan, *Mani pulite,* had become a well without a bottom. To many it came as encouraging proof of the necessary assertion of the rule of law, with opinion polls showing a large majority hoping that the 'positive' work of Di Pietro and his colleagues would go the whole way. The practical difficulties involved in handling so many cases and the moral question of individual guilt in a corrupt environment gave rise to the much larger problem of the proper relationship that the judiciary should have with the political branch of government.

Because of the sheer scale of wrongdoing being uncovered, a rough consensus began to take shape towards the end of February, shared by many party leaders (Martinazzoli, Occhetto, Bossi), some of the overworked and exhausted magistrates and even, from comments he made, the President, around the idea of a 'political solution' to the corruption investigations – a solution, in other words, that would distinguish between different degrees of guilt and help to accelerate the judicial process. In particular, it had been suggested that those who had flouted the law on party financing, but not personally gained from it, should not be subjected to the disgrace of preventative detention. To this end, the new justice minister, Giovanni Conso (a former president of the Constitutional Court), took the lead in talks between politicians and judicial officials about a new legal framework, including a proposed decree-law depenalising violations of the 1974 law on the financing of political parties, making it an administrative offence or irregularity rather than a crime, subject to the sanction that, if culprits confessed, they would have to repay the sum three times over and be barred from public office for up to five years. In cases of future corruption, a similar arrangement for plea bargaining would apply, to be dealt with by government-appointed regional prefects. A decree was also envisaged introducing tighter guidelines covering the distribution of public sector contracts, which would also allow for the unfreezing of existing, currently blocked agreements.

Approved by a parliamentary committee on 2 March, the depenalising decree (with its heavy overtones of Catholic guilt and repentance) came under heavy attack from the head of the *Mani pulite* team, Borrelli, who said that all the judges were adamantly opposed to any political settlement that might override legal sanctions, hinting that the decree was only a way for the political class to save their own skins. The proposal to remove detention on remand (which was primarily intended to prevent tampering with evidence or flight from justice but had been so successful in getting suspects to talk) was especially unpopular. The investigations, it was said, were being neutralised just as they were reaching 'the danger level'. When the Council of Ministers discussed the measures on 5 March, the proposal to abolish detention on remand was dropped but, after an 18-hour discussion, the decision was made to otherwise press ahead and issue the decree laws, to come into force the moment they were published.

The parliamentary, press and public response was one of fury at the granting of what was widely seen as 'an amnesty for those who had pillaged this country' (Occhetto). One cabinet member, Carlo Ripa di Meana, resigned in anger, making it clear that in his view the government had lost all touch with opinion at large. Even the Christian Democrats officially cooled to the idea. Concerned that the politicians would try to hide behind the judiciary, one of the *Mani pulite* pool of magistartes put things bluntly: 'The political class in power has absolved itself, by itself. Don't let's hear them say that we, the judges, asked for this'.[29] Conso, taken aback, admitted that the author of the depenalising decree, and in particular the provision for it to take retroactive effect, was the prime minister. After receiving Amato and the presidents of the two chambers of parliament, Scalfaro brought the initiative to a halt by declining to sign the offending decree, arguing that it suffered from 'a problem of constitutional relevance' as it clashed with one of the forthcoming referenda, now set for 18 April, on whether to abolish the 1974 law on party financing, and he asked the prime minister to re-examine the question. It was a finely judged move, designed to help the government off the hook without tarnishing the Presidency, and Amato – though resignation crossed his mind – was urged to persevere, at least until the referenda were safely negotiated.

After further cabinet discussion, Amato announced that the measures would be reintroduced in the form of a bill to be put before parliament, and he defended his actions before the taunts and jeers of opposition Senators, admitting he had been wrong to overrule Conso but arguing that it had been genuinely meant as a means of avoiding 'never-ending trials'. His special scorn was reserved, however, for his coalition partners who had at first encouraged him and were then frightened off by the outcry; the time had come to put a stop to the 'double language' of the coalition parties, some of whom vowed total support in private and then kept on publicly pretending they were ready to depart. Once his mandate was fulfilled, Amato declared, he would leave politics for good. By 143 to 99 votes, with one abstention, the issue was resolved in a vote of confidence and the government's approach was endorsed in the Senate, as it was in a similar, less noisy debate in the Chamber (by 295 to 248, and 7 abstaining), without in any way consolidating Amato's position. A final humiliation resulted from the parliamentary defeat of the last surviving element of the depenalising package – the unfreezing of public sector contracts – on 18 March, sparked off by a minor DC revolt, underlining how much the government was at the mercy of uncontrollable forces.

CONCLUSION: THE ISSUE OF REFORM

The downfall of the governing parties heralded the prospect of system change of an exceptionally radical kind. Because the parties had played so central a part in postwar politics, their decline was bound to have far-reaching effects on the particratic distribution of power and patronage. Indeed, according to one persuasive view,[30] corrupt party financing in the North and mafia clientelism in the South were both manifestations of the same co-mingling of party interests and public power, rendering the political class not only delegitimised by scandal but fundamentally illegitimate, never having had the right to claim popular consent.[31] The overriding concern was whether such a fundamental political transformation could be brought about without imperilling democratic norms, a danger to which the President, warning that further instability could end in dictatorship, was acutely aware.

Scalfaro's own position had become vital. Without taking a pickaxe to the constitution – in the style of his predecessor – Scalfaro had acted on the public demand for change, promising Italians in his end-of-year message that there would be no political solution to *Tangentopoli*, or in other words no painless resolution to wrongdoing. Above all he had given his consistent support to the Amato government, constantly looking for ways to shore up its morale and, in so doing, managing (for the first time in the history of the Republic) to detach the life of the government from the fortunes of the parties. It was this distancing which made it easier for Amato to hold on to power, in spite of coalition rivalries and in spite of losing even his theoretical parliamentary majority. The budget for 1993 had been got through largely unamended and in record time, being finally approved on 22 December, on the strength of which the EC furnished a loan of 8 billion ECUs. By good luck, the benefits of the forced devaluation of the *lira* were also beginning to make themselves felt, the cheaper *lira* providing a competitive boost to exporters who were already profiting from a reduction in inflationary pressure. Interest rates, though lower, had not – however – reduced in real terms, since the government had to ensure that Treasury bills remained attractive to investors, which in turn complicated the control of the budget deficit. Even so, the root problems were not caused by economic nor would they be cured by economic factors alone. Whatever difference the economic adjustment plan might make, it was still likely to be determined by ongoing political uncertainties.

A stronger economy could only spring from a newly constituted government, for which fresh elections, at least in the medium term, were unavoidable. But a general election would have to wait until reform of the electoral system – the second of Amato's initial objectives – was complete; otherwise, Amato believed, only the smaller extremist parties would gain. Following Scalfaro's (uncommon) call for joint parliamentary action, a 60-member *Bicamerale* commission of eminent figures drawn from both the Senate and the Chamber had come into being in September, under the chairmanship of Ciriaco De Mita. Resembling a scaled-down constituent assembly with a six-month remit to examine the full range of constitutional issues and put forward recommendations, the commission was able to make only slow progress. The principle of a switch to a more majoritarian voting system was overwhelmingly endorsed, yet delaying tactics and premeditated walkouts made certain that the specific details of a new system were not.

Initially, Mario Segni was excluded from the commission, which existed, as De Mita explained, 'to represent the parties and not the Holy Ghost'.[32] In November, after he had announced his new movement for reform, Segni was belatedly co-opted, without changing his view that parliament was too slow and divided to take the necessary action on electoral reform. Instead, on 16 January, the Constitutional Court gave its approval to the holding of 10 of the 13 referenda which Segni's followers had submitted in the Summer of 1992, including the main proposal altering the law relating to elections for the Senate, thereby effectively creating a predominantly majoritarian voting arrangement. The referenda would have to be held between 18 April and the close of the parliamentary session on 13 June, unless and only unless parliament decided to legislate in the meantime. A delighted Segni, who had seen a similar proposal rejected two years earlier, resigned from the *Bicamerale* forthwith. He had badly fallen out with the leader of *La Rete*, Leoluca Orlando, who no longer favoured the weapon of popular referenda, convinced that the old party structures were collapsing of their own accord (and that the minor parties, like *La Rete*, would be at a disadvantage in a predominantly first-past-the-post electoral system). On the other hand, Segni had started to establish an understanding with reforming elements in the PDS and the Republican and Socialist parties, all of whom could see the benefit of reinforcing the majoritarian trend towards alternative coalitions. For the moment, however, the prospect of the referenda obliged the main party leaders – as they had been obliged in 1991 – to publicly take sides, and Martinazzoli moved speedily to align the DC with the cause of voting reform.

Notes

1. M. Caciagli, 'Italie 1993: vers la seconde république', in *La Revue Française de Science Politique* (1993) especially pp.254–5.
2. On the Death of the PSI, see M. Rhodes 'The "long wave" subsides: the PSI and the demise of *craxismo*', in S. Hellman and G. Pasquino (eds), *Italian Politics: A Review*, Vol. 8 (1993); M. Rhodes, 'Reinventing the left: the origins of Italy's progressive alliance', in C. Mershon and G. Pasquino (eds), *Politics in Italy: A Review*, Vol. 9, (1994).
3. In August 1995, Amato denied the claim of Carlo Ripa di Meana (his environment minister) that he had told him in August 1992 that Craxi was not wrong to resist the 'political designs' of the magistrates and that the heads of the secret services and the police wanted to stop Di Pietro 'before it was too late'. *Il Corriere della Sera*, 31 July 1995, p.8, and 1 August 1995, p.8.
4. Mino Martinazzoli (1931–). Lawyer DC Senator since 1972. Former floor leader of the DC in the Chamber of Deputies. Oversaw the transformation of the DC into PPI beginning in Summer of 1993.
5. R. Mannheimer, 'The electorate of Lega Nord' (1993) p.92.
6. B. Poche, 'La Ligue Nord Face à L'Etat Italien', in *La Revue Politique et Parlementaire*, November–December 1993, especially pp.27–28.
7. 'Ugola profonda', in *Panorama*, 21 February 1993, pp.36–9.
8. Raul Gardini (1933–93). Corporate buccaneer and international yachtsman. Took over control of the Ferruzzi agricultural group in 1979, developing it into a powerful but debt-ridden holding company before being ousted by the Ferruzzi family in 1991.

9. Enimont was jointly created by the private Montedison chemicals concern, run at the time by Gardini, and the state petrochemicals company, ENI, with each taking a 40 per cent stake and the remaining 20 per cent being floated on the stock exchange. After months of long-running conflict, it was wound up when ENI was instructed to buy out the 40 per cent held by Montedison and the 20 per cent in the hands of shareholders. The over-inflated price paid in the buying-out raised suspicions of a 'political' commission.

10. J. Glover, 'Italian government near collapse as two resign', in *The Guardian*, 20 February 1993, p.7.

11. S. Acciari, 'Di Riina non ne posso piu', in *L'Espresso*, 20 September 1992, p.27.

12. E. Vulliamy, 'Inside the empire of evil', *The Guardian* (Review) 18 January 1993, p.11.

13. *Commissione Parlamentare Antimafia, Mafia e Politica – relazione del 6 Aprile 1993* (republished by Saggi Tascabili Laterza, 1993).

14. See the interview in *Le Monde*, 21 January 1993, p.4.

15. P. Allum, 'Il Mezzogiorno', in I. Diamanti and R. Mannheimer (eds), *Milano a Roma – guida all'Italia elettorale del 1994* (1994) p.109. A number of investigations had been in progress since late 1989.

16. A. Vito (1946–). Formerly 'an obscure auditor with ENEL in Caserta' (G. Bocca, *L'Inferno – profondo sud, male oscuro* (1992) p.225). Excelled in vote-buying following the curbing of the preference vote in 1991, which had intensified the rivalry between candidates of the same party and faction.

17. Ranging from the distribution of relief funds for the November 1980 earthquake and the construction of the unfinished metro in Naples to the disposing of toxic waste from Tuscany and the public works for the 1990 World Cup.

18. Antonio Gava (1930–). Son of the DC notable Silvio Gava. Member of the regional and then central direction of the DC since the 1960s. Leader of the Grand Centre faction in the DC and a former interior minister. Paolo Cirino Pomicino (1939–). Surgeon. DC MP from 1976 to 1994. Occupied key posts in the distribution of post-earthquake relief funds in the Irpinia area. Promised to build a 'new Naples'. Budget minister in 1989–92. Vincenzo Meo (1937–). DC Senator and political lieutenant of Gava. Raffaele Mastrantuono PSI MP. Former president of the parliamentary justice commission.

19. Commissione Parlamentare Antimafia, *Camorra e Politica – relazione approvata dalla commissione il 21 dicembre 1993*, pp.198–203.

20. 'Richiesta di autorizzazione a procedere nei confronti di P. Cirino Pomicino et al.', reprinted in a special supplement on 'Camorra e Politica' in *La Repubblica*, 15 April 1993, p.8.

21. Dossier Andreotti–Il testo completo delle accuse dei giudici di Palermo: le dichiarazioni di Leonardo Messina.

22. Caselli replaced Giammanco as the chief prosecutor in Palermo. he played a prominent part in the defeat of the Red Brigades in 70s and early 80s.

23. The referenda of April 1993 is the subject of the next chapter.

24. 'Le dichiarazione di Francesco Marino Mannoia' in *L'Espresso*, special insert.

25. P. Arlacchi, in the introduction to the special supplement on 'Camorra e Politica', in *La Repubblica*, 15 April 1993.

26. L. Pedrazzi, 'Andreotti e gli amici', *La Repubblica*, 7 April 1993, p.12.

27. *La Repubblica*, 20 February 1993, p.7.

28. Quoted by R. Graham in 'When honesty means sharing your bribes', *The Financial Times*, 27–28 February 1993, p.1.

29. E. Vulliamy 'Anger sweeps Italy over "licence to steal" decrees', in *The Guardian*, 8 March 1994.

30. D. Hine, 'Italy conspires against itself', in *The Times*, 2 April 1993, p.18.

31. F. Camon, 'Le Parlement est illégitime', in *Le Monde*, 14 April 1993, p.2.

32. M. Franco, 'Tiro al Ciriaco', *Panorama*, 7 February 1993, p.52.

6 *Vox Populi*: The Referendum of April 1993

REFORM AND THE REFERENDA

It was the shock outcome of the referendum on the curbing of the multiple preference vote in June 1991 (see Chapter 1) which persuaded those campaigning for institutional reform of the referendum's system-busting potential. The first attempt to also obtain a referendum on the introduction of a major-itarian voting system at both national and municipal level, proposing to delete the stipulation that candidates could only win a seat in the Senate outright if they secured at least 65 per cent of the validly cast votes,[1] had been turned down by the Constitutional Court in January 1991. Unperturbed, in the autumn Mario Segni's Committee for Electoral Reform (COREL) set about collecting the necessary signatures for a second challenge.[2] This time electoral reform was not the only item on the agenda. The newly-formed Committee for Democratic Reform (CORID) began pressing the case for further proposals to abolish the Ministry of State Participation, to put a stop to the Treasury's control over ap-pointments to the boards of savings banks, and to bring to an end the flow of extraordinary economic assistance to the *Mezzogiorno*. State financing of political parties also came under attack from the Radicals. Taken together, these refer-enda amounted to a formidable assault on some of the most conspicuous levers of party-power.[3]

The prospect of a pending popular consultation had cast a shadow over the slow-moving deliberations of the *Bicamerale* commission on electoral reform, without causing any of the squabbling participants (Gianfranco Fini of *Alleanza Nazionale*, Gianfranco Miglio of Northern League and Segni himself had all staged walkouts) to rush to find common ground over future institutional change. But once the Constitutional Court recognised the admissibility of ten referenda (out of 13) in

January, and the President duly fixed a voting date for 18 April, leading parliamentarians expressed the hope that this would add weight and urgency to the work already underway.

By employing decree-laws to extend majoritarian voting to towns of more than 5000 inhabitants, and to terminate all further extraordinary aid to regions in the South, parliament took steps in time for two of the ten referenda issues to be annulled. Eight referenda remained. On the central, symbolic issue of a new voting system, the most that the joint commission could agree on was a general acceptance of the majority principle. Beyond that, it 'threw in the towel',[4] as each party tried to make sense of how the various outcomes might affect their standing. While the nature and implications of the eight referenda propositions were highly complex and technical, we have simplified the core issues to show what a vote of 'yes' would mean (see Table 6.1).

Table 6.1   The eight 1993 referenda

---

1. Reform the law (1948) designating the Senate's electoral system so that 75 per cent of its seats are allocated through a majoritarian system with the remaining 25 per cent of seats allocated through proportional representation.
2. Reform the law (1978) on state financing of parties, so that political parties no longer receive a yearly monetary contribution by the State in proportion to their number of MPs.
3. Reform the law (1990) on possession of drugs, which made it a criminal offence to hold more than the legally defined 'average daily dose' of drugs, therefore imposing more severe sanctions on consumers of drugs.
4. Abolition of the law (1938) whereby the nomination of presidents of local banks were the subject of ministerial discretion.
5. Reform the law (1978) that allows local health boards a role in environmental protection, therefore allowing for a definitive separation between health and environmental concerns.
6. Abolition of the Ministry of State Holdings (law of 1956).
7. Abolition of the Ministry of Agriculture (law of 1929).
8. Abolition of the Ministry of Tourism (law of 1959).

Reformers were in no doubt about the strength of anti-party sentiment, fanned over recent months by the stark facts of institutionalised corruption and economic mismanagement which were powerfully contributing to the message of change. There was, understandably, a temptation to promote voting reform as a cure-all for the manifest ills of *partitocrazia*. The excessive proportionality of the current voting system took the brunt of the blame for the revolving-door instability of coalitions, mafia infiltration and even the alarming state of Italy's high public debt.[5] Moving to a predominantly majoritarian form of voting would, by contrast, facilitate the development of two or three new, more stable and moderate poles or alliances that could alternate in power directly in response to the will of the electorate, just like in Britain, France and the United States.

Unpopular governments could be kicked out, ensuring greater responsibility to the electorate. The *conventio ad excludendum* which had been slapped on the old communist party and the far right to keep them out of government would no longer operate. As the 'Yes' camp proclaimed, a 'Yes' vote was a vote to replace the 'Italy of parties' with an 'Italy of citizens'. A 'Yes' vote was the only available means for bringing about a modern, cleaned-up system of government equipped to tackle the problems of the economy and organised crime. If the 'No' vote triumphed, however cleverly the partisans of 'No' rationalised their objections, everything would stay the same.

The relative merits of proportional and majoritarian systems of voting were exhaustively debated, but without really conveying their full complexity. This was hardly surprising. Academic literature exploring the relationship between particular voting systems and party systems has a long and involved history, in which the search for universal and demonstrable laws has been paramount. Valid comparisons have, however, always been hampered by the need to take account of the distinctiveness of each country's political environment. It is agreed that there is no ideal voting method, that the desired criteria vary, and that certain methods tend to facilitate multiparty politics more than others. Any connection between electoral systems and governability or economic success is, as sceptics tried to point out, still unproven.

To this extent, the claims of reformers were not subject to the kind of searching examination that was required. There

was, for one thing, a failure to distinguish between the electing of a legislature, to be judged by the standard of fairness or
representativness, and the choosing of a government, which
calls for efficacy. The wish to bring greater stability was considerably qualified by the existence of a new but growing regional
party identity which was likely to benefit further from any
voting proposals. Most of all, the issue of electoral reform did
not stand by itself; it was part of a much larger discussion
about wider institutional change, touching on practically the
whole of the institutional order, and about which there were
as yet no clear views.[6] Having said that, the approach which
Segni and his supporters took was essentially a pragmatic one.
After much organisation and effort, the opportunity for voters
to express a real will for change now presented itself.
Abrogative referenda might not be everybody's first choice,
but a start had to be made somewhere, and if reformers could
only have one wish, changing the voting system would be it.
Rightly or wrongly, the electoral system was the natural focus
of discontent. Italians were urged to seize their chance, if they
were sincere in wanting to allow the emergence of new political forces and new political leaders.

PARTY ALIGNMENTS

The difficulty of being forced to choose also had a disorientating effect on party alignments and outlooks. The new DC
secretary, Mino Martinazzoli (who had only been at his post
since October), while trying to weaken the hold of traditional
party factions and acknowledging criticisms of 'the old ways of
doing politics',[7] was determined not to be outsmarted by
Segni. Now that the referendum on voting reform was to take
place, the DC would officially support it, even though many
DC MPs were of two minds on this question. On the news that
Andreotti was under investigation for mafia association, Segni
resigned from the party. This move had the tactical object of
showing that a 'Yes' vote need not also mean a vote for 'the
parties which had ruined Italy',[8] opening up a serious rift in
Catholic ranks.

But Segni had lost an important ally in Leoluca Orlando,
one of the original sponsors of electoral reform who had since

become its most vocal opponent and had swung *La Rete* round to the same position. Orlando contemptuously pointed out that he had left the Christian Democrats back in 1990, when Segni was still hoping to change the DC from within. After the 1992 general election the political context had altered and, in Orlando's view, the old party structures were already falling apart; what the proposed reform would actually do would be to prop them up. He was obviously aware, too, that under 'winner-takes-all' rules smaller parties like his own faced extinction. His advocacy of a 'No' vote had the curious result of grouping the leftist *La Rete* not only with Communist Refoundation and the Greens but also the normally isolated and isolationist (neo-fascist) MSI, all of whom were demanding immediate general elections instead.

Having misjudged the mood in June 1991, the leader of the Northern League Umberto Bossi was not going to make the same mistake twice and welcomed the referendum, even though this meant rubbing shoulders with the same parties that the Northern League specialised in denouncing. The only consistent advocate of reform was Occhetto, though in this case also there were ambiguities. The PDS favoured two-round voting, which was plainly not Segni's stated preference. Furthermore a sizeable left-wing section of the party was hostile to reform altogether, making much of the fact that all of the old ruling parties (including the post-Craxi PSI) were backing it.[9] As Marcello Fedele commented, all sides supposedly wanted change and chided others with blocking it.[10] The kaleidoscope of unlikely alliances and internal divides, which became more and more strained as the campaign neared its conclusion, shook still further the party loyalties of voters.[11]

THE RUN-IN AND RESULTS

Wild talk of a *coup d'état* (allegedly led by Cossiga) during the run-in to the vote, and the smearing of Segni in a masonic conspiracy, should not distract from the extreme gravity of the moment. Because of parliament's failure to act, and because of the almost daily revelations of high crimes and misdemeanours,[12] so much more was hanging on the popular verdict. Parliament was effectively at the mercy of public opinion, finally draining it of any credibility.

The Amato administration was only able to see things through until 18 April, when the Prime Minister had promised he would step down, by the continued commitment of the President, who was actively sounding out possibilities for a more widely-based coalition to take office. But Scalfaro was also the target of increasing hostility. His refusal to sign the depenalising decree, which would have acquitted many MPs from charges of corruption, had infuriated many of the old guard, who felt betrayed by the erstwhile defender of the centrality of parliament. Scalfaro had then, in the immediate aftermath, publicly reaffirmed what he had said on previous occasions that whoever breaks the penal code 'must pay'.[13] Each subsequent burst of round-ups and confessions were further confirmation that the 'untouchability' of the political and business class had been irreversibly breached.

Opinion polls indicated clear though not overwhelming support for the 'Yes' campaign, although there was a large number of undecided voters. As Segni appreciated, the need for a high turnout and a convincing margin of victory was not simply academic. The more emphatic the result, the stronger the reforming signal being sent and the less the likelihood of a further period of unstable jockeying. Some of Segni's followers went so far as to argue that a decisive victory would also strengthen the case for reform of the Chamber of Deputies along the same one-round voting lines as the Senate. Either way, given that MPs were being hounded in the streets and MSI activists briefly besieged the parliament building, an uncertain outcome might have only aggravated an already tense situation. The sheer range and shadowy implications of the proposals on offer made many observers question whether the remedy of the referendum was not worse than the evils it was intended to correct. The startling aspect was the obvious lack of a well thought-out, constructive and coherent plan for a reconstructed polity.

In the event, the majority for change exceeded even the most optimistic expectations of the reform movement (see Table 6.2). With an average turnout of 77 per cent (the 50 per cent quorum having already been passed during the first of the two days of voting) and in spite of the convoluted phrasing of the proposition, a revision of the law on voting for the Senate was overwhelmingly, and incontestably, endorsed by 28 937 375 votes (82.7 per cent) to 6 038 909 (17.3 per cent).

The majority in favour of ending state financing of the parties was higher still. A clean sweep also saw votes for abolishing the ministries of agriculture, state participation and tourism.

A strong 'Yes' was apparent in all parts of the country and across all social classes and age groups. But although the Senate reform was endorsed in all 95 provinces, the results did disclose a characteristic regional pattern (see Table 6.3) – the further North, the greater the turnout and the heavier the vote in favour. In some parts of the centre and the South, a sizeable minority (almost as much as one-in-two in Orlando's home base of Palermo) were opposed, particularly to the abolition of the agriculture ministry. Indeed, the 'Southern' constituency opposed to reform was calculated to have grown by some 930 000 votes since the election of April 1992.[14]

Table 6.2   Results of the 1993 referenda – final results (%)

	Turnout	Yes	No
Reform of the law relating to elections for the Senate	77.0	82.7	17.3
State financing of political parties	77.0	90.3	9.7
Abolition of the ministry of agriculture	77.0	70.1	29.9
Abolition of the ministry of state participation	76.9	90.1	9.9
Abolition of the ministry of tourism	76.9	82.2	17.8
Nomination of directors of savings banks	77.0	89.8	10.2
Removing environmental protection from health boards	76.9	82.5	17.5
Depenalising the personal use of drugs	77.0	55.3	44.7

Source: Adapted from R. Salvato, documentary appendix in C. Mershon and G. Pasquino (eds) (1995) p.232.

Table 6.3   Reform of the law relating to elections for the Senate – geographical breakdown of voting (%)

	Turnout	*Yes*	*No*
North	85.1	87.4	12.6
Centre	81.1	81.8	18.2
South	64.4	76.5	23.5
Islands	64.8	72.7	27.3
Total	77.0	82.7	17.3

On the other hand, there was also evidence from the exit polls of a weakening of party allegiances on which reformers had set their hopes. Support for change from government party voters (89 per cent of DC and 84 per cent of PSI voters) far outweighed the half-hearted backing of coalition leaders, while many others (56 per cent of Refoundation, 59.5 per cent of *La Rete* and 44 per cent of MSI voters) ignored their own party's instructions to vote 'No'.[15] Most Italian and foreign commentators had no hesitation in describing it as the latest stage in the process of dismantling and renewal set in train by the 1991 referendum and the 1992 election, attributing to people-power the decisive push in the direction of wider constitutional change. From today, as Segni announced, the parties count for less and the citizens more.

DIRECT DEMOCRACY

It is perhaps not surprising that the last blow to particracy took the form of a popular referendum. Being primarily issue-based, referenda do not easily fit into the logic of party polit- ical debate, indeed that was their usefulness to the reforming lobby.[16] This in part explains why a large number of voters dis- regarded the stated preference(s) of the party they otherwise claimed to support. The referenda, one might say, provided an escape from party-conditioned choices.

A referendum is also an instrument of direct democracy, which appeals to a plebiscitary (rather than particratic) form of government. It is also important to reflect on the type of political culture which openly embraces the referendum as a legitimate decision-making institution. The referendum may not be used consciously as a challenge to representative government, but its constant use nevertheless reflects a predilection for direct democracy. Of course, it is an error to consider the ideal of direct democracy as an exclusive alternative to the familiar notion of representative democracy. Even the more impassioned advocates of wider democratic participation like C.B. Macpherson and Carole Pateman concede that the former cannot be wholly substituted, *tout court*, for the latter, and that one should instead be looking for ways of integrating forms of direct democracy into the general framework of representative government.[17] This is the position recently adopted, for example, by Robert Dahl, who makes the case for greater democracy in the workplace.[18] A blend of both can contribute to the translating of individual wills into a collective choice.

Participationists define direct democracy as 'a form of decision-making in which a citizen body makes an unmediated impact on the shape of binding collective policies'.[19] Popular deliberation on important matters is held to be open and uncoerced. All those qualified to participate engage in informed persuasion before a decision is taken and no decision can be trumped (for example by military force) afterwards. Seen in this light, direct democracy is a necessarily imperfect, procedural decision rule which does not guarantee the best or the right answers but which allows for authoritative choices which accord with the directly expressed wishes of the majority. The essential assumption behind a popular referendum is that it is in and of itself the most direct and undistorted form of democracy and therefore, by definition, the most purely and meaningfully democratic.

These statements are attractively simple but – we want to explain – innocent and oversimplistic. There is more to democracy than the formal symbolism of popular voting in a referendum. In a modern, mass society, direct democracy is not only hard to attain but, even if it were practicable, might not in any case be desirable. It makes no difference whether voting on an issue is abrogative or consultative.[20] In the last analysis, the problem with the referendum as the quintessential instrument of direct democracy is that it carries with it a number of attendant risks, all of which cloud the exercise of democratic decision-making and which, more importantly, were all exemplified in the mixed package of referenda in April 1993, illustrating how difficult it is to graft direct popular balloting onto the representative mode of government. These are the risks of agglomeration, manipulation and legitimation.

Agglomeration. By agglomeration we refer to the common experience that although proposals which successfully reach the point of a popular vote are very different in nature, and not necessarily part of the same political project, they are nevertheless liable to be treated by the electorate as parts of a whole, to be accepted or rejected *en bloc.* There is no question that such lumping together of an eclectic catalogue of proposals occurred in April 1993, and was indeed encouraged by the partisans of a 'Yes' vote. The electoral reform proposal was the key proposal, taking up most of the publicity before and after the campaign, yet it was assumed that most of the other issues at stake tended in the same direction. A 'Yes' vote was deemed to be progressive, and a 'No' vote as reactionary. Thus it was that, with the single exception of the referendum on the personal use of drugs, the overall votes in favour of change were of a similar order of magnitude, in spite of the fact that they concerned matters about which the full implications were obscure and about which the experts disagreed. There was, it could be said, a concurrent majority of a surprising level of conviction.

Manipulation. The possibility of manipulating a vote is directly correlated to the technical complexity and/or moral sensitivity of the question(s) being posed. In other words the more complicated or contentious a question is, the greater the risk of manipulative appeals by those claiming expertise, or by those employing rhetorical skills or television advertising. Studies of human rationality indicate that, when presented with conflicting information, people are more likely to be flexible (and therefore open to suggestion) about technical points on which there is loosely-held disagreement, and stubborn about matters of opinion deriving from emotional beliefs which they find hard to alter.[21]

The point about manipulation is that the abstract notion of 'the people's will' needs careful handling. Manipulation may well be a trademark of mass society, and therefore present in all forms of democracy, yet the risk of manipulation is more accentuated for plebisceterian forms of democracy. A referendum is an instrument of plebiscetarian democracy, and although it has been argued that plebisceterian forms of democracy can be reconciled with liberal democracy, as for example in the case of presidential elections in France and the US,[22] plebiscitary calls for change may sit uncomfortably with the ideal of liberal democracy.

Legitimation. Mark Donovan has argued that although the referendum, as an instrument of direct democracy, may challenge the very principle on which modern democracies are built, namely representation or indirect democracy, 'in postwar western Europe such a direct challenge to representative democracy has not been witnessed'.[23] While we share Donovan's views, overuse of the decision-making instrument of the referendum is bound to diminish the authority of parliament. If all disputed issues are to be determined by popular vote, then why have an elected assembly in the first place? Norberto Bobbio rightly remarked that the referendum is an exceptional tool which ought only to be utilised in exceptional circumstances. That clearly has not been so in Italy. Since 1987, Italians have passed judgement on no less than 32 different proposals, on six separate occasions, with some of the same issues cropping up more than once.

THE REFERENDUM ON ELECTORAL REFORMS

The referendum on electoral reform for the Senate opened up a debate on the merits and vices of the different electoral systems. The majoritarian system was upheld by its supporters on at least three different grounds: first, it would promote greater political stablity, since governments would not be formed on unsustainable coalitions. Second, it would induce parties to act more responsibly, since there would be a clear distinction between the parties in government and the parties in opposition. Third, under the majoritarian system the *conventio ad excludendum* would be seriously challenged, therefore bringing Italy in line with other Western democracies by easing the conditions of governmental alternation. On the other hand, supporters of proportional representation argued that this electoral system is more democratic by ensuring equity of party representation in parliament, therefore reflecting more faithfully the will of the people.

The significance of this reform should not go unnoticed. Because of the question on electoral reform this referendum became identified with a vote for radical change. As Corbetta and Parisi point out, the referendum was not about a choice between two electoral systems (proportional vs. majoritarian system), instead the referendum was about a choice between defending the status quo, characterised by particracy, corruption and organized crime, and the possibility of starting all over again from scratch, with a new electoral system that will give rise to a new way of doing politics. It was believed that the reform of the electoral system for the Senate would form the basis for a wider electoral reform which would include also the Chamber of Deputies.

It is important to recall that the debate on the appropriate electoral system was founded on a preliminary basic assumption, namely, that the institutional rules of the game were the cancer within Italian politics. In particular, it was the specific rules that define the way in which political representatives are elected that were believed to be the seed of all political evils in Italy. In what follows we want to argue that holding this position is, in part, equivalent to barking up the wrong tree.

While we share the view that extreme forms of proportional representation may be problematic, and that in fact proportional representation is not more democratic than the majoritarian system,[24] we also feel that the electoral system is the least of the problems in Italy. In a recent book, Diego Gambetta and Steven Warner have argued that we should view such reforms with some caution and scepticism. First of all, it is illusory to think that as a result of an electoral reform Italy's political system will change, indeed that political life in Italy can come to resemble that of the country from which the electoral system was imported.[25] Secondly, the hype which has accompanied the electoral reform has given rise to unrealistic expectations.

Gambetta and Warner go on to argue that no electoral system can resolve the political problems of a country, above all the problems of the Italian political system. The point is a crucial one. First of all, it is unrealistic to expect that a new electoral system could deliver immediate results. Each system has its own mechanical logic, and it takes time for the electorate to come to terms with it. When a new system is introduced, there is always going to be a transitional period (perhaps of two or three electoral turns) before the chief actors in the political system – politicians, parties and the electorate – come to reassess their respectives roles. But secondly, it is unrealistic to expect that nearly fifty years of particratic domination could be erased almost by magic simply by institutional tinkering. Political institutions can only function as well as the people that work within them, so that it would take much longer than expected before the fruits of the new political institutions would become apparent. The assumption that all the problems in Italy will vanish if only the right institutional formula could be found was a chimera; time, effort and much patience would be needed before the defects resulting from half a century of corrupt maladministration will be corrected. Finally, the unleashing of unrealistic hopes can have dangerous consequences. The risk is that people become dissatisfied with key institutions when these seem unable to bring about an improvement. It is almost trivial to point out that Italy has already had recent experience of a type of government that held democratic norms in contempt.

THE FORGOTTEN REFERENDUM: STATE SUBSIDY TO POLITICAL PARTIES

The results of the 1993 referendum were greeted with jubilation by virtually every newspaper in the country.[26] The results were not simply seen as foregone conclusions but as desirable results that few would dare contest. Yet, there is little doubt that the phenomenon of agglomeration played an important role in the April 1993 referenda. While the referendum on the electoral reform was the star attraction of the campaign, and the one that got most publicity before and after the results, one should not forget that there were seven other issues on which the Italian electorate were asked to vote. The fact that the other issues lived in the shadow of the vote on the electoral vote for the

Senate (with the possible exception of the referendum on drugs) raises some important questions on the desirability of the referendum as a legitimate democratic institution, or at least the fact that at any one referendum more than one question can be put to the electorate. In what follows, we will look at one of the neglected questions in the referendum, namely the public financing of political parties.

In the eyes of the electorate, ending the annual state subsidy to political parties in proportion to their number of MPs took the form of a deserved punishment for the existing parties, who were anyway heavily in debt and losing popular favour. It is not a coincidence that this single referendum attracted the highest number of consents (90.3 per cent). Yet the fact that 9 out of 10 voters voted 'Yes' does not necessarily mean that they were right in doing so. That is to say, the numerical support for a principle does not guarantee its validity (or truth).[27] Indeed it could be argued that voting 'Yes' on the issue of state financing of political parties was a grave error of judgement which may have unwelcome repercussions on all future elections.

An important principle is at stake. Supporting state subsidy for political parties finds justification in the substantive idea of democracy, whereby democracy is captured by the notions of autonomy and reasoned public deliberation. The emphasis here is on the fact that in a democracy all individuals ought to be free and equal in determining the conditions of their own association. The sense in which individuals are free and equal defines their autonomy, that is to say, the ability to exercise self-governing capacities. The distribution of resources plays a vital role in determining degrees of individual autonomy. As Joshua Cohen and Joel Rogers argue in *On Democracy*, the belief that individuals ought to be autonomous goes a long way to justifying a fair distribution of resources in a society. If the absence of material deprivation is a precondition for free and unconstrained deliberation and a capacity for political action, then a basic level of material wellbeing for all becomes an unavoidable requirement for a fully-fledged democracy.

The same line of argument can be extended to political parties. Unless all parties enjoy equal access to resources that can help them to compete in the political arena, pluralistic diversity is constrained, making a mockery of the ideal of democracy. The importance of state financing of political parties has been recognized amongs others by Charles Beitz,[28] who regrets the domination of American elections by rich individuals and lobbies. Beitz suggests that substantial background inequalities, especially though not exclusively of a financial nature, will be reflected in the outcomes of the political process, making it imperative to eliminate unfair material advantages. Of course there are different ways of achieving this goal, and we are not claiming that there are easy solutions to what is a very complex and technical question. Nevertheless public financing of political parties is undoubtably a step in the right direction, and its restriction may do incalculable harm to Italian democracy in the long run.

The backlash against party corruption overcame the elementary justice of basic fair competition. Reforming the present law on state financing of political parties is not only likely to inhibit the formation of new political groupings (the chief goal of electoral reformers), but it may force both the 'old' and the 'new' parties into soliciting for voluntary, and unverifiable, sources of income. It would appear that voters were expressing the aspiration for renewal, without the financial means with which to give effect to it.

Most political commentators argued that the 1993 referendum was a sign of democratic maturity in Italy. Unfortunately that may not be the case. Weakening the public financing of political parties may prove to be a serious blow to the aspirations of nurturing forms of liberal democracy in Italy. As a result of this referendum on state financing of political parties, equality and fairness suffered while rich individuals stand a better chance of being elected.[29]

CONCLUSION

The risks associated with the instrument of the referendum are sufficient to dent the widely-held view that it was the popular thrust of people power that was driving the motor of reform. One can continue to insist on the special, epoch-making nature of the anti-party rebuke by the voters, and the truth that they were not picking a system of rules so much as entering a plea for salvation. At the same time, one must also be prepared to recognise the inconsistencies and dangers bound up with the act of voting in a direct democracy.

We can summarise this by saying that the enthusiasts for 'referendum democracy' were wanting a sense of the tragic limitations of politics.[30] They operated on the assumption that the institutional rules of the game, and especially the way in which representatives were elected, were at fault, and that a different institutional fix would have different, more desirable effects. Unfortunately, as we shall see in the next chapter the exaggerations accompanying reform gave rise to wildly unrealistic expectations.[31]

Notes

1. The effect of this alteration being to create a mixed but mainly majoritarian system, with three-quarters of Senators (238 out of 315) to be elected on the basis of the highest number of one-round votes in single-member constituencies.

2. The Court can declare as 'inadmissible' any proposals which deal with excluded topics (taxation, treaties) or lack a clear, rational basis.

3. Of course Segni's object was not to undermine the authority of the Italian parliament or to threaten, in the manner of Bossi, an apocalyptic break-up. The whole purpose of Segni's rolling strategy was simply to compel parliament itself to do what it otherwise would not do by bouncing party leaders into acting in advance of a pending popular consultation. See M. Donovan, 'The politics of electoral reform in Italy', *The International Political Science Review* (1995) p.55.

4. P. Clough, 'Italians take a do-it-yourself approach to electoral reform', in *The Independent*, 27 January 1993, p.10.

5. According to the results of an analysis of the relative success of majoritarian and proportional governments in containing and reducing public debt since the 1970s – 'Conti sani con il maggioritario', in *La Repubblica*, 26 March 1993, p.9.

6. A. Manzella, 'Des partis tout-puissants', in *Le Monde des Debats*, April 1993, p.19.

7. *La Repubblica*, 7 April 1993, p.3.

8. Cited in the diary by one of Segni's (anonymous) collaborators in *L'Espresso*, 11 April 1993, p.48.

9. S. Rodotà, 'Ma non é la strada giusta', in *La Repubblica – Guida ai Referendum*, 7 April 1993, p.I. For a defence of the principle of proportionality in capturing the spread of political opinion, see M. Bovero, 'La grande manipolazione', in *Il Manifesto*, 18 April 1993, zp.12.

10. M. Fedele, *Democrazia Referendaria – l'Italia dal primato dei partiti al trionfo dell'opinione pubblica* (1994) p.119.

11. For other accounts of the official party positions on the eight referenda, see J. Newell and M. Bull, 'The Italian referenda of April 1993:

real change at last?', in *West European Politics* (1993) pp.607–15, and *Capire i Referendum: Guida ai quesiti referendari del 18 Aprile.*

12. The knife-edge decision by the Chamber on 18 March to lift the immunity from prosecution of Francesco De Lorenzo was an explicit condemnation of vote-buying.
13. Quoted in *Il Corriere della Sera*, 13 March 1993, p.9.
14. P. Corbetta and A. Parisi, 'The referendum on the electoral law for the Senate: another momentous April', in C. Mershon and G. Pasquino (eds), *Italian Politics – Ending the First Republic* (1995) p.88. The authors make the point that what makes the South different is not its 'Southerness' but its 'marginalisation', so that if the Southern electorate rejects the rules of the central state this is because it feels geographically marginalised, not because its culture is intrinsically conservative or reactionary – a point well worth taking further. Parisi, incidentally, was one of Segni's principal policy advisers.
15. P. Corbetta and A. Parisi, op. cit. (1995) p.85.
16. See Gordon Smith's 'The functional properties of the referendum', in *The European Journal of Political Research* (1976) pp.1–23.
17. C.B. Macpherson, *The Life and Times of Liberal Democracy* (1977); C. Pateman, *Participation and Democratic Theory* (1970).
18. R. Dahl, *Democracy and its Critics* (1989) Ch. 23.
19. This is the definition of M. Saward, 'Direct democracy revisited', *Politics* (1993).
20. There has been only one recent instance of a consultative referendum in Italy, namely the experimental referendum of guidance, or *d'indirizzo*, on the drafting of a treaty for the European union in 1989.
21. See especially S. Sutherland, *Irrationality – the enemy within* (1992).
22. See A. Panebianco, 'Plebisciti e Democrazia', in his *Il Prezzo della Libertà* (1995).
23. M. Donovan 'The referendum and the transformation of the party system', in *Modern Italy* (1995) p.54.
24. On this point see C.Beitz, *Political Equality* (1989) ch.6.
25. See S. Warner and D. Gambetta, *La Retorica della Riforma* (1994) p.8. For an English version of the key arguments in this book, see D. Gambetta and S. Warner 'The Rhetoric of Reform Revealed', *Journal of Modern Italian Studies* (1995).
26. The left-wing newspaper *Il Manifesto* was one of the few exceptions.
27. This is one of the lesson we learn from reading J.S. Mill's *On Liberty* (1972). Mill says that 'If all mankind minus one were of one opinion, and only one person were of the contrary opinion, mankind would be no more justified in silencing that one opinion, than he, if he had the power, would be justified in silencing mankind .... the opinion which it is attempted to suppress by authority may possibly be true. Those who desire to suppress it, of course deny its truth; but they are not infallible' (p.85).
28. C. Beitz, op. cit. (1989).
29. See Berlusconi's electoral victory of 1996, analysed in Chapter 8.

30.   G. Ionescu, *Politics and the Pursuit of Happiness* (1984).
31.   It would be difficult to deny that in political matters Italy has always had a sense of inferiority towards, and a great admiration for, the British parliamentary system. But as Brian Barry remarks in *Justice as Impartiality* (1995), things are not always the way they seem: 'A few years ago a senior political scientist remarked to a conference in New Delhi that the 'Westminster model' had not served India well; I could not forbear to comment that it had not done too well at Westminster either' (p.106).

7 Which Way Forward? (April 1993–December 1993)

By endorsing all of the main reforming referenda, by such clear margins and on such a high turnout, the Italian electorate was regarded as having signalled a plebiscitary desire for far-reaching change. Reformers argued that the political elites were morally bound to respect the voters' *diktat*. The principle of popular sovereignty, as opposed to party sovereignty, had been strikingly affirmed. But the referenda could not and did not prescribe what form or direction this change would take. Even an overwhelming majority in favour of modifying the law relating to elections for the Senate, as the President of the Constitutional Court had indicated in February, need not be binding, since, apart from being unable to reinstate any law which is abrogated, 'everything else is open to interpretation'.[1]

Reform of voting for the Senate had implications for the Chamber of Deputies, as well as for the future balance of power between the legislature and the executive. An already disgraced parliament was being compelled, in effect, to reconsider the ground-rules by which it was constituted. On all of these issues, moreover, there were marked differences of view, not least among the allies of the referendum pact. However unsatisfactory a way this might have seemed of having to proceed, and however ambiguous the real state of public opinion, the April referenda turned the key that unlocked the wider issue of institutional reform.

FROM AMATO TO CIAMPI

On 22 April the prime minister, Giuliano Amato, gave a valedictory address to the Chamber of Deputies, asserting

146

(controversially) that the results of the referenda brought to an end the party–state model inherited from fascism 50 years ago. Having completed his work, Amato tendered the resignation of his crisis-stricken, ten month-old government.

An interim administration to see through new electoral rules and prepare fresh elections was now imperative, and President Scalfaro also wished to install a less party-coloured, more broadly-based government. The manoeuvring which followed Amato's resignation saw, instead, a reversion to the old habits of intense party infighting. Opinion polls suggested that the outgoing coalition parties only commanded around 27–28 per cent of the popular vote, which made a resurrection of the DC, PSI, PLI, PSDI four-party coalition (*quadripartito*) politically unsustainable. But the Christian Democrats were determined not to yield, blocking any idea that Segni should become Prime Minister and looking for time to regroup and regenerate. Although Occhetto had already spoken of the PDS's availability for government, there was much rank-and-file hostility. A possible DC–PDS grand accord fell through, however, complicating the President's consultations. The Northern League in the meantime kept up its claim as the only authentic anti-system antagonist, with Bossi threatening that unless elections were called soon he would provoke a mass mobilisation of his supporters.

Scalfaro eventually fell back on a 'technical' choice, asking Carlo Azeglio Ciampi, the Governor of the Bank of Italy, to try to form a government – the 52nd government since the war, the first to be led by a non-parliamentarian, and the first (in accordance with the letter of Article 92 of the Constitution) to be put together without prior consultation with party leaders. Ciampi immediately announced that he would make voting reform an 'absolute priority', along with continuing to rectify the state of the economy. Barucci was reappointed to the Treasury, and several other experts were brought into the cabinet. The DC retained the foreign and interior ministry portfolios. Segni refused a post, saying that he would only participate in an administration more in keeping with the reformist spirit. But in the boldest break with the past, three PDS MPs, and one PDS sympathiser (Luigi Spaventa, the new Budget minister) were included, the first ministerial appointments from the PCI/PDS since 1947.

The Ciampi government was almost over before it started. Only hours after it had been sworn in, a series of votes took place in the Chamber of Deputies rejecting the request by the *Mani pulite* judges for the lifting of the parliamentary immunity of Bettino Craxi on four corruption charges (two charges to do with violation of the law on party financing were approved), against the earlier recommendation of a Chamber committee and in apparent defiance of the temper of the times. Scuffling broke out amongst Deputies, members of *La Rete* walked out in protest, and after a meeting of the PDS executive, the three PDS ministers stood down. While accusations were traded that some forty opposition MPs had deliberately decided to protect Craxi, in what was still a secret vote, it was also plain that a large number of DC and PSI Deputies were quite ready to defy the magistrates, reviving the old belief that the political class had made themselves invulnerable.[2]

Craxi's 'absolution' was strongly attacked by Borrelli, the Chief Prosecutor in Milan, and by the CSM, sparking off a renewed parliamentary confrontation with the judiciary. Stiffened by the President, Ciampi issued a statement explaining that his task remained unaffected, and he still evidently hoped to entice the PDS members back into his team. Demonstrations broke out in a number of cities. Shrewdly, Andreotti – after at first putting up a fight – chose the moment to ask for his own parliamentary immunity to be lifted, even though new allegations about his mafia connections had recently been made, including a recollection by Baldassare Di Maggio that he had seen Andreotti meet and receive the mafia kiss of honour from 'Toto' Riina at a hideout in Palermo in 1987.

Once again, Scalfaro's role was decisive. Not only, he said, should the Ciampi government consider the abolition of parliamentary immunity; it should do everything in its power to speed electoral reform, respecting the outcome of the referendum 'to the full'. Therefore when Ciampi went before the Chamber of Deputies and Senate to secure a vote of confidence, he knew he could count on the opposition parties. Confirming what had been 'positive' about the past fifty years of Italian history, he went on to make it plain that he would actively press for a Senate-type mixed, mainly majoritarian voting system for the Chamber, which he hoped would be realised by the end of the session in July, making possible an autumn election. By 309 votes to 60 in the Chamber of Deputies, and 162 votes to 36 in the Senate, the Ciampi government was confirmed in office, aided by the benevolent abstention of the PDS and (abandoning its customary counter-vote) the Northern League. It was, as a consequence, an unusual government by any standards, enjoying only grudging backing from the majority parties and owing its existence in large measure to its ostensible opponents.

The controversy over the fate of Craxi and Andreotti was not caused purely by the actions of those politicians, once linked to the PSI and DC, fighting for their political lives. Party politics in general had fallen into a confused and confusing state, following the awkward and unwelcome choices of the referendum campaign. Most of the DC notables were also at risk (DC's De Mita had finally been told he was part of the investigation into the Naples earthquake fraud), the party's parliamentary cohesion was breaking up, and both Segni and Orlando (*La Rete*) were hopeful of benefitting. Giorgio Benvenuto, leader of the PSI since March, departed after failing to overcome the resistance of Craxi-ite loyalists, taking the party president and several members of the party executive with him. The leader of the Liberal Party, Renato Altissimo, was implicated in illegal party financing. The Republican Party too fell under further suspicion in the wake of the arrest of Davide Giacalone, the postal ministry official who helped draft the controvertial Mammí media law (which was highly favourable to Berlusconi's media empire) and then landed a consultant's job with Berlusconi's Fininvest. Continuing disagreements and divisions in the PDS hindered Occhetto's aim of constructing a broad, and electable, 'pole of the left', just as damaging revelations about the party's own involvement in bribe-taking and ownership of foreign bank accounts were attracting press attention. And the Northern League, federalist by now in all but name (Bossi was toying with renaming it the Italian Federal League), still had no credible federal programme.

A NEW MAFIA BOMBING CAMPAIGN

The uneasy party political transition was made still more perilous by the ongoing and not unconnected conflict with powerful mafia interests which the Pope, denouncing the 'culture of death' and defending the right of people to live in peace, had attacked in the course of a visit to Sicily. Michele Zaza, head of the Neapolitan Camorra, was arrested a few days later. A car bomb in Rome on 14 May, believed to have been targeted at a popular television presenter, injured several passersby. Then, on the 18 May, in a dawn raid, police captured 'Nitto' Santapaola, supposedly the second-in-command to Totó Riina and wanted for numerous homicides. Two further unclaimed car bombs on the 27 May, one close to the Uffizi Gallery in Florence, killed five people and destroyed valuable, irreplaceable art works. These latest outrages, coinciding with the first anniversary of the death of Giovanni Falcone, revived speculation about the 'grey area' of collusion between *Cosa Nostra*, masonic circles and deviant secret service agents, and lent substance to the view that Falcone may have been silenced because he had got too close to hidden centres of state power.

'Look at the condition Italy was in a year ago and at what has happened since', Judge Vito D'Ambrosio (a colleague of Falcone) told a meeting in the capital, 'and you can see that it need not be just the mafia who may have found it necessary to mount such a murder'. Several separate lines of inquiry had begun to converge on what Bruno Siclari, the chief anti-mafia prosecutor, called 'a web of intrigue'. 'Masonry', according to Judge Cordova, was the 'transversal *superpartito*' linking people in almost all of the political parties and in a vast number of posts of power'.[3] 'It is not an organisation', one of the Milan magistrates was to tell reporters, 'but an environmental situation in which mafia clans, terrorists, big companies and corrupt politicians wallow', involving the large-scale laundering, recycling and transfer of illicit funds, based in Italy but international in scope.[4]

THE JUNE MUNICIPAL ELECTIONS

On 6 June, in the largest electoral consultation since April 1992 taking in 1192 communal councils across Italy, the decline of the parties of the old coalition was dramatically substantiated. Though it remained the largest single party, the Christian Democrats' share of the national vote fell by a half, to 18 per cent, and really only held up well in the South and

Sicily. The PSI (hit by splits and breakaways) was almost wiped out, failing to win a single seat in its former stronghold in Milan, and, together with the other lay parties, managed to muster only 5.6 per cent all told.[5]

The biggest victories went to the Northern League (showing further strong progress by emerging as the leading party in the North), the PDS (which did badly elsewhere but retained control of its traditional area in central Italy) and, challenging in the South, *La Rete* and a host of unfamiliar independent, civic and local lists. But the most interesting results concerned voting for the mayoralties of the larger urban areas, which – as a result of the new electoral law of 27 March 1993 – were to be filled by candidates directly elected by majority vote (rather than being chosen by the parties), with a second round run-off between the two leading contenders in cases where no candidate obtained more than 50 per cent of the vote. The party or coalition of parties supporting that candidate would then be awarded a majority premium of sixty per cent of the seats on the council.

In Milan, the Northern League's candidate, Marco Formentini, took 38.8 per cent, 8 per cent ahead of Nando Dalla Chiesa of *La Rete*, who had the support of the PDS and the Greens, and other Northern League candidates also headed the field in Novara, Pavia, Pordenone and Vercelli. But in Turin the Northern League's Domenico Comino could only come third, behind Diego Novelli (*La Rete*–Greens–Refoundation–Pensioners) and Valentino Castellani (supported by the centre-left Democratic Alliance, the PDS, and the Green Alliance). In the only major contest in the South, Enzo Bianco, with Segni's support, came out ahead in Catania. Bossi declared that a new bi-polar politics was taking shape, with the Northern League occupying the centre ground against the left-wing. At the same time the importance of forming rainbow alliances was already becoming obvious, threatening to hold back any further advance by the Northern League so long as it insisted on fielding candidates in its own right.

THE REFORM OF THE VOTING SYSTEM

After several months of inconclusive stalling, the *Bicamerale* committee for electoral reform was enjoined to make haste, even though a basic consensus about how the majoritarian principle should be translated into legislative form was still lacking. Many had maintained that parliament's hands were tied by the magnitude of the referendum result. However, it remained unclear whether the revised Senate law[6] was workable, whether the balance between majoritarian and proportional seats was acceptable, and whether one-round voting *all'inglese* or the French double ballot should be employed. In the event, the codifying of rules for the Senate turned out to be relatively straightforward and uncontroversial. The bigger quarrel concerned the electoral law for the Chamber of Deputies which had also to be altered so as to bring the two constitutionally co-equal chambers into conformity again.[7]

In the absence of a common position, a bill containing outline proposals for the Chamber of Deputies was drawn up by the vice-chairman and rapporteur of the *Bicamerale*, Sergio Mattarella (DC), and put before the Chamber on 14 June. The Mattarella bill envisaged a mixed, mainly majoritarian system in which voters would still have two votes, with 70 per cent of the seats (the DC had initially favoured 60 per cent) to be awarded by simple majority in 474 single-member colleges and the remaining 30 per cent allocated – with a mechanism devised to compensate the smaller parties – on a proportional party list basis in 26 larger constituencies. Voters would be free, if they wished, to 'split' their vote. In order to reduce party fragmentation, a 4 per cent threshold for representation was to operate. But it would be left up to Parliament, in the normal course of its legislative deliberations, to determine the final shape of the bill. By resorting to this expedient, as Pappalardo has observed, the *Bicamerale* was virtually ridding itself of any surviving authority.[8]

In a series of decisive votes on 16 and 17 June, the Chamber endorsed a 75:25 ratio of majoritarian to proportional seats, but the demand for a double ballot was roundly defeated, disappointing the PDS and Segni, who had both championed the French alternative. Although the conjectured effect of this new arrangement in promoting two-party politics was open to much dispute,[9] the Christian Democrats, the Northern League (Formentini had just triumphed in the mayoral run-off in

Milan), MSI, *La Rete* and most of the PSI saw enough advantage in it to give the bill its final approval on 30 June, and it passed (overcoming the opposition of the PDS, the Republicans and the Liberals) by 311 votes to 124, with 99 abstentions. Segni abstained, unconvinced that the legislation went far enough. A last minute amendment promoted by the MSI enfranchising two million Italian expatriates – which would require an amendment to the constitution – ensured that the bill would have to return to the Chamber at a later date.

Four months were set aside for the drawing up of new electoral boundaries, adding to the likely delay. The bill then transferred to the Senate, where it met with further obstacles. It was only by going to the point of carrying a vote of confidence tied to a law ending the practice of *lottizzazione* (the sub-dividing of posts among the parties) in RAI, the public broadcasting corporation, that Ciampi had been able to clear the decks for the Senate to begin its consideration in the first place. The Senate subsequently adopted an amendment limiting any elected candidate to no more than three parliamentary terms, which by itself would have disqualified most of the incumbent party leaders. All of these incidents helped to hold up the passage of the legislation and the prospect of a general election, especially for the more than 150 parliamentarians who, once stripped of their seats and their immunity, faced instant arrest.

Interrupted by three further, unclaimed explosions – two in Rome and one in Milan[10] – the new electoral laws completed their parliamentary passage with only a day to spare before the deadline of the close of the session, the Senate approving the bill by 128 votes to 29, with 59 abstentions, on 3 August, and the Chamber by 278 to 78 (with 153 Deputies abstaining) on 4 August. Jubilantly greeted by the prime minister's office as a clear signal of the capacity for expeditious change through existing constitutional and parliamentary channels, a committee of experts was appointed to draw up a new map of electoral colleges and constituencies consistent with the new legislation. As if to underline the new course, the Chamber also finally voted by a large majority to lift Craxi's parliamentary immunity in connection with 46 separate corruption charges, which Craxi had fought to the end, before leaving for his villa in Tunisia.

THE FOUNDING OF THE ITALIAN POPULAR PARTY

The reform of the electoral system was only one of many political episodes in the summer of 1993. Two other significant events of these months were (once again) the investigations on corruption, and the founding of the Italian Popular Party from the defunct DC.

After more than seven months on the run, the former chief executive of Ferruzi-Montedison, Giuseppe Garofano, was arrested in early July at Geneva airport and extradited to Italy. Garofano's testimony blew open the Enimont affair.[11] Gabriele Cagliari (the former head of ENI) was already being held in preventative detention in Milan on charges of illegal party funding, but had so far refused to implicate others. Despite a promise by a judge that he would shortly be released, Cagliari's petition to be freed was turned down, and – after 133 days in incarceration – he committed suicide on 20 July, complaining in several suicide notes that he had unfairly been made the target of public resentment and the scapegoat of what was a national tragedy. Three days later, Raul Gardini, discovering that he was soon likely to be taken into custody, shot himself at his home. Two prominent DC politicians, Forlani and Pomicino (the latter already being investigated for mafia collusion), were also named by Garofano.

The impression this gave – taking into account the recent confessions of other captains of industry like Gianni Agnelli (Fiat) and Carlo De Benedetti (Olivetti) about corrupt past practices – was not simply of bribe-taking by the political parties in the awarding of public sector contracts, which many entrepreneurs had been claiming they had had no choice about proffering. Instead it painted a picture of agreed and regularised under-the-table payments designed to protect home industry from foreign competition in return for the consolidation of political power and personal enrichment, creating 'an unholy alliance where industrialists and politicians joined as allies, one making sure the markets remained closed and the other to make sure that the same political parties stayed in power'.[12] The rigged economy and polity which resulted was, as De Benedetti remarked, 'closer to an Arab *souk* than to Brussels'.

On 23 July (the very day of Gardini's suicide), the Christian Democrats convened a long-awaited constituent assembly in Rome, at which Martinazzoli announced his intention to renew the DC (without renouncing its past or its white shield symbol), by giving birth to a new Italian Popular Party. Deputies and Senators tainted by scandal were not invited. Financially and organisationally, the old party structure was on the verge of disintegration. In obtaining full powers to carry through the change, sanctioned by all but one of the delegates, Martinazzoli managed to avoid a harmful split with more active-minded reformers grouped around Rosy Bindi, the regional secretary in the Veneto, who were pushing for a thorough purge of the party's ranks.

Such reinventing of the DC on the move was shot full of imponderables. It would not be easy for the party, even in the longer-term, to shake off its large share of responsibility for Italy's current state.[13] In the draft of the final agreed statement, reference was made to the possibility of the party passing into opposition, although the equally pressing question of future alliances was circumvented altogether.[14] The poor Christian Democrat showing under new voting rules in the June local elections had very much shaped the party's damage-limiting preference for the mixed, one-round voting reform going through parliament, on the assumption that the new system would still allow it to survive as the largest single party with a national presence.

CIAMPI'S ECONOMIC POLICIES

Ciampi's own reputation for sound finance had been a deciding factor in his initial appointment as Prime Minister, but his technical economic team – Barucci, Spaventa (budget) and Gallo (finance) – enjoyed the benefit of greater freedom from party political pressures, while the cabinet as a whole operated with more collective cohesion. Once established in office, it was also spared the string of embarrassing resignations that had dogged Amato. Ciampi's was an 'institutional' and not a 'party' government,[15] not wholly unresponsive to parliamentary or political influences but with a clear determination to

restore international trust and credibility at a point when industrial output had dipped and unemployment had climbed
above 11 per cent of the economically active population – over
a quarter of a million had been laid off in the first quarter of
1993 alone.

Economic circumstances were not entirely unfavourable.
The depreciation of the *lira*, which had nominally lost 22
per cent of its value against the *Deutschmark* by the middle of
the year, had encouraged a sharp surge in exports and a
healthy trade surplus. This had not, moreover, had any detrimental effect on the rate of inflation which, at just over 4
per cent, was the lowest it had been since the 1960s. Interest
rates had fallen progressively as a result, benefitting manufacturing industry. But there had been no easing of the
problem of public debt (112–14 per cent of GDP) and of
the budget deficit (10.2 per cent of GDP, and almost twice
the European Community average), requiring real interest
rates to remain relatively high so as to attract new pur-
chasers of government stock and facilitate debt servicing.
Even floating outside the EMS, the currency was not
immune to speculative attack. A mini-budget in May (fore-
seen by Amato) brought in L12 500b through tax increases
and spending cuts, in accordance with the terms for the
release of the second tranche of the EC loan. But this still
left Ciampi with a further L45 000b to find in the full
budget for 1994, if he was to keep close to the target deficit
for the coming year.

One confidence-boosting achievement was the reaching (at
the beginning of July) of a new, four-year joint accord between
employers and trade unions, confirming the abolition of the
indexation of wages and setting in motion twice-yearly meetings to determine wage settlements that would harmonise with
the main objectives of government policy – instituting in all
but name a national incomes policy. Followed up by a further
interest rate cut, Ciampi was able to promote the accord as a
vital sign of Italian intent at the July summit of the G7. In the
short-term, it made wage inflation less likely, since the unions
were placing job security ahead of pay increases. But the issue
of the reform of state pensions, which currently accounted for
half of the annual budget, had still to be addressed.

Ciampi took a personal hand in settling on a basic budget calculation which, in contrast to the previous year, emphasised cost-cutting rather than tax-raising.[16] The complexity of the new minimum tax on the self-employed was causing an outcry, but added to this was a belief by Treasury ministers that the tax burden (taxes were taking up 42.4 per cent of GDP)[17] was already too high. The main reductions in spending were sought through a package of measures aimed at the reorganisation of public administration,[18] topped off with an across-the-board 3 per cent cut in departmental spending. Along with other modifications in health and educational services, this brought total anticipated savings to L31 000b (£13.25b), fixing the deficit at L144 200b, or 8.7 per cent of GDP. The final shape of the proposals was approved by the cabinet on 11 September before being sent on to parliament. Compared with past budget practice, however, there had been little or no 'party intermediation'.[19] One senior Christian Democrat politician commented 'the first we knew of the details was from the newspapers'. In Parliament the budget, or Finance bill, was being exposed to an unusually extended examination. First Spaventa and then Barucci declared that they would leave office should the budget not be passed by the deadline of the end of December, and it was generally assumed that Ciampi might do the same.

A key element in economic restructuring was the privatisation programme. Much preparatory groundwork had been carried out under Amato, especially in depoliticising the boards of state concerns. Not all obstacles were of a political kind. The Milan stock market was not well developed. The economic slowdown had put off potential buyers. Debts owed by EFIM had still not been rescheduled. The precedent of the Montedison sale, a privatisation which ended up as a renationalisation, was not encouraging.[20] Rather than setting aside the proceeds of any projected sell-offs for the current account, Ciampi created a special fund for debt reduction.

Strong disagreements remained about the best way to disengage the state from significant holdings. The incoming chairman of IRI, Romano Prodi,[21] favoured turning those enterprises in the first wave of selling (principally the two state banks, Credito Italiano and the Banca Commerciale Italia) into fully-fledged public companies with a large number of smaller shareholders (and with a 3 per cent upper limit on ownership). Alternatively, a *nocciolo duro* or hard nucleus of existing, successful private sector groups should be constructed, orchestrated by Enrico Cuccia's Mediobanca,[22] which would take a controlling stake.[23] Ciampi declared his 'full confidence' in Prodi, and in late September a cabinet decree laid down the first course, on a case-by-case basis.[24]

Powerful interests, and rival philosophies, were clearly at stake. The leading 'family' businesses were anxious to conserve their private power and pre-eminence, whereas the advocates of the public company model preached the benefits of wider share ownership and the democratising of the economy. When shares in Credito Italiano went on sale in December, they were heavily oversubscribed. It only subsequently came to light that groups close to Mediobanca had gained control of the bank's new board by pooling shares. It was clear that privatisation did not just involve a technical transfer of state holdings. It heralded important structural changes for the Italian economy just when many major companies were in severe financial difficulties.

For once, however, the chronic instability of the executive did not obtain. Instead, it was parliament – racked by scandal and increasingly undisciplined – that was the weaker branch. Many MPs nominally of the government fought a long rearguard action designed to prolong the life of the 11th legislature for as long as possible. Passing of the budget legislation and completion of arrangements for the new electoral laws would clear the path for a general election, the exact timing of which was President Scalfaro's decision, whose preference for early elections was widely known.

In September, in an attempt to pressurise him, a death threat was made against his daughter. The following month, when the Chamber of Deputies voted to lift the parliamentary immunity of Gava but not that of Francesco de Lorenzo, the President went out of his way to show his disgust by announcing that, had the Ciampi government already accomplished its tasks, he would have dissolved parliament forthwith. Then, on 29 October, the recently arrested former director of SISDE (the civilian secret service), Riccardo Malpica, backed up earlier claims that SISDE had operated a slush fund of illicit payments to prominent politicians, including a monthly salary to the interior minister since the early 1980s, a post which the current President Scalfaro had held from 1983 until 1987. Other former SISDE colleagues suspected of embezzlement bore this out. Refusing to be pushed into resigning, Scalfaro appeared on evening television to condemn concerted attempts at 'the slow destruction of the country'.

THE NOVEMBER MUNICIPAL ELECTIONS

Anxieties concerning the longevity of Ciampi's government were exacerbated by the spectacle of a party system in the throes of full-scale organisational and ideological mutation, evident in the outcome of the first round of voting in municipal elections for 424 towns and cities and the mayoralties of several major regional capitals (Venice, Trieste, Genoa, Rome, Naples and Palermo) on 21 November. Bereft of electoral allies or a cohesive Catholic constituency, and lacking in candidates of stature, the Christian Democrat party's nationwide support collapsed and dispersed, leaving it with 8.2 per cent of the vote in communes of less than 15 000 inhabitants and 11.2 per cent in communes of more than 15 000 inhabitants. Only one DC-sponsored candidate, Riccardo Illy in Trieste (exceptionally with PDS support), made it through to the second round run-off on 6 December.

In the centre and the South, there was an astonishing quintupling in the vote for the MSI to 31 per cent, with the party leader, Gianfranco Fini, in Rome, and Alessandra Mussolini (the granddaughter of Benito Mussolini), in Naples both coming second in their mayoral race.[25] In Palermo Leoluca Orlando's *La Rete* triumphed with 75.2 per cent of first-round votes. But the undisputed victor of these elections was the PDS, which made modest electoral gains by virtue of tactical alliances with a variety of other left and centre-left groupings – the Greens, *La Rete*, and the Democratic Alliance[26] – all of its mayoral candidates winning through to the second round.

Even with the second round run-offs still to come, two observations could be made. Firstly, the 'radicalising' of the vote between June and November. Partly, this was explained by the very different terrain in which the later contests were fought. But there was no doubting that the long-standing centrality of the Christian Democrats had turned into a liability.[27] The effect of the results was to invest those 'clean' parties who had been excluded from or most antagonistic towards the organisation of party power with new found electoral legitimacy.[28] The new politics was not just post-Communist or post-Cold War, it was essentially post-particratic.

Secondly, the geographical fracturing of party support. In each case, the Northern League, the PDS and the MSI were stronger where they were already strong, accentuating the three-way split between the Northern League in the North, the central 'red belt' of the PDS and the MSI from the capital southwards. In fact, in Diamanti's view,[29] the MSI was a kind of Lega Sud, both the Northern League Nord and the MSI having established themselves as the natural parties of oppositional protest. Yet the views of the Northern League and the MSI were antithetical in the extreme, with the Northern League's economically liberal and federalist programme quite at odds with the welfarist, nationalist outlook of the MSI. Their joint electoral ascendancy called into question the rationale of an interventionist state fostering national unity through extensive economic redistribution, marking the end of the political understanding of which the DC had been the recognised guarantor.

It is interesting to note that the Northern League, the MSI and the PDS both attracted *and* repelled voters. The Northern League did much better than the mayoral fights implied, consolidating its support wherever Northern voters were voting for a party list. But its advance no longer looked irresistible, and Bossi was minded to change strategy and eradicate any lingering separatist tendencies in order to overcome its electoral isolation. Furthermore anti-left opinion was not persuaded that the Northern League constituted a sufficiently credible alternative. The MSI, building on its traditional nationalist–populist appeal to the marginalised urban voter, had undergone a political rehabilitation, helped by the presence of high profile candidates. It had been less successful in convincing others about the authenticity of its democratic credentials, particularly since the party had not renounced its fascist past and a large majority of its own activists still did not accept the legality of republican institutions.[30] The PDS, meanwhile, and despite its title to be the only remaining viable national party that could hold the country together,[31] laboured to reassure those who had reservations about entrusting it with government. Occhetto hoped that recent successes justified the difficult choices that had been made after 1989, not least in rejecting an alliance with the PSI.[32] Yet as we shall see in the next chapter, to get the fissiparious forces of the left to agree on a common programme for the forthcoming election would be a very different matter.

An early opportunity for the PDS to underline its respectability arose in the week after the first round of municipal voting, when rumours were circulating that sections of the Christian Democrat and Socialist parties, shattered by the latest events, were on the verge of pulling out of the Ciampi coalition, jeopardising the budget and panicking investors (the *lira* fell below the psychological threshold of 1000 to the DM).

After calling together parliamentary leaders, Ciampi was confident that a majority still existed in favour of price and monetary stability, above all because the PDS and the Northern League (by its policy of active abstention) reaffirmed their commitment to the approval of the budget by year's end. A major feature of the new economic strategy of the PDS was, indeed, that if and when it came to power it would continue the work of the Ciampi administration, holding down spending, demanding shared sacrifices and pushing ahead with the privatising of state assets.

THE RUN-UP TO THE MARCH 1994 GENERAL ELECTIONS

In the second round of voting in the municipal elections on 6 December, PDS-backed candidates made a clean sweep of the five big mayoralties, so that, with the single exception of Milan, all the main regional capitals were in the hands of the left or held by leftist-influenced coalitions. The PDS also did well in the run-offs in the larger towns and cities (of over 15 000 inhabitants) where victory carried with it the right to appoint two-thirds of the council. Occhetto was aware that, with any cross-party arrangement for the full general election, there would be a cost in terms of party unity and distinctiveness. But if there was to be a deal (Segni apart), it was now obvious that it would be his party that would be the central pivot, around which a broad alliance of the centre-left could then combine.

The ominous advance made by the leftist alliance finally convinced one interested onlooker – the media proprietor Silvio Berlusconi – that the time had come to make his move. His own Fininvest empire was heavily in debt, the Mammí law which regularised his profitable monopoly control of private television was due to be revised, and his political allies and benefactors were all disgraced. Notwithstanding repeated denials about having any political ambition, Berlusconi had been paying close attention to the unfolding drama, adjusting the editorial line of his broadcasting and publishing outlets to give coverage to Bossi and the Northern League and doing everything to combat what he characterised as the malign influence of the Scalfari-de Benedetti-PDS lobby.[33] Diakron, an opinion research and marketing arm for Fininvest, had already been created in June. This was followed in November by the formation of the first *Forza Italia!* clubs (from the football slogan, 'Come on, Italy', which even the Pope had recently used),[34] also utilising the organisation and personnel of Fininvest. Though many had warned him against going into politics,[35] Berlusconi had been having meetings with Martinazzoli, Segni and others about the feasibility of a PDS-blocking alliance and was evidently waiting for the right moment to 'descend onto the field of play', ready and able to convey an image of honesty, transparency and competence.

While the left were imposing their programme on the voters, Berlusconi's pollsters would cross-question people to find out what it was *they* wanted.[36] In a series of press interviews on the morrow of the first round of voting, he spoke of the Italy which 'works, produces and saves' and 'does its duty', and when he was asked who, if he were living in Rome, he would support in the second round, he astonished everyone by replying that he would certainly vote for Fini 'because he represents the values of the moderate block in which I believe'.

With the budget about to be passed, and a general election no more than a matter of weeks away, a frantic phase of forming up and manoeuvring for position ensued. On 26 November, the leader of the MSI Gianfranco Fini – denying any nostalgic sympathy with fascism – announced his intention to establish a National Alliance (*Alleanza Nazionale*, or AN).

Apart from incorporating the MSI, Fini's National Alliance would attract former DC supporters, show the will to govern constitutionally and 'bar the route to the left'. The MSI was reconstituted by merging it into the AN on 11 of November, the speed of the change raising questions about its authenticity.[37] The PSI, rejecting a last fling by Craxi, threw in its lot with the progressive left. The Northern League, in the meantime, had convened its annual assembly, in the wake of allegations by the ex-President of the Northern League that Bossi had accepted an undeclared L200m donation from the Montedison chemical giant in the Spring of 1992, and that 120 000 militants had been 'invented' as a way of inflating membership to cover this and other irregular sources of income. Bossi offered his resignation, which was turned down by delegates, and some of the missing money was collected by contributions from the floor,[38] after which he unveiled a draft plan (devised by the Northern League ideologue, Gianfranco Miglio) for the division of Italy into three self-governing republics of 'Padania', 'Etruria' and the 'South'. Segni was putting his faith instead in his *Popolari della Riforma*, launched in October, which promised a pact for national rebirth for all those unattracted by either the Northern League ('the new centre', Bossi was claiming) or the PDS but which, unless it could quickly establish organisational roots, threatened to leave him looking like 'a general without an army'.[39]

CONCLUSION

The shaping and reforming of alliances was also likely to have important economic consequences. The closing act of the Ciampi government was played out in the week of the 18–24 December, when the budget cleared its final obstacles in the Senate and the Chamber of Deputies, signalling, in Ciampi's expression, a new credibility and confidence about the recovery of Italy. The inflationary effects of devaluation had been offset by the wages accord, and although still serious, the economic position was improving. Most of all, because of the efforts of Ciampi and Amato before him, there had been a turning around of the public finances, with control over the growth of public spending and a reduction of the public debt

– the first absolute decline in the debt stock for more than a decade. The longer-term doubt was whether a future, 'party' government was likely to pursue similar policies.

To the dismay of Bossi and Berlusconi, the president of the Employers Association *Confindustria* Luigi Abete had already effectively dropped his organisation's objections to the PDS, even though the party was still markedly interventionist. Whatever the outcome, the old state-guaranteed equilibrium was unlikely to persist. Deficit-financing had, in the past, provided for economic expansion in the North while defending less efficient industries in the South.[40] This mutually sustaining economic relationship had been broken, after the abrupt cessation of 'extraordinary economic intervention' in the *Mezzogiorno*, in March 1993, and the freezing (in September 1993) of loans to predominantly southern, state-owned enterprise. The pattern of political relations was now also altering. The objective consensus between the two Italies, incarnated by the postwar Christian Democrat party, had come to an end. Opinion was ideologically and geographically polarising, prefiguring a new politics of society, economy and the state.

Notes

1.   F.P. Casavola, quoted in M. Fedele, *Democrazia Referendaria – l'Italia dal primato dei partiti al trionfo dell'opinione pubblica* (1994) p.121.
2.   M. Andreoli, 'Dov'é finito il 18 Aprile?', *Panorama*, 9 May 1993, p.43.
3.   A. Cordova, 'La loggia rapita', *Panorama*, 12 September 1993, p.79.
4.   P. Clough, 'Milan judge offers to return bribes', *The Independent*, 7 September 1993, p.9.
5.   For a detailed analysis of these elections, see G. Di Franco and R. Gritti (eds), *L'Italia al Voto: analisi delle elezioni amministrative del 1993 e delle prospettive del sistema politico italiano* (1994).
6.   Effectively turning three-quarters of the seats in the Senate into majoritarian ones.
7.   D. Hine, 'The New Italian Electoral System', in the *Association for the Study of Italy Newsletter* (1993) p.28.
8.   A. Pappalardo, 'La nuova legge elettorale in parlamento: chi, come e perché', in *Rivista Italiana di Scienza Politica* (1994) p.292.
9.   R. Katz, 'The 1993 Parliamentary Electoral Reform', in C. Mershon and G. Pasquino (eds), *Italian Politics: a review*, Vol.9 (1995) p.100. Mattarella called it 'the best of all possible electoral systems', but critics like Giovanni Sartori and Giorgio Galli argued that it combined the worst of both worlds, and was unlikely to either encourage the

formation of stable, alternating blocs or bring about a turnover in the political class.

10. According to Ciampi, these latest attacks were designed to 'create disorder' and 'thwart renewal'. Following these events, Ciampi assumed personal control of the Italian security service, the SISDE.

11. See the conclusion of Chapter 3 for a brief account of the Enimont affair.

12. G. Sapelli, quoted by P. Semler, 'Elite face music in corruption scandal', in *The Sunday Times*, 14 November 1993, Section III, p.9.

13. D. Wertman, 'The Last Year of the Christian Democrat Party', in C. Mershon and G. Pasquino (eds) op. cit. (1995) p.142.

14. M-C. Decamps, 'La Democratie chretienne se transforme en "Parti populaire"', *Le Monde*, 28 July 1993, p.6.

15. G. Pasquino and S. Vassallo, 'The government of Carlo Azeglio Ciampi', in C. Mershon and G. Pasquino (eds) op. cit. (1995) p.68.

16. R. Graham, 'Dolorosa vita in the public sector', in *The Financial Times*, 14 September 1993, p.17.

17. C. Guimbard, *Ou va l'Italie?* (1994) p.262.

18. These included conversion of the ministry of posts and telecommunications into an independent agency; abolition of all interministerial committees; new restrictions on the eligibility of civil servants for a state pension; a pay freeze; and the encouragement of competitive appointment and promotion.

19. The words of the Prime Minister, as reported in *Il Corriere della Sera*, 6 September 1993, p.2.

20. G. Ragozzino, 'Soldes d'état, état des soldes', in L'Italie Postmoderne, *Peuples Méditerranéens*, April–June 1994, p.123.

21. Romano Prodi (1939–). Professor of Economics. Chairman of IRI 1982–9. Reappointed as successor to Nobili in May 1993. Currently Italy's Prime Minister.

22. Enrico Cuccia (1908?–). Founder, managing director and then honorary president of Mediobanca, a public and private sector merchant bank with financial interests in several important Italian companies. According to legend, 'What Cuccia wants, God wants too'.

23. The 1936 banking law had been revised to allow banks to buy in to the private sector.

24. R. Rosati, 'Commerciale di fuoco', in *Panorama*, 24 October 1993, pp.18–19.

25. In Naples, the maladministration of former viceroys like Gava (DC) and De Lorenzo (PLI) was acutely felt.

26. Mario Segni had joined Democratic Alliance, hoping the PDS would merge into it, and which he then abandoned.

27. C. Lombardo 'Alla ricerca del centro perduto', in G. Di Franco and R. Gritti (eds), *L'Italia al Voto* (1994).

28. In the case of the PDS, the party was only relatively 'clean', since it too was tarnished by mounting allegations – aided and abetted by Craxi – of illicit financing from the Soviet Communist party, import–export activities with Eastern Europe, and the cooperative movement.

29. I. Diamanti, 'Geopolitica del bluff federalista', in *Limes*, October–December 1994, p.39.

30. P. Ignazi, 'La force des racines – la culture politique du mouvement social italien au seuil du gouvernement', in *La Revue Française de Science Politique*, December 1994. An MSI survey of its own youth wing, carried out in 1991, found that fascism was the historical reference point for 88 per cent of them but that only 13 per cent were content to define themselves as 'democratic'.

31. Though it too was much smaller in size, the number of employees in the central party apparatus having fallen from 5000 to roughly 600.

32. See the interview with Occhetto, in 'La gauche italienne est prête à assumer le pouvoir', in *Le Monde*, 3 December 1993, p.6.

33. Eugenio Scalfari is editor of *La Repubblica*.

34. 'Forza Italia! grida il Papa', *La Stampa*, 13 April 1993, p.6.

35. When Indro Montanelli, the editor of *Il Giornale* (owned by Fininvest), pleaded with him not to go into politics, Berlusconi countered: 'You haven't understood that I am tired of being Silvio Berlusconi. I want a heroic life'. Quoted in *Index on Censorship*, September/October 1994, p.25.

36. G. Riotta, 'Il segreto della vittoria e 'la strategia da judo', *Il Corriere della Sera*, 30 March 1994, p.3, reporting on the strategy meetings of Berlusconi and his advisers in the Summer and Autumn of 1993.

37. At the following general elections of March 1994, 95 per cent of AN's candidates were MSI MPs. See C. Valentini 'Alleanza Nazionale: la componente "storica" del Polo della libertà', in P. Ginsborg (ed.), *Stato dell'Italia* (1994).

38. Bossi returned the money in person to Di Pietro, who observed that the Northern League had been implicated in the web of corruption 'just like all the others'.

39. G. Sartori, in *Panorama*, 11 December 1993, p.31.

40. C. Trigilia, 'Nord e Sud: se il belpaese si spezza', in *Limes*, October–December 1994, pp.81–94.

8 The General Election of March 1994

THE ELECTORAL CAMPAIGN

President Scalfaro announced on 16 January that a general election would be held on 27 March. He justified his reasons for calling an election on the following grounds. First, the referendum of April 1993 had profoundly modified the operation of the electoral system. Second, the subsequent municipal elections in June and November had portrayed a large discrepancy between the forces represented in parliament and the popular will. Third, the work of the judiciary was exposing the 'pathologies' in the management of public affairs.[1] Firmly resisting unsettling attempts to force the creation of an entirely new government, which might have delayed the holding on an election until the Summer, Scalfaro asked Ciampi to stay at his post with full powers up until the day of voting. Ciampi had already justified the record of his administration, which, having only a limited duration and clear goals, had acted he said as a 'national guarantee' at a time when the dramatic evolution of the party system could have had damaging economic effects. But he ruled out associating himself with any of the newly emerging political forces.

The imminence of the election sparked off a frenzied burst of regrouping and repositioning. To start with, Berlusconi threw down an ultimatum that unless all moderate, 'constitutional' forces came together to combat the left he would enter the contest himself, at the head of his network of *Forza Italia!* clubs. The Christian Democrat party, however, officially split into two the very next day. A smaller grouping, the Christian Democratic Centre (CCD), going off to ally with the Northern League, while the larger grouping was reborn as the Popular Party of Italy (PPI). The PPI was led by Martinazzoli, who had refused to 'abdicate' in favour of the Northern League in the North. Mario Segni, the hero of the 1993 referenda, launched

167

his own political movement, Pact for Italy, on a programme of liberal democratic reform.[2]

With a range of left-wing parties (comprised of the Democratic Party of the Left (PDS), Communist Refoundation, the Greens, *La Rete*, the Democratic Alliance and the new Italian Socialist Party) about to form a first-ever campaigning alliance on a common platform of cautious reconstruction, Berlusconi finally took the plunge, renouncing his role as a publisher and entrepreneur and offering to help to establish a 'credible alternative' to a Communist-dominated government of the left inevitably tied to a 'bankrupt past'. In an address on one of his own television channels, he said that he was not going to constitute an 'umpteenth' party, but a force that would bring together those with their head on their shoulders and a certain innovating experience to create a more just, modern and prosperous Italy.

Berlusconi moved quickly to show how exactly this would be done. First reaching an agreement to fight in a common front with the Northern League in the North of Italy, creating the Pole of Freedom, he then teamed up with the *Alleanza Nazionale* – the recently reconstituted MSI, now self-proclaimedly post-fascist – in central Italy and the South, forming the Pole of Good Government. In spite of Bossi's protestations that he would never ally with the fascists, Berlusconi signed a joint deal on the dividing up of candidates and colleges on 12 February.

It was an astonishing masterstroke by Berlusconi, indicative of how far arch-rivals were willing to make common cause in the quest for political power. At one go, it isolated the centre and targeted the now united left, and in the last few days before the provisions on parity of treatment in the media came into force,[3] Berlusconi used his broadcasting outlets to drive home the attack on those he branded as 'Communists, former Communists and post-Communists', openly exploiting what remained of what was once the central divide of Italian politics.[4] The bitter tone of the campaign had been set, and notwithstanding the new law, claims and counterclaims about media bias were a strong feature of the electioneering that followed.

The hybrid nature of the new, mixed voting system did, it should be noted, pull in contradictory directions. Straight-fight majority voting compelled parties to combine, yet at the same time proportional representation encouraged them to divide.[5] The uneasy unity of the Pole of Freedom and Pole of

Good Government on the right and of the Progressive Alliance on the left led to much internal bickering, which intensified with the approach of polling day. Northern League's activists were unhappy at the *Forza Italia!* candidates who were parachuted into Northern constituencies, and often refused to campaign on their behalf. Bossi, by the closing stages, was denouncing Berlusconi (whose support had grown at the expense of the Northern league) as a 'false friend'. Similar tensions were felt in the left-wing alliance. When the leader of Communist Refoundation, Fausto Bertinotti, called for the taxation of interest on state bonds, the PDS, which had been anxiously cultivating the City of London, accused him of trying to lose them the election. The growing likelihood of a victory for the Berlusconi coalition even induced Occhetto to invite those who could not bring themselves to vote for the Progressive Alliance to opt instead for the PPI.

All parties aspired to be part of, or to be in a position to affect, whatever governing majority might eventually come about. But the shaping of any absolute majority would be determined by the relative strength of its composing parties. As such, the mechanics of the new voting system complicated the efforts of the parties and bewildered the voters, many of whom were baffled by the unfamiliar alignments and personalities. The Italian Employers' Confederation, or *Confindustria*, adopted what it called a 'vigilant neutrality', while the splintering of the Christian Democrats destroyed any concerted clerical influence. Party programmes tended to be declarations of intent rather than fully worked-out statements of policy, the ideological differences between them typically being exaggerated.[6] No future government would be able to ignore the economic reality of the public debt, the budget deficit and wage restraint. The hope, therefore, that a more adversarial election would empower the voter – by offering a genuine choice – was not conclusively borne out. Compared with the unstable but largely static electoral politics of the First Republic, all those participating in the election of March 1994, either as buyers (the electorate) or as sellers (political parties and hopeful candidates), were genuinely uncertain about the final outcome. According to one distinguished commentator, the most open and truly unpredictable election since 1948 turned into 'a great national lottery', which risked throwing up all kinds of surprises.[7]

THE RESULTS

The unexpected duly materialised. On a slightly lower than average turnout of 86 per cent of eligible voters, the right wing alliance triumphantly obtained an absolute majority of seats in the Chamber of Deputies (366 out of 630) and only fell three short (155 out of 315) in the Senate, the three alliance partners together winning 42.9 per cent of the national vote, (see tables 8.1. and 8.2). *Forza Italia!* ended up with the largest share of support, proving to be especially popular among female, professional and younger voters,[8] and even outpolling the Northern League in its own Northern heartland, the Northern League only prospering because of the favourable pre-election sharing out of seats. The AN also made a strong showing, particularly in Rome and the South. For the Progressive Alliance it was a bitter defeat, the PDS holding on to its traditional areas of support but taking a beating in Lombardy and Piedmont, the attempt to demonise Berlusconi making it seem to be opposed to the forces of reform. *La Rete* won no representation, falling short of the parliamentary threshold, while Segni, defeated in his home seat in Sardinia, only returned thanks – ironically – to one of his Pact's four proportional seats. Berlusconi's message of economic liberalism – tax cuts, privatisation, and a million new jobs in the medium term – had had an electrifying appeal, tapping the mood of many people who felt excluded from and alienated by the old political elite.[9] By concentrating and polarising partisan opinion, albeit it in surprising ways, an unmistakeable verdict had been arrived at.

Table 8.1   Results of 1994 election in terms of seats in the Chamber of Deputies

Progressives	202
Communist refoundation	11
Pole of freedom + pole of good government	366
Pact for Italy	46
Others	5
Total	630

Table 8.2   Results of 1994 election in terms of seats in the Senate

Progressives	122
Pact for Italy	31
Pole of freedom + pole of good government	155
Pannella list	1
Others	6
Total	315

Progressives = Democratic Party of the Left; Socialist Party; Socialist Rebirth; Communist Refoundation; Greens; Democratic Alliance; The Network; Christian Social

Pole of Freedom = Forza Italia; Northern League; Christian Democratic Centre; Union of the Centre; Pannella List

Pole of good government = Forza Italia; National Alliance; Christian Democratic Centre; Union of the Centre

Pact for Italy = The Segni Pact; Italian Popular Party

Sources: Adapted from S. Burgess, 'The New Italy and the General Election of March 1994', *Representation*, Vol.32, No.118, 1994.

A number of important aspects of the results are worth commenting upon. To begin with, the 1994 election was the first in which the new electoral laws applied, and these new rules-of-the-game had a non-negligible effect on the results. One way of measuring the effects of the new electoral system is by looking at what is known as the level of distortion between the percentage of votes each party won, and the percentage of parliamentary seats each party was awarded. The greater the disparity between the two sets of percentage numbers, the greater the level of distortion. In the Chamber of Deputies the Right (FI, Northern League, AN) won 42.9 per cent of the votes but 58.1 per cent of the seats, the Left (PDS, RC, Rete, Verdi, Democratic Alliance (AD)) 34.4 per cent of the votes and 33.8 per cent of the seats, and the Centre (PPI and Patto Segni) 15.7 per cent of the votes but only 7.3 per cent of the seats. Roughly the same pattern can be found in the Senate, with the Right winning 40.4 per cent of the votes and 49.2 per cent of the seats, the Left winning respectively 33.1 per cent and 38.7 per cent, and the Centre respectively 16.7 per cent and 9.9 per cent.[10] The source of the seat-vote distortion is not hard to find – for example, of the 475 simple majority winners for the Chamber, only 151 collected over half of the vote.

Of course, it was to be expected that the new electoral system would create a high level of distortion, since switching from a purely proportional to a predominantly majoritarian voting system was inevitably going to benefit the major parties. Yet the supporters of the reform had argued that this was a price worth paying in order to reduce the number of parties in parliament and, consequently, to create a more solid parliamentary majority. In fact the desired outcomes did not come about. There are two indicators which reflect this reality. First, the number of parliamentary groups did not change as radically as had been hoped, with 8 groups in the Chamber of Deputies and 11 in the Senate, compared with 13 and 10 respectively in 1992.[11] As a result, the winning right-wing coalition was made up of 6 different parties (FI, AN, Northern League, CCD, CDU and Lista-Pannella), which is hardly an improvement on the recent past. Italians, as Sartori joked, managed to find a way of proportionalising the majoritarian vote. Secondly, comparing the total percentage of votes gained by the two major parties in the 1994 elections (FI and PDS) with the two major parties in previous elections (DC and PCI), one can see in table 8.3 that the largest parties were relatively less 'large' than in the past.[12]

The contrast with the 1992 election – when the signs of incipient collapse first became evident – was instructive, two important changes having since then occurred: there had been a technical change to the voting system,[13] and there had been a changearound in the leading protagonists. By this we are not only referring to single individuals, the politicians that symbolised the old regime such as Craxi and Andreotti, but also to the number and character of political parties themselves, which had ceased to exist in their former configuration.[14] Voters had switched votes, not only but not least because of the change in whom and what they could vote for.

The electoral campaign was dominated by the theme of novelty and change. All political forces, notwithstanding their location on the ideological spectrum, made strenuous efforts not to be associated with the politics of the First Republic.[15] All political parties, and especially hopeful individuals

Table 8.3   Index of bipolarism (Chamber of Deputies)

Year	DC	PCI	Total
1948	48.5	31.0	79.5
1953	40.1	22.6	62.7
1958	42.3	22.7	65.0
1963	38.3	25.3	63.6
1968	39.1	26.9	66.0
1972	38.7	27.1	65.8
1976	38.7	34.4	73.1
1979	38.3	30.4	68.7
1983	32.9	29.9	62.8
1987	34.3	26.6	60.9
	DC	PDS	
1992	29.7	16.1	45.8
	FI	PDS	
1994	21.0	20.4	41.4

campaigning for the first time, were keen to present themselves as the legitimate ambassadors of change. This atmosphere of renewal encouraged political analysts to understand the 1994 election by considering what they took to be the 'new' factors. In other words, many commentators tended to assume that if there were new results, these must be due to new variables, and therefore that an original explanation of the outcome must start by looking at what was different about the 1994 election from all earlier elections.

In what follows we are going to resist this widely held tendency of correlating new results with new factors. Our argument is the very different one that the classics (as always) have something to teach us, and that even when confronted with a new reality, there is much to be learned from going back to, and drawing upon, the timeless texts that shaped the discipline of politics – in this case, the pathbreaking account of *Capitalism, Socialism and Democracy* composed by Joseph Schumpeter.[16]

In this landmark work, Schumpeter rejected the so-called classical theory of democracy, 'centred in the proposition that "the people" hold a definite and rational opinion about every individual question and that they give effect to this opinion – in a democracy – by choosing "representatives" who will see to it that that opinion is carried out'.[17] In lieu of this, Schumpeter put forward an alternative account of democracy, according to which 'the democratic method is that institutional arrangement for arriving at political decisions in which individuals acquire the power to decide by means of a competitive struggle for the people's vote'.[18]

The important difference between the classical theory of democracy and what Schumpeter calls the *another* theory of democracy, is that the former puts greater emphasis on the demand side of politics (that is the electorate), whereas the latter gives prominence to the supply side of politics (that is the competition between political actors). This is an insight of great theoretical value, since, as we shall see, the most important aspect of the 1994 elections was the fact that there was a marked shift from the demand side to the supply side of politics, rewarding those parties who anticipated this shift and penalising those which did not.

THE SIGNIFICANCE OF THE 1994 ELECTION

The outstanding feature of the 1994 election was that it marked the advent of a competitive political market, something Italy has perhaps never had. For the first time since the war, the electoral contest was 'open' and 'competitive', rather than 'closed' and 'static'. There was a real sense of open political competition, rather than oligopolistic tendencies.[19]

The opening up of the political market to competitive forces had a number of profound repercussions on the political system. Above all, in the electoral arena there was a marked turn away from political demand (coming from the electorate) to political offer (political actors, parties, organization and programmes). It would be wrong to believe that the change in the electoral system was sufficient by itself to explain the swing all the way from one extreme (political demand) to the other extreme (political supply). We should not jump to the erroneous conclusion that the voters had simply become consumers, since the political identity of the voter still plays a major role in their political choices.[20] That said, there was a clear move in the direction of a fully competitive electoral marketplace.

As Ilvo Diamanti and Renato Mannheimer remarked,[21] one important factor which reflects the opening up of the electoral market was the way in which the 1994 political campaign was conducted. Open competition for votes required a different approach to the electoral market. It was not a coincidence that campaigning gave greater prominence to individual politicians. This change of emphasis, with individual political actors being at least as important as the political party/movement which he or she represented, had profound implications for the final results.[22]

First of all, it was easier for new political personalities to make an impression on the electorate. To this extent, the new faces in the political scene had a non-negligible advantage over the old guard, who struggled to come to terms with the new requirements of an open and fluid market for votes. The experienced politicians were not only shackled by the tradition of the political parties they represented, but also by the traditional ways of electioneering.

Secondly, the opening up of the electoral market and the increasing personalisation of electoral competition meant that the role of the media became increasingly important. The mass media in general, and television in particular, have been identified as one of the determining factors behind the success of Silvio Berlusconi and his right-wing alliance. For the moment, let it suffice to point to the fact that the mass media become instrumental both in creating political personalities and in presenting the political campaign under the guise of a personal duel between individual actors as supposed to political parties presenting their traditional points of view. The increasing personalisation of the new electoral campaigning, accentuated by the increasing prominence of the mass media, seemed to bring out emotional rather than rational motivations from the voters. Thus the political actors were not being judged for their political programmes, but for the level of trust or hope they embodied.

On the basis of what has been said so far about the opening up of the electoral market, with the corresponding shift away from the demand side towards the supply side of politics, and the market personalisation of the campaign which concentrated more on the political actors than the political parties, we can now focus on the protagonists of the election, beginning with the undisputed star of the campaign: Silvio Berlusconi.

BERLUSCONI

There is little doubt that this election will be remembered for the meteoric rise to power of Silvio Berlusconi and his *Forza Italia!* movement. There were two dominant explanations given for Berlusconi's success: the view that Berlusconi personified change, at a time when change and novelty was seen as intrinsically desirable, and the (not unrelated) view that Berlusconi's control of the mass media was decisive in clinching victory for *Forza Italia!* In what follows, we shall critically analyse – but reject – both explanatory approaches.

The first approach argued that people voted for Berlusconi simply because he represented something 'new'. This naively realistic explanation of Berlusconi's electoral popularity was based on the assumption that the electorate was out to punish the old political order. The assumption that in the eyes of the electorate Berlusconi was seen as a political virgin, new to the game of politics, and therefore untainted by the corrupt political regime of the first republic, could be seen as insulting the intelligence of the electorate. The close friendship between Berlusconi and Craxi had been documented many times already, and Berlusconi's recent charges of corruption would indicate that he was not exactly a newcomer to the political world. Furthermore Berlusconi was not the only politician to play the 'novelty' card during these elections. Mario Segni (*Patto Segni*) and Umberto Bossi (Northern League) had the best claim to have been the real agents of change. If the electorate wanted something new, why did they overwhelmingly choose to vote for Berlusconi as opposed to Segni or Bossi? Something else is needed to supplement this approach, something that set Berlusconi apart from other adversaries.

This brings us to the second explanatory approach to Berlusconi's success. This approach points to Berlusconi's almost monopolistic control of the private mass media. Gundle and O'Sullivan suggested that 'the political rise of Berlusconi was a consequence both of Italian television and popular culture, and of the previous *laissez-faire* approach to concentration in media ownership'.[23] In what follows, we will try to argue that the role of the mass media has been exaggerated, and that this variable is not sufficient to explain the success of Berlusconi. The rather simplistic affinity between Berlusconi the winner of the elections, and Berlusconi the media tycoon, was assumed but never really examined in any depth.[24] There seemed to be an untested belief that all those who watched Berlusconi's channels and read his newspapers inevitably voted for him. Yet there is no reason why the causal chain could not be reversed, such that those who watched his television channels did so because they were already predisposed in his favour.[25]

Even if there was a grain of truth in the emphasis placed on Berlusconi the 'redeemer' of Italian politics and Berlusconi the media tycoon, both approaches fall short of a completely comprehensive answer. In order to explain Berlusconi's success, it is imperative to take into consideration what has been said already about the opening up of the electoral market. The success of Berlusconi's *Forza Italia!* was due to the fact that Berlusconi was able to swing on to his side the more mobile sectors of the electoral market. Thus we must try to understand why Berlusconi was more successful in this operation compared to his competitors in the electoral market. In particular, we believe that the role of the mass media in this election must be analysed in the light of what has been said before, namely, the opening up of the electoral market, and the personalisation of political debates. What is needed is an explanatory framework in terms of electoral mobility, party competition and the market for votes. In what follows, we will argue that a re-reading of Schumpeter's seminal work on *Capitalism, Socialism and Democracy* provides important help in trying to understand the politics of electoral success.

THE SCHUMPETERIAN/DOWNSIAN MODEL

The most valuable intuition in Schumpeter's analysis concerns what is required of political parties during electoral confrontation.[26] This aspect of Schumpeter's analysis is related to his *another* theory of democracy, which he defines in the following famous formula:

> [T]he democratic method is that institutional arrangement for arriving at political decisions in which individuals acquire the power to decide by means of a competitive struggle for the people's vote.[27]

As we argued above, the significance of the 1994 electoral turn lies in the changes in the structure of the political offer. As the electoral market opens up, we move closer to what Schumpeter identified as a position in which political parties engage in a competitive struggle for the votes of the electorate. Because of this competitive struggle, it becomes important to recognise (still following Schumpeter) that political parties actively attempt to shape the so-called will of the people.

It is in the light of Schumpeter's analytical framework that Berlusconi's electoral triumph must be explained. Berlusconi had the entrepreneurial know-how to appreciate that the electoral marketplace was opening up, while the parties of the left were slower to see this.[28] But in addition to this, Berlusconi was more successful in influencing the outlook of the electorate than the opposition. Of course Schumpeter's views are essentially of a theoretical and speculative nature. More work must be done in order for us to see how Schumpeter's model translates to the real world. Fortunately, much of this work has been done for us. Schumpeter's idea of the party's competitive struggle for people's vote is the cornerstone of Anthony Downs' influential *An Economic Theory of Democracy*, first published in 1957, which represented the dawn of a new methodology in political science: rational choice theory.

The central assumption of Downsian analysis, indeed of rational choice theory in general, is that political actors are essentially rational actors, with political parties behaving like firms in a competitive market and the voters operating as consumers. On the basis of this assumption Downs builds his explanatory model, the fundamental hypothesis of which is that 'parties formulate policies in order to win elections, rather than win elections in order to formulate policies'.[29] It follows that in the competitive struggle for peoples' votes the political parties will want to attract as many voters as they can manage. Political parties will assume that voters have as their goal the attainment of a government responsive to their wants, therefore they will vote for the party that advocates policies closest to their goals.[30]

If we assume, hypothetically, that the views of each voter can be depicted along a single left-right ideological dimension,[31] each voter will vote for the party closest to his or her most preferred position. If, for instance, we assume a frequency distribution of political orientations on a left-right ideological spectrum which is unimodal (that is voters are massed near only one point on the spectrum) and symmetrical (that is there are an equal number of voters on each side of this one point), with only two parties in competition for people's votes, namely party A and party B, we will find that the parties will converge towards the centre, that is the median voter. This is depicted in Figure 8.1.

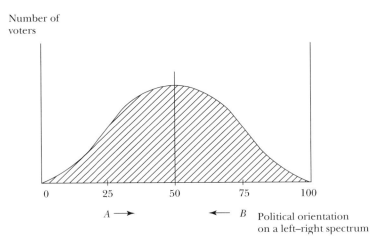

Figure 8.1 Distribution of political orientations on a left–right ideological spectrum (unimodal)

However, if we alter the distribution, and we assume that voters' preferences are distributed so that they are massed bimodally near the extremes, as in Figure 8.2, the parties will not move away from their original position, since they would lose more voters at the extremes than they could possibly gain in the centre.

While the limits of Downs' model have been exposed many times already,[32] there is still much to be learned from this analysis. In particular, Downs' model can be applied to the Italian context of 1994 in two ways. First, it helps to explain the opposing coalitions' electoral strategies and their contrasting success. It will be clear from our analysis of the electoral strategies adopted by the opposing electoral alliances that while the right-wing Pole of Freedom alliance took a more extremist position, successfully appealing to the right and the left, the left-wing Progressive alliance made the strategic mistake to assume that the election was going to be won in the centre. In other words, the Progressive alliance seemed to be converging towards the median voter in the centre at a time when the voters were abandoning the centre. The voters' preferences are reflected by measuring the electoral strength along a left-right axis between 1987 and 1994 (see Figure 8.3). This shows that in 1994 there was a reinforcement of the extremes and a weakening of the centre.

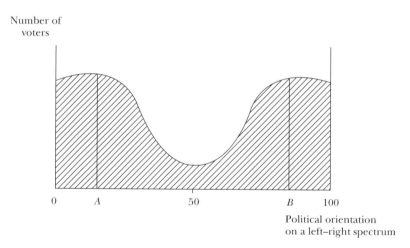

Figure 8.2 Distribution of political orientations on a left–right ideological spectrum (bimodal)

181

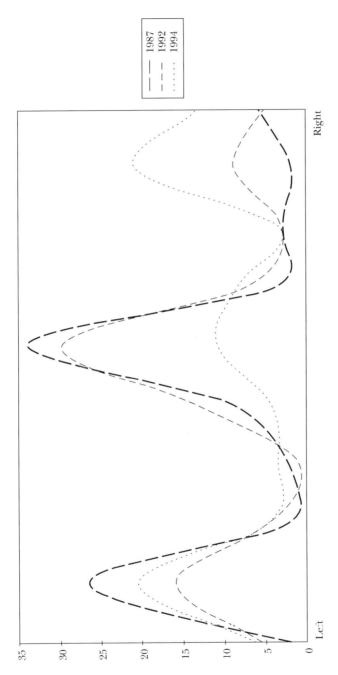

	1987
	1992
	1994

Right

Left

Figure 8.3 Electoral strength of political parties along a left–right continuum

This figure is adapted from L. Morlino, 'Crisis of party change and party system in Italy', *Party Politics* (1996). Morlino explains that 'the poles have been measured simply by placing the various parties, with their electoral strength, on a 10-point scale on the grounds of their traditional self-placement along a left-right continuum' (p.28, n30).

The second way in which Downs' model applies to the 1994 election concerns the origin of new parties. Downs distinguishes between two types of new parties, those designated to win elections, and those designated to influence already existent parties to change their policies, or not to change them. Like old parties, new parties cannot survive without gaining the support of a sizeable fraction of the electorate, thus the all-important location of the new party on the ideological spectrum is dependent upon where other parties are and upon where voters are.

According to Downs, 'new parties are most likely to appear and survive when there is an opportunity for them to cut off a large part of the support of an older party by sprouting up between it and its former voters'.[33] New parties have an important advantage over old parties, namely, 'they can select the most opportune point on the scale at which to locate, and structure their ideologies accordingly',[34] while older parties are ideologically immobile.

The points Downs raised concerning the origin of new parties are of especial relevance to the Italian election of 1994. A new political party such as *Forza Italia!* had an advantage over older parties not just because it represented something new. Being a new party gave *Forza Italia!* a tactical advantage in respect to other parties, since it had relatively greater freedom to locate itself on the ideological spectrum at a point judged to be the most advantageous. Furthermore, *Forza Italia!* had a structural or institutional advantage over the older parties, since it was in a position to create a more flexible party structure to fit with the times.

The latter point is not an insignificant one. The new reality of Italian politics, centred on political offer rather than political demand, required a new approach by the political parties towards the electorate. While the older parties had a structure that was tuned towards political demand, *Forza Italia!* was the first party that had a structure tuned towards political supply. Patrick McCarthy points out that Berlusconi, using his Fininvest empire (and especially the publishing arm of Publitalia), 'conducted market surveys to discover what sort of political conduct the electorate wanted and how it could supply it'.[35] This was done by setting up 4000 *Forza Italia!* clubs, which invited citizens to participate by providing the input to the programmes of *Forza Italia!*, a procedure which was very different from the local party organisations and policy-formulation typical of the old regime.[36]

The setting up of *Forza Italia!* was, above all, an exercise in political marketing, which was exactly what the opening up of the political market was poised to reward. It has been argued that Berlusconi did nothing more than to follow step by step the basic teachings of a political campaigning textbook, including market research on what the electorate perceived as the most pressing problems a government was expected to deal with, continuous opinion polls which ensured fine-tuning with the demands of the electorate, and a careful selection procedure for the candidates who were expected to sell the *Forza Italia!* product.[37] On this last point, it is worth quoting at length Gino Bedani's account of how Berlusconi chose his team of candidates:

> By October 1993, unbeknown to the Italian public, the Director of Publitalia, Lo Jucco, had identified 2000 potential candidates for Forza Italia ... Candidates underwent successive company screening operations to ensure their suitability. Successful candidates then had their images checked out and if necessary revamped in terms of dress and appearance. Berlusconi doesn't like men with beards, for example, with long hair or sloppy dress. They should look like successful executives. Candidates were then sent to Segrate in Milan, where they underwent telegenic tests and training in presentation, techniques of communication and good image projection. The final hurdle was the meeting with Berlusconi himself at his luxurious villa in Arcore, in Northern Italy. He later boasted: 'I met 400 people in these months – all new to politics, all ready to throw themselves into the fray with one word from me'. Clearly, this was not a party preparing policy, but a publicity machine selling itself: the living embodiment of Marshall Macluhan's dictum: 'the medium is the message'.[38]

There is little doubt that the competence of *Forza Italia!* in political marketing was crucial to its success in the 1994 elections. Nevertheless one ought to remember that while parties are in open competition for votes, there is still room for influencing the electorate to vote in a certain way, all the more so in regard to voters who are unsure about how to vote. This is an aspect of political competition that Schumpeter was very much aware of. Schumpeter explains the political opportunities for groups 'with an axe to grind'[39] in the following terms:

> The only point that matters here is that, Human Nature in Politics being what it is, they are able to fashion and, within very wide limits, even to create the will of the people. What we are confronted with in the analysis of political processes is largely not a genuine but a manufactured will. And often this artefact is all that in reality corresponds to the *volonté générale* of the classical doctrine. So far as this is so, the will of the people is the product and not the motive power of the political process.[40]

If we accept Schumpeter's views on social psychology as generally correct,[41] it follows that the victory of *Forza Italia!* must, at least in part, be measured in terms of Berlusconi's success in influencing the wishes of the electorate. Control of or free access to the media was obviously helpful in this context, and while no one would want to deny that the use of these resources is important, it is at least as important to know how to make the most of them.[42]

The success of Berlusconi's strategy can also be appreciated in one other important way – by looking at the ability of the Pole of Freedom to hold together the seemingly anatagonistic forces of the Northern League and AN while enlarging and maximising its potential support.[43] Geographically, socioeconomically and attitudinally, the junior partners in the alliance were poles apart; but combined with the broad-based appeal of *Forza Italia!*, they were all-encompassing.[44] Furthermore, the Pole was not only more effective in attracting former supporters of the old ruling parties; it even exerted a pull on many voters hitherto attached to the left. The polling organisation, BVA, calculated that 9 per cent of those who had voted for the PDS, 10 per cent of those who had voted for Communist Refoundation and 25 per cent of those who had supported *La Rete* in the general election of April 1992 switched to voting for one of the Pole of Freedom parties in March 1994.[45] 'Berlusconism' proved to be the most attractive electoral package on offer; whether it had the makings of a long-lasting governing coalition had yet to be shown. Berlusconi's political skill in influencing voters to trust him and his political movement can usefully be set against the campaigning style of his principal foe, Occhetto's PDS.

THE PDS – OR HOW TO LOSE AN ELECTION

It is difficult to disagree with Martin Bull's claim that with the 1994 elections the PDS had missed its greatest opportunity to win office since the war.[46] The fact that this is an election that the PDS felt it could (and should) have won is perhaps the best starting point for an explanation of its defeat.

Above all, the PDS paid the price for being complacent. Having survived the corruption scandals virtually untouched, and being the front runner in all the opinion polls a few months prior to the election, the PDS never considered the possibility of defeat. Such optimism was perhaps accentuated by a touching belief that virtue would be rewarded. By adopting a form of logic which had great affinity with the most vulgar conceptions of historical determinism, the PDS felt that its time had come and victory was inevitable. Over the last 50 years, and in all the previous eleven elections, the PCI/PDS had been the traditional runner-up to the Christian Democrats. The DC having vanished in the most humiliating of circumstances, the leadership of the PDS were convinced, particularly after the local elections in November 1993, that the way was now open for a government of the left.

Unfortunately for the PDS, it failed to fully exploit the collapse of the DC and PSI.[47] Effort was required to secure the votes of those who in the past had supported the governing coalition, and in this respect the PDS failed miserably. Considering that in the last 40 years, with the exception of 1976, the potential left-wing electorate has never been above 40 per cent, the PDS should have known that it had its work cut out. Arguing for the benefits of alternating parties in government may convince some scholars in political science, but not necessarily the mass electorate.[48]

The left presented itself to the electorate under the banner of the Progressive Alliance, which was constituted by eight different parties (PDS, Communist Refoundation, *La Rete*, Greens, Socialist Party CSI, *Rinascita Socialista*, Democratic Alliance, Christian Social). In order for the Progressive Alliance to present itself as a united front, it needed a decisive leadership, but this was never achieved. Occhetto assumed that since the PDS was the largest party in the Progressive Alliance, he was automatically the leader. In fact this assumption only aggravated the tensions within the Progressive Alliance, especially between the PDS and Communist Refoundation. The fact that the Progressive Alliance appeared leaderless and consumed by internal feuds did not go unnoticed by the electorate.[49]

But above all, the left failed to realise that the nature of political competition had radically changed. The opening up of the electoral market meant that a successful party coalition would have to win voters on both the left and the right. This is exactly what Berlusconi was able to do, and what the left did not. Berlusconi's skillful mobilisation of lower-middle-class interests[50] can perhaps be seen in terms of his ability to play the ideological card by denouncing communism as the number one public enemy, while at the same time exploiting the vanishing line which distinguishes the right from the left. Berlusconi was able to target the voters of the left, pledging to create one million new jobs in the next three months. The parties ostensibly of the right made good use of the arguments and programmes normally associated with the left, such as employment, unemployment and social security, while embracing the rhetoric of the right, in defence of the free market.[51] Berlusconi's unholy alliance of parties and mixing of policies deprived his opponents of ideological clarity.

On the other hand, the left seemed to be more concerned with providing a realistic picture of the hard times to come, especially on the question of economic issues. Occhetto went out of his way to reassure industrial and business leaders, which failed to convince the right and alienated the left. The most clear-cut example of this was his lecture at the London School of Economics in February 1994 ('The Italian Elections: The Left-Wing is Ready to Govern'), just one month before election day, in which he explicitly sought to reassure the City of London financial world that his party was not a threat to economic interests. The bleak picture of the prospects for the Italian economy drawn by Occhetto did nothing to inspire people to vote for the PDS. Ultimately, Occhetto failed to grasp the new factor in democratic politics. When opposing parties compete for the people's vote, it is not always a good idea to be hyper-realistic.

CONCLUSION

The holding of the 1994 general election was generally considered to be a trial operation of the new electoral system, and there was a tendency, particularly amongst those hostile to the move in favour of majoritarian voting, to consider the final outcome as a vindication of their doubts about the merits of electoral reform. It was argued that the principle of proportional representation had been sacrificed in order to bring about 'strong government' which, in the event, had not been attained. This seemed somewhat harsh, both because of Berlusconi's undoubted victory and subsequent investiture in office (see Chapter 9), and because the debate about what constitutes the ideal voting rules carried on even after the election, so that it was not impossible that further reforms would follow.

Notes

1. M-C. Decamps, 'Les elections legislatives devraient avoir lieu le 27 mars', in *Le Monde*, 18 January, p.7.
2. Segni succeeded in securing an electoral accord with Roberto Maroni, the parliamentary leader of the Northern League, but 24 hours later it was disowned by Bossi.
3. The law of 10 December 1993, apart from establishing equality of access to both the publicly-owned and privately-owned broadcasting media in the 30 days prior to polling, also introduced a ban on all opinion polling in the 15 days prior to voting day and laid down specified spending limits for candidates and parties, backed up by fines for any violations of the law. See C. Fusaro, 'Media, sondaggi e spese elettorali: la nuova disciplina', in *Rivista Italiana di Scienza Politica* (1994) pp.427–64.
4. G. Pasquino, 'The birth of the 'Second Republic'', in *The Journal of Democracy*, (1994), p.109. See also G. Pasquino (ed.), *L'alternanza Inattesa: le elezioni del 27 Marzo 1994 e le loro conseguenze* (1995).

5. For the Chamber of Deputies, 475 seats were to be allocated on a first-past-the-post constituency basis, and 155 by collegiate proportional voting.

6. M. Bull and J. Newell, 'Italy changes course? The 1994 elections and the victory of the right', in *Parliamentary Affairs* (1995) pp.72–99.

7. S. Romano, 'La rivoluzione politica passa attraverso il voto', in Come Si Vota, special insert in *Epoca* magazine.

8. See the socio-demographic voter profiles in G. Calvi and A. Vannucci, *L'Elettore Sconosciuto – analisi socioculturale e segmentazione degli orientamenti politici nel 1994* (1995).

9. R. Graham, 'A prima donna's great performance', in *The Financial Times*, 2–3 April 1994, p.1.

10. See L. Bobbio 'Dalla destra alla destra, una strana alternanza', in P. Ginsborg (ed.), *Stato dell'Italia* (1994). See also G. Sani 'Dai voti ai seggi' in I. Diamanti and R. Mannheimer (eds), *Milano a Roma* (1994).

11. See A. Agosta, 'Maggioritario e proporzionale', in I. Diamanti and R. Mannheimer (eds), *Milano a Roma* (1994).

12. This is known as the index of bipolarism. See A. Agosta, op. cit. (1994) and G. Sani, op. cit. (1994).

13. See Chapter 7.

14. The DC was replaced by two centre parties the PPI (Italian People's Party) and the CCD (Christian Democratic Centre). The old PSI was replaced the new PSI, the CD (Social Catholics) and the AD (Democratic Alliance). The old PSDI and PLI did not survive the momentus changes.

15. This is also true of the two most extreme political movements, the extreme right-wing *Alleanza Nazionale*, and the extreme left-wing Communist Refoundation.

16. I. Diamanti, 'La politica come marketing', *Micromega*, 2/1994, pp.60–77, briefly refers to Schumpeter in his analysis of the 1994 election results.

17. J. Schumpeter, *Capitalism, Socialism and Democracy* (1954) p.269. See also the recent *Joseph A. Schumpeter – his Life and Work* by R. Swedberg (1991).

18. Ibid.

19. This point has been made by I. Diamanti and R. Mannheimer in 'Introduzione' to I. Diamanti and R. Mannheimer (eds), op. cit. (1994).

20. This point has been made by I. Diamanti and R. Mannheimer, ibid., (1994).

21. Ibid.

22. The personalisation of political competition is not the result of changes in the electoral system. The protagonists of the campaign are all of a national stature, not local as one might have expected considering the new first-past-the-post electoral system.

23. S. Gundle and N. O'Sullivan 'The mass media and the political crisis', in S. Gundle and S. Parker (eds), *The New Italian Republic* (1996) p.206.

24. With the exception of L. Ricolfi, 'Elezioni e mass media. Quanti voti ha spostato la TV', *Il Mulino*, Nov/Dec 1994. Ricolfi argues that Berlusconi's private television channels influenced at least 13.7 per cent of the electorate.

25. This view is echoed by J. Farrell, 'Berlusconi and Forza Italia: New Force for Old?' in *Modern Italy*, Autumn 1995, p.47.

26.   The originality of Schumpeter's views have been under close scrutiny, and there is a suspicion that Schumpeter was doing little more than echoing the views of Max Weber. See D. Beetham *Max Weber and the Theory of Modern Politics* (1985) pp.111–12. For our purposes, we need not bother with this question, indeed it is best to leave this debate to scholars of Schumpeter and Weber.

27.   J. Schumpeter, op. cit. (1954) p.269.

28.   Of course, it could be argued that Berlusconi was not a political fox, instead he was lucky that the system was ready to reward someone with his skills. We shall not pursue this line of thought, and give Berlusconi the benefit of the doubt.

29.   A. Downs, *An Economic Theory of Democracy* (1957), p.28.

30.   Ibid. p.137.

31.   This requires the assumption that each voter has a single peaked political preference, which in fact may not be the case. See P. Dunleavy, *Democracy, Bureaucracy and Public Choice* (1991).

32.   See D. Mueller, *Public Choice II* (1989); P. Dunleavy, op. cit. (1991); D. Green and I. Shapiro, *Pathologies of Rational Choice Theory* (1994).

33.   A. Downs, op. cit. (1957) p.128.

34.   Ibid, p.129.

35.   P. McCarthy 'Forza Italia: the new politics and old values of a changing Italy', in S. Gundle and S. Parker (eds), *The New Italian Republic* (1996).

36.   Ibid., p.139.

37.   See R. Mannheimer, 'Forza Italia' in I. Diamanti and R. Mannheiher (eds), op. cit., 1994, p.40.

38.   G. Bedani, lecture, University of Manchester 1995, p.21.

39.   Namely, groups that consist of 'professional politicians or of exponents of an economic interest or of idealists of one kind or another or of people simply interested in staging and managing political shows' J. Schumpeter, op. cit. (1954) p.263. Some would argue that Berlusconi is a perfect example of someone 'with an axe to grind'.

40.   J. Schumpeter, op. cit. (1954) p.263.

41.   It ought to be pointed out that although Schumpeter entertains the idea of a manufactured will, his views should not be associated with the more extreme and simplistic views of N. Chomsky. Unlike Chomsky, Schumpeter is not a conspiracy theorist, furthermore Schumpeter is more aware of the limits of his position, hence his views become more plausible. For example Schumpeter admits that 'there is truth in Jefferson's dictum that in the end the people are wiser than any single individual can be, or in Lincoln's about the impossibility of "fooling all the people all the time"' (p.264). Yet the point is that while Jefferson and Lincoln stress the long-run aspect, Schumpeter wants to argue that in the short-run people can be fooled into something they do not really want.

42.   See I. Diamanti and R. Mannheimer (eds), op. cit. (1994).

43.   There were other important protagonists in the 1994 elections, from the parties of the centre post-DC, to the other left wing parties in the Progressive Alliance. For an analysis of the PPI, see M. Follini, *C'Era Una Volta la DC* (1994); V. Belotti 'Il patto per l'Italia', in I. Diamanti

and R. Mannheimer (eds), *Milano a Roma* (1994); C. Warner, 'The new catholic parties: the Popolari, Patto Segni and CCD', in R. Leonardi and R. Nanetti (eds), *Italy: Politics and Policy, Volume One* (1996). For an analysis of the other major parties in the Progressive Alliance, see J. Foot, 'The "Left opposition" and the crisis: Rifondazione Comunista and La Rete', in S. Gundle and S. Parker (eds), *The New Italian Republic* (1996); M. Rhodes, 'The Italian left between crisis and renewal', in R. Leonardi and R. Nanetti (eds), *Italy: Politics and Policy, Volume One* (1996).

44.   G. Calvi and A. Vannucci, op. cit. (1995).
45.   Figures reported in *Liberation*, 31 March 1994, p.18.
46.   M. Bull 'The great failure? the Democratic Party of the Left in Italy's transition', in S. Gundle and S. Parker (eds), *The New Italian Republic* (1996).
47.   Ibid., p.168.
48.   The PDS seemed to have committed the same mistake as the Labour Party in Britain, whose 1992 campaign was based on the slogan 'it's time for change'. What the Labour party in Britain, and the PDS in Italy, failed to understand is that the arguments for change must be made, not assumed.
49.   Perhaps what the Left required was two leaders, one for the Progressive Alliance and one for the PDS. On this point, see G. Pasquino 'Un leader nuovo? no, ce ne vogliono due' and G. Bosetti 'Professionisti del presente', both in *Reset*, June 1994, No.7.
50.   See P. McCarthy, op. cit. (1996).
51.   See I. Diamanti and R. Mannheimer (eds) op. cit. (1994).

9 Who Governs? The Trials of Berlusconi's Government (March–December 1994)

One of the central themes of this book is the conjecture that the liberal political culture has struggled to set roots in Italy. A close analysis of Berlusconi's term in office reveals this lacuna in Italian politics. Although Berlusconi championed the liberal creed during his electoral campaign, there is little doubt that some of his political acts reflect rather poorly on his understanding of liberal procedures and liberal culture.

As we shall see, the illiberal nature of Berlusconi's government is illustrated by a series of political acts and unfelicitous remarks made by Berlusconi during his premiership. These include his failure to understand that the parties in opposition have a right (if not a duty) to oppose the parties in government; his belief that the people had granted him a right to govern undisputed; that all state institutions, including the Presidency, should bend to the majority will; his unwillingness to accept defeat in parliament, reflected by his attempt to antagonise political conflict by making constant direct appeal to the people; his lack of respect for institutional procedures, as when he felt he had the right to dissolve parliament and call the next election, a right which constitutionally rests with the President of the Republic; but above all, Berlusconi's attempt to curb the powers of the judiciary, and to bring this under the control of the executive, is a clear indication of his failure to appreciate that a liberal democracy is based on the division of powers between the executive, the judiciary and the legislative.

HOW (NOT) TO CREATE A CABINET IN 30 MINUTES

Italy had spoken, Berlusconi remarked, and it was now up to
the politicians to form the government demanded by the
voters, clearly implying that he had acquired a personal and
political mandate of a kind which was not typical under the
pure proportionality of past elections.[1] Instead of registering
the relative strength of different party forces, voters had been
asked to discriminate between rival governing coalitions, an
all the more novel choice in that the available alternatives
were new and untried. But if the result was clear-cut, the
outcome was not. Constructing a successful coalition of interests in order to gain office was not the same thing as convert-
ing that coalition, made up of contradictory policies and
irreconcilable philosophies, into a credible, effective and
lasting administration.[2]

'The great seducer's'[3] own position was surrounded with
difficulties. Berlusconi had appealed to the electorate by
promising that what he had done as a private businessman
(and as president of Europe's most successful football team of
the decade, A.C. Milan) he could do in public office. Entering
the election so late in the day, with a message of simple and
optimistic populism, it was unclear whether he had the patience and perseverance, and not just the presentational skills,
to give an effective lead once in government.[4]

His task was complicated by the squabbling which had
broken out between the ally-enemies in the coalition, even
while the election campaign was still underway. The Northern
League's strategy had been to join forces with Berlusconi and,
making itself indispensable to any governmental alliance, to
then drive a hard bargain. Since the Northern League had the
largest number of MPs, Bossi started out by stating that the
new prime minister should not be Berlusconi and that, whatever the case, he would not enter into power with 'the fascist
pigs' of AN.[5] He later recanted on this, while setting new conditions. Bossi even criticised Berlusconi's victory, won because
of television manipulation.

Finally, on 10 April, a deal was reached between representatives of the Northern League and the AN designed to satisfy
their respective positions, a plan to create a federal Italy being
offset by the move to a directly-elected head of government

(the latter being the only way by which the AN would agree to swallow the former), the whole project to be put to a national referendum. The Northern League unilaterally insisted on a six-month deadline for progress on the changes. That such far-reaching reforms were settled by post-electoral negotiation, hardly having been discussed during the election itself, was more than disconcerting.

When parliament reconvened on 15 April, there was no certainty that the Pole of Freedom would be able to impose its own candidates in the voting for new speakers of both chambers. It was not so much of a problem in the Chamber of Deputies, where the favoured nominee, the Northern League's 31-year-old Irene Pivetti[6] was elected on the third round. It was a different story in the Senate, where the Pole of Freedom was, on paper, eight votes short of a majority and where the outgoing speaker, Giovanni Spadolini, was standing for re-election. It was only on the fourth round of voting, and even then by only a single vote (159 to 158) that Carlo Scognamiglio[7] won the post, accompanied by a bitter speech from Spadolini in defence of the prestige of the Senate against the arrogance of the new majority. Berlusconi's threat to force an election if his nominees were rejected having already been denounced by President Scalfaro as a breach of conduct.[8] The composition of new parliamentary groups subsequently completed, Berlusconi had obviously to try and reach out to MPs in the two main centre parties, namely the Pact for Italy and the Italian Popular Party,[9] if his alliance was to be sustainable.

Formation of the cabinet was no less awkward. The Northern League demanded the interior ministry (and a non-portfolio ministry for institutional reform) which Berlusconi was reluctant to concede. He had also approached the *Mani pulite* magistrate Antonio Di Pietro, offering him the post of minister of justice, in spite of the fact that the magistrate was still conducting an investigation into another bribery case involving Fininvest. Di Pietro duly refused. When, on 28 April, after consulting with parliamentary and party leaders, Scalfaro officially called on Berlusconi to attempt to form a government, he was very far from settling the issue in 'half an hour' as he had boasted.

But the most formidable obstacle to overcome was the constitutional safeguard exercised by the President, who on the eve of receiving the cabinet nominations took the remarkable

step of writing to Berlusconi (and then publishing the exchange of letters) setting out the essential criteria that the
members of the new government should observe, guarantee-
ing national unity,[10] social solidarity, and respect for Italy's existing overseas alliances and (peace) treaty commitments.
Further to this, the President was widely credited with blocking a number of proposed appointments, though he publicly
denied this, as well as expressing reservations about others,
adding to the delay in finalising a cabinet.

The President's anxieties were obvious. Postwar Italy had
never known a genuine, majoritarian-style changeover of
power. Nor had it had a government which was not controlled
by Christian Democrats. There were real fears that a
Berlusconi government might strike out in a radical free
market or Eurosceptic direction, or that its national integrity
might be endangered.[11] The whole thrust of the President's
action was to remind the incoming administration that there
were permanent democratic values that were part of the
country's recent history which could and should transcend
any temporary popular majority.

The new cabinet of 25 was a balancing of party affiliations –
seven posts went to *Forza Italia!*, including three of
Berlusconi's own employees (Cesare Previti, Berlusconi's per-
sonal lawyer and a board member of Fininvest; Gianni Letta,
Fininvest's head of public relations; and Giuliano Ferrara, the
talk-show host), six to the Northern League, including the
Interior Ministry to Roberto Maroni,[12] five to the National
Alliance (three of these MSI), two each to minor CCD and the
CDU and an assortment of technical figues, chief amongst
whom was Lamberto Dini, appointed to the treasury.[13] A new
ministry of the family was created, pleasing Catholic opinion.
One of the only two appointees with previous ministerial experience, Alfredo Biondi (of the CDU, but formerly in the
Liberal party), took over at justice, after Previti (reportedly
vetoed by the President) was moved to defence. Under-secretarial appointments reflected a similar careful apportioning.
In his first television interview as prime minister, Berlusconi
defended and justified his new team, dismissing concern in
European capitals as the result of bad faith and disinforma-
tion, and arguing that the best people had been chosen for
the job in hand. Berlusconi reiterated that his government

believed in the principles of liberal democracy, and there was nothing that others in Europe, uneasy with the presence of post-fascists,[14] should be fearful about.

POWER AND POLICY

In his speech opening the crucial debate in the Senate for the government's vote of confidence at the beginning of the following week, Berlusconi granted that the new government represented an 'absolute novelty', willed for by the majority of voters under the new electoral law and not by the habitual game of the political parties, although on all the key issues – the democratic values of liberty and tolerance, the indivisible unity of the country, its loyalty to NATO and to the European union – he and his ministers remained fundamentally attached. He emphasised several urgent objectives, lifting the tax burden on firms so that they could employ more workers, while increasing temporary and part-time work, as well as pressing ahead with the further privatisation of state industries. The law covering the use of *pentiti* (supergrasses) would also be reviewed, to prevent any 'excesses'.

Berlusconi rammed home his message in a closing statement, claiming that the majority had a 'pact with the voters' which they could not go back on, and that although it was up to the Senate to confirm or overturn that majority, another majority could only be had by holding another election – which *Forza Italia!*, riding even higher in the opinion polls for the European elections, would be bound to benefit from. It was always going to be a close call. The loyalty of the eleven life senators[15] was uncertain, as was that of the PPI, until it finally resolved not to support him unless he dropped AN and coalesced with the centre. Yet on the evening of 18 May – while Berlusconi's AC Milan were winning the Champions Cup in Athens – his government was voted in the Senate by 159 votes to 153, with two abstentions, the margin of victory helped by the departure from the chamber of five PPI MPs, who were immediately expelled by the PPI leadership. After this closely fought battle, victory in the Chamber of Deputies two days later was more of a foregone conclusion, by 366 votes to 245 (without any abstentions). Fours months after *Forza*

Italia! was first launched, six weeks after the election, and 22 days since Berlusconi had been asked to form a government, the Pole of Freedom had been invested with the power to give effect to its policies. Privately, Berlusconi commented that eighty per cent of the task (preventing the left from winning) had been accomplished, all that was left was to govern.

CONTROLLING STATE INFORMATION

The manner in which the government of Silvio Berlusconi chose to approach the problems of its first hundred days set the tone for its whole existence. They were all problems which any incoming government would probably have had to tackle, but their handling illustrated a mystifying sense of priorities, not made any easier by the evident confusion of the prime minister's public and private involvements. As the most perceptive commentators pointed out, there was a need to contrast the 'false fears' (of a resurgence of neo-fascism) with the 'real dangers' of an unacceptable concentration of power.[16]

The popularity of *Forza Italia!*, and the personal standing of Berlusconi, were fully reconfirmed in the elections to the European parliament on 12 June, lifting *Forza Italia!* to over 30 per cent of the vote while both the Northern League and AN slipped back, as did the PDS.[17] All of these developments might have been expected to strengthen the prime minister's hand. He had, however, already suffered his first defeat in parliament, over the election of the presidents of the 13 committees of the Senate, as well as being preoccupied by the erratic behaviour of Bossi. Barely one month after entering office, Berlusconi was telling an audience of businessmen that he 'could not govern with the way the new electoral law worked', because it had not given the winning coalition a clear majority in both chambers.

Although there had been no wholesale clear-out of top officials (such as some members of the AN were pressing for),[18] Berlusconi's advisers took it for granted that the change of government logically involved changes in the most important posts in the civil service and state industry. One institution singled out for special treatment was the state broadcasting corporation, RAI.[19] RAI had been saved by Ciampi from the threat of bankruptcy in the Summer of 1993, and the team of experts known as the 'professors', brought in as an administrative council to draw up a plan for its longer-term economic restructuring were about to report back to parliament. Before this occurred, however, Berlusconi criticised the 'absurd' way in which RAI, as an endebted company, should continue to have recourse to state aid, referring to the 'anomaly' of there being no other democratic state in which the public broadcasting station is against the majority from which the government is formed.

The controversy was rekindled when Giuseppe Tatarella (AN), the Minister of Posts and Telecommunications, expressed his dissatisfaction with the work of the RAI administrative council, and when the Ciampi decree came up for renewal before parliament, the cabinet had attached modifications to it, such that if parliamentary approval was not forthcoming the whole council would have to retire, effectively handing the nomination of the board of RAI to the executive arm. The administrative council and the director-general of RAI refused to accept this, and they resigned in protest, followed by the refusal of President Scalfaro to sign the 'unconstitutional' decree in its new form (an existing Constitutional Court ruling negated the possibility of government control of public information).

A way out was found with a new draft of the decree re-affirming that responsibility for the overseeing of appointments and the scrutinising of the management of RAI remained the exclusive competence of the presidents of the two chambers of parliament. The new five-person board nevertheless was composed of individuals proposed by the three main coalition partners, doing nothing to further the principle of organisational autonomy.[20] The disclosure a few days later by the former director-general that the prime minister had suggested a carving up of the audience and advertising by RAI and his own three private television channels hinted at his real methods. Berlusconi maintained, as if this was sufficient justification in itself, that most Italians agreed with him that so long as RAI was to be state-financed then it should reflect the governing majority. More than this, that all other institutions, including the Presidency, should bend to the majority will. 'This is not the Ciampi government. It is a question of knowing who at the moment, the president of the republic or the prime minister, governs Italy!'[21]

Italy since 1989

CONTROLLING THE JUDICIARY

In mid-July a second major political tumult arose in relation to the judicial attack on corruption. Berlusconi had not made many direct references to the issue during the election, and his advisers believed that public interest had waned. Even so, the main defendant in the Enimont trial, Sergio Cusani, had just been sentenced to imprisonment for eight years, the pursuit of Craxi was continuing, and magistrates had gained fresh impetus by looking into the realm of fiscal evasion – a field in which Berlusconi's Fininvest was already under suspicion. Di Pietro had in fact spurned Berlusconi's offer of a cabinet post on the grounds that he wanted to carry on with the work of his colleagues. Critics claimed that the judges had become too political, and that they had been abusing their investigative powers; Berlusconi had his own reasons for feeling hounded by them. Despite the uproar that had been provoked by the Amato decree in the Spring of 1993, the prime minister was determined, in a particularly ambiguous phrase, to 'restore legality'.

With surprising haste, a 14-article decree was introduced by the prime minister and the justice minister, Alfredo Biondi, on 13 July (on the evening that many Italians were distracted by Italy's match in the World Cup semi-final against Bulgaria), apparently with the full backing of the cabinet, revising the penal code so as to withdraw from magistrates the right to pre-trial, preventative detention in 'less serious' cases like bribery and corruption, as well as shortening the period for conducting inquiries and prohibiting the release of details to the press – all vital tools in the successful conduct of the *Mani pulite* team over the last two years. The decree was also countersigned by President Scalfaro.[22] The well-publicised release from prison of many suspects began the next day, including some of the most notorious, like De Lorenzo, pictured leaving Poggioreale prison in Naples. According to Berlusconi, the prisons were overcrowded with people who had been detained on minor charges but were forever waiting to go to trial, incarcerated by judges who had abused their powers without respecting the law. As many as 3000 remand prisoners seemed likely to be affected, of whom about 200 were being held on charges of bribery and corruption.

(handwritten margin note: clashes w/ mani puli. investigation)

At first muted, the attacks then started to mount up, fanned by a joint statement from the *Mani pulite* investigators, read out by Di Pietro, explaining that the provisions of the decree no longer permitted them to pursue serious work and asking to be assigned to other tasks. Caselli and Cordova made it clear that the effect of the decree would be to hinder their anti-mafia activities. It was past judicial experience of never-ending (or politically hampered) investigations which made preventative detention, in their eyes, so useful. The press and public clamour obliged some of Berlusconi's coalition allies to think again. The interior minister, Maroni, who had signed the decree, now backtracked, saying that he had been 'mistakenly persuaded' – tricked – by government colleagues into giving his approval, admitting that the government had given the impression that it wants to protect its friends. Unless the decree was modified or rescinded, he would feel compelled to step down. Both Bossi and Fini were critical of the decree. Bossi saw it as a chance to recover some lost ground, while Fini, sensing the change of mood, also distanced himself from Berlusconi's 'untenable' position. Even Tiziana Parenti, who had left the *Mani pulite* team to enter politics with *Forza Italia!*, contested the very substance of the decree, which, by distinguishing between serious and less serious crimes, would mean rewriting the entire penal code.

The outcome was that, when a parliamentary committee came to examine the decree, both Berlusconi and Biondi left it open to improvements, providing that it was not dispensed with altogether. Using prison to obtain confessions was illegal and unacceptable in a civilised country, Berlusconi insisted, and he would stick to his guns even at the risk of unpopularity; if parliament rejected the decree, the government would resign. After a meeting of the cabinet on 19 July, nevertheless, it was announced that the government had decided after all to drop the decree, opting instead to legislate with a full bill. A large majority in parliament subsequently rejected the decree too, though not before deputies from *Forza Italia!* and the Northern League had exhanged insults and come to blows. The *status quo ante* was restored, and those already released were gradually rounded up and put back into custody. Berlusconi, angered by the way his 'good faith' had been twisted by press polemics, warned that that was not the end of

the matter, seeming to suggest that, despite the unprecedented verbal assault by the executive on the judiciary, a
further attempt to re-establish a proper institutional equilibrium would be made.

Just 24 hours later, warrants were issued for the arrest of
several Fininvest employees, including – for the second time –
Silvio Berlusconi's brother Paolo, in connection with inquiries
into the bribing of the financial police. Berlusconi then held
an emergency meeting ('between friends') at his villa on the
outskirts of Milan, with Cesare Previti, Gianni Letta and
Fedele Confalonieri (the president of Fininvest since
Berlusconi's departure), apparently to discuss how best to deal
with the legal, financial and political troubles of the group,[23]
raising once again the apparent mixing of his business and his
political interests after he had long since said he would no
longer concern himself with the affairs of Fininvest. Once his
brother had confessed to paying bribes to the *Guardia di
Finanza* (the finance police) on the 29 July, Berlusconi
renewed his onslaught on 'the government of magistrates'
which, by failing to limit their own activities, risked having a
devastating impact on society. Berlusconi's associates asserted
that the judges were out to get him, indeed they were being
used as a front by those old political forces which had never
accepted the verdict of the ballot box.

The episode was unmistakeably damaging to Berlusconi.
Hoping to rush the decree through without any fuss, he had
had to make a fight of it, before backing down. His own prestige was hurt, the coalition had split apart, the opposition
parties were revitalised and public opinion had swung against
him. The government did not seem capable of normalising
the treatment of cases of corruption if its proposals did not
first have the consent of prominent members of the judiciary.

The clash between Berlusconi and the pool of magistrates in
Milan was not, evidently, just a juridical tussle. The magistracy
had moved in and filled the void left by the disappearance of
the old political class, and the new majority-minded government of Berlusconi was, by questionable means and for
dubious motives, anxious to assert its popularly-derived authority. For Berlusconi, the power of the judges, who had
become celebrities revelling in the limelight, had to be
curbed; it was time to bring to a close the moral crisis that Italy

had been living through. His opponents pointed out that he should learn to govern, and not pretend to command. New judicial accusations and arrests against former notables soon followed.[24]

The clash between Berlusconi and the judiciary is perhaps the clearest example of Berlusconi's failure to respect one of liberalism's basic creeds, namely, the independence of the judiciary from the executive and the separation of powers.[25] The importance of the separation of powers for a liberal culture is high-lighted by the former prime-minister Giuliano Amato.[26] Amato argues that although Italy is no longer governable without recourse to the majoritarian principle, 'we must ensure a commensurate, high fusion of independent powers and articulations that can guarantee that we do not allow ourselves to sanction an exclusive power through the majority principle'.[27] In other words, Amato argues that a majoritarian system, with its tendency towards a monist culture, must be counterbalaced by strengthening those institutions that guarantee pluralism, and he singles out 'the crucial role played by the judiciary, the media and social interests in the name of pluralism'.[28]

Was Berlusconi a threat to liberalism in Italy? If we accept Amato's analysis, then the clash between Berlusconi and the judiciary can be interpreted as a clash between a monist culture versus a liberal culture. In fact, it is hard not to read a direct reference to Berlusconi in the following remark Amato makes at the end of his article:

> The media, social interests and their clients are, and will be, an excellent litmus test. As soon as we see that traditional clients run to the new victor and that this victor also runs the media, we know that the monist culture has invincibly survived.[29]

THE ECONOMY TAKES (YET ANOTHER) TURN FOR THE WORSE

Management of the economy, and the preparation of the all-important budget for 1995, provided Berlusconi's government with its greatest credibility test, both with the voters and with the financial markets. Economic circumstances had been highly favourable. Inflation remained at an all-time low, unemployment had started to fall and there were many signs of a growth in industrial output, most of the praise for which had to go to the exalted tenureship of Carlo Ciampi. With Berlusconi's election victory, the stock market soared. The programme of no increases in taxes, deregulating of the labour market and the encouragement of wealth creation had a business-oriented leaning, and the new economic ministers – Lamberto Dini, Giancarlo Pagliarini, and Giulio Tremonti – were chosen primarily for being well-qualified.

By removing barriers to enterprise, the government intended to stimulate economic recovery and to moralise economic life, excessive regulation being cited as the main cause of corrupt practices.[30] Greater money-raising freedom was also to be given to the regions, thereby liberalising and decentralising economic activity. The central difficulty with this plan of action was that it sat ill with the persisting need to control and restrain the budget deficit and the consolidated debt, which continued to cast doubt on Italy's political commitment to European economic and monetary union. The lack of decisive early steps had already led to a capital outflow in June.

Internal differences in the coalition had prevented rapid progress from being made. Bossi had denounced the AN vote as a vote for prising open the wallets of the North. Furthermore he argued that welfare had to be 'regionalised' and loss-making public industry sold off, combined with anti-trust legislation (which would strike at Berlusconi's own holdings). But AN were hostile to deep cuts in social spending, and opposed to the privatisation of strategic industries, which were heavily concentrated in the South. Mastella (CCD), the minister of labour whose brief included the pensions system, feared for the social consequences of further austerity. By the end of July, only the broadest of three-year plans for debt reduction had been outlined, foreshadowing an overall reduction of L45 000b to hold the deficit down to L139 000b, without any precise indication of how this target was to be achieved. A pardon on illegal construction and a tax amnesty was expected to raise part of the required sum, but the vexed question of pensions reform (aggravated by a recent Constitutional Court ruling)[31] was put off until after the summer recess – a decision *not* to decide which, in the absence of central bank intervention, left the *lira* to fall below the psychologically significant 1000 *lira* to the Deutschmark. The Governor of the Bank of Italy, Antonio Fazio, added his weight by criticising the temporary, one-off nature of the savings to be made through the two amnesties in the face of a systematically rising debt, and disclosed that L20 600b of capital had been moved out of the country in the second quarter, L11 700b of it in the month of June alone.[32]

In a parliamentary debate on 2 August, Berlusconi – responding to doubts about his recently unveiled idea to nominate a special commission to supervise the administration of Fininvest and to disassociate him from possible conflicts of interest – denied that there was a government crisis or any governing alternative, avowing that he was an 'incurable optimist'. A television commercial extolling the government's achievements in various fields of policy, ostensibly to do with a campaign of public information (and which objectors succeeded in getting withdrawn), seemed to imply that it had simply failed to communicate what it had been doing. But the speed with which the post-election euphoria faded away was startling. On 11 August, to counteract increasing currency speculation, the Bank of Italy was forced to raise the discount rate by half a per cent to 7.5 per cent, the first hike since September 1992 and one which fixed Italian interest rates fully four points higher than German ones. Once more, the prime minister sought to calm the markets, blaming critics for talking down the *lira* and assuring people that they could 'go serenely on holiday'.

The next day he had to rush back from Sardinia to meet with Bossi, sealing their new understanding with a handshake in the early hours of the morning and putting an end for the time being to talk that the Northern League might be about to ally itself with the opposition parties. Internal squabbling was accompanied by an unpleasant search for scapegoats: Mastella identified 'the Jewish lobby' in New York which controlled international financial markets; another undersecretary wanted to bar the merchant bankers, Morgan Stanley, from trading in Italy; and Tatarella, interviewed by *La Stampa*, spoke of 'invisible powers', made up of freemasons and former ministers, who were working against the government.

These outbursts showed how instinctively remote some ministers were from the free market outlook publicly espoused by Berlusconi. They also represented a wider reality. If any Italian government could claim to represent a fresh start, this was it. But financial and foreign exchange traders had yet to be convinced that the Pole of Freedom coalition had the will and the cohesion not only to act on its promises but to take the strong measures deemed to be necessary.

The extreme urgency of the economic situation was made abundantly clear by Dini, on the 24 August, when he announced that the budget deficit for 1995 was projected to reach L189 700b, an increase of L31 000b on that for 1994 and way above the L138–140 000b total (8 per cent of GDP) that they had been working to. Spending had overshot, and it was vital in the treasury's view that corrective measures be taken to reduce the deficit by as much as L51 000b. 'Welfare abuses', notably in the form of false invalidity benefits paid out as a means of disguised assistance or clientelistic recompense (one-in-three were said to be irregular), were singled out for particular attention. Abolition of wage indexation had, according to economists, knocked the equivalent of two percentage points off the cost-of-living index, easing fears of inflationary pressure, and in talks with the trade union confederations there was a degree of agreement about the primacy of pensions reform, providing that more steps were taken to clamp down on both direct and indirect tax evasion (the building and tax amnesties obviously favoured the small businesses on whom Berlusconi was depending).

But the unions had still not dropped the threat of strike action unless the government tried to seek more in savings instead of additional spending cuts. Dini was also acutely aware of the timetable for European monetary union (EMU), to which he was personally committed. Fear of exclusion meant that free-riding, which had its attractions (Amato admitted as much in October 1992), was all but ruled out.[33] In a policy document, the governing German Christian Democrat party observed that, given the Maastricht convergence criteria and given the present state of the Italian public finances, Italy was unlikely to qualify for the inner core of EMU – a judgement which enraged the foreign minister Antonio Martino,[34] but which Italian industrialists regarded as an objective evaluation of the facts. Invited to a 'last supper' with several senior business figures, Berlusconi was told by Gianni Agnelli that the economic growth rate of the 1950s and 1960s was unlikely to return, making it unwise to depend on growth in order to boost tax revenues. Without a tough budget, he stood no chance of winning international credibility, let alone retaining the continuing support of the business community that he claimed to represent.

The warning had its effect. Berlusconi's resolve was stiffened, and the cabinet eventually fell in with the treasury's hardline demands, acquiescing in a much harsher budget package with the specific aim of sticking to the originally envisaged deficit of L139 000b. Pension entitlements were the hardest hit. The raising of the retirement age for men and women (first initiated by Amato) was speeded up, the increase in pension payments was halted, and the rate at which pensions accrued each year was to be lowered. To break up the state-only monopoly, private pension schemes were to be promoted. Cuts were also made in health care. Needless to say, the unions were not impressed. The general secretary of the CGIL, Sergio Cofferati, called the latest proposals unfair and unacceptable, and a general strike was earmarked for 14 October. The magnitude of the reduction was only just over half the size of that secured by the Amato budget of 1992, but it was favourably viewed by other EC finance ministers, even though there were many doubts about its attainability, particularly since it was based on the assumption of a 2.5 per cent inflation rate for 1995.

BERLUSCONI, THE JUDGES AND THE UNIONS

Opposition MPs had scarcely begun to study the bill in detail before the stand-off between the government and the senior judiciary flared up again. In an interview with *Il Corriere della Sera*, on 4 October, Francesco Saverio Borrelli, the head of the *Mani pulite* inquiry, let it be understood that their investigation of the Tele+ pay-television network, in which Finivest supposedly had only a 10 per cent stake, was approaching a crucial stage and that it could reach 'the highest financial and political levels' – implying that the prime minister himself was implicated. Borrelli also commented on the 'imprudence' of

Biondi, the justice minister who had been critical of their activities, adding that Biondi had been guilty of procedural cheating when acting for one of the defendants in the Banco Ambrosiano affair in the early 1980s. Biondi resigned on the morning that the story broke.

The cabinet convened, rejected the 'intolerable' insinuations, and agreed to a signed exposure (drafted by Ferrara) to be sent to President Scalfaro and to the CSM asking that Borrelli be censured for a breach of article 289 of the penal code for interfering with the legitimate work of the government. For several hours the markets were in a state of turmoil, only placated by a comment from Borrelli that there was no *avviso di garanzia* being readied for the prime minister. Berlusconi then denied wanting to proceed against Borrelli, and Biondi decided to remain at his post. Not for the first time, the finance police (*Guardia di Finanza*) visited the Milanese headquarters of Fininvest, taking away documents and computer discs. Berlusconi reiterated that all the allegations against him were unfounded, and that he had no intention of resigning, pointing to 'a mandate from the voters' which nothing could alter.[35] The CSM subsequently cleared Borrelli of any misconduct, but Biondi by that time had set in motion a countermove, instructing a team of inspectors from his ministry to investigate the Milanese pool of magistrates, and leading anti-mafia judges, for 'possible irregularities', including violation of the rights of defendants. Borrelli remarked that such an unprecedented interference had not even happened during the Fascist era.

Battle was also joined over the finance bill, against a background of growing social unrest. The all-out, four hour general strike on 14 October mobilised an estimated three million workers in street marches, protests and shutdowns, with the promise of further action to come so long as the government declined to contemplate any budgetary modifications. 'One, ten, a hundred general strikes won't make any difference', the prime minister told reporters. Business leaders were rumoured to have given up on Berlusconi, and his coalition partners, having gone along with him so far, began to consider how much longer he could, and should, last. Bossi, who had made an art of weakening the coalition without ever quite precipitating its downfall, turned against *Forza Italia!*, describing it as the Northern League's 'mortal enemy', and insisted that the terms of the alliance would have to be re-negotiated the moment the budget had been passed, but not before. In a rowdy debate on the future financing of RAI, the interior minister Maroni denounced the 'conquest' of the new board by nominees of *Forza Italia!* and AN. Gianfranco Fini's (AN) own popularity now surpassed even that of Berlusconi, encouraging speculation that he had almost become a prime minister-in-waiting. A further massive national anti-budget demonstration took place on the weekend preceeding parliamentary discussion of the bill, suggesting that even the wage agreement of 1993 was not safe. In order to overcome a large number of spoiling amendments, the government had to resort to successive votes of confidence. 'It's incredible', Berlusconi remarked. 'I have everyone jumping on me – the judges on one side, the newspapers on the other, on the other the industrial groups'.[36]

Chairing a United Nations conference on organised crime in Naples on 22 November, the prime minister received the news he must have been anticipating – notification that he was under investigation on suspicion of corruption, together with a request to appear for interrogation (*ordine di comparizione*). Berlusconi is the first serving head of government to be investigated in the history of the postwar Republic.

The former tax director of Fininvest, Salvatore Sciascia, had just told the *Mani pulite* team about the bribing of the finance police in return for a favourable tax audit for three of the companies' subsidiaries (Mondadori, Mediolanum and Videotime) in the period between 1989 and 1991, and the prime minister's name had been added to the list of suspects at the last moment after the discovery of a secret bank account used exclusively for illicit payments. But several other investigative leads were also being pursued. Berlusconi defended himself in an eight-minute message on one of his own television channels, swearing on the head of his five children that he had never corrupted anyone, and refusing to resign of his own accord; only a vote of no confidence in parliament would make him. As he reiterated, the 'first law of democracy' is that 'he who has the votes to govern should govern'.

Colleagues contended that the alleged offences had supposedly occurred when Berlusconi was a private citizen, so they could have no bearing on his current responsibilities. Yet while AN gave Berlusconi its full support, the Northern League, refusing a *verifica* (a get-together of the leaders on whether or not to continue their alliance), would only say that Berlusconi should go once the finance bill was law. Mastella was more forthright – 'the coalition no longer exists'. A *second* notification of investigation soon followed, this time in relation to an equally serious but more recent allegation to do with an abuse of office in attempting to divide up the advertising and audience between RAI and Finivest. The more divided the government seemed, the more unpredictable the possible permutations of parties and factions.

With fresh fears of a budget delay, the *lira* sunk to a new low of 1035 to the deutschmark. Only Scalfaro's stipulation that the destiny of the Berlusconi government had to be 'entrusted to the free determination of parliament' offered a lifeline. To all intents and purposes the government and the prime minister were politically finished.

BERLUSCONI RESIGNS

Encircled and embattled, Berlusconi fought to the last to save his premiership, throwing out accusations of conspiracy and betrayal, and insistent to the end that he was the head of a government which had been duly elected.

In a final, decisive meeting with trade union leaders on 30 November–1 December, Berlusconi succeeded in securing an accord which granted a number of further important concessions to union demands, such as pushing back the finalising of the pension plans to June 1995, in return for which a second general strike scheduled to begin 24 hours later was called off. Giving ground in this way created a shortfall of L4000b in budget savings which, added to the amendments dictated by the Chamber, undermined the turn towards budgetary rigour which the IMF and financial opinion already judged to be insufficient. He also tried to buy further time by giving a push to plans for federal reform in lengthy roundtable talks with members of the Northern League.

Voting in the second round of municipal elections, however, provided a new setback. Government-backed candidates won only two of the mayoralties of the six large cities being contested, there was a drop in the level of support for the governing parties more generally, and, ominously, there were signs that the teaming up of centrist candidates with the left[37] found favour with the electorate.

No date had yet been set for Berlusconi to meet with magistrates, but in a new twist, the Italian Supreme Court ruled that in another similar case involving the bribing of the finance police the trial should be transferred from Milan to the notoriously overworked law courts in Brescia, effectively taking responsibility for the Finivest investigation away from the *Mani pulite* inquiry. This proved to be the catalyst, and on 6 December Di Pietro handed in his resignation, not just from the *Mani pulite* inquiry but from the judiciary altogether, frustrated by the fact that all of his actions were interpreted as a move for or against others in a political game, when all he had been trying to do was to carry out his work in as objective a way as possible.

By stepping down, he hoped that the investigations would become less 'personalised', restoring calm and tranquility to the institutions. Even Scalfaro tried to persuade him to change his mind, but without success. Borrelli declared that, notwithstanding Di Pietro's departure, their investigation would continue, and it was announced soon afterwards that the prime minister would be meeting members of the Milanese pool on 13 December. Before this could take place, the president of the Supreme Court, Arnaldo Valente (complaining of a smear campaign), and the inspectors from the ministry of justice who were examining the work of the magistracy, also resigned. Berlusconi was eventually questioned by Borrelli, Davigo and Colombo for a total of seven hours, after which he went on television to denounce the case against him as 'an incredible theory' lacking in evidence or testimony which had been cooked up to discredit him because he had committed 'the original sin' of having been the president of Fininvest. Unusually, there were no press leaks, and the inquiry team maintained a strict silence, preoccupied with considering whether or not there were any grounds to proceed further.

Manoeuvring by the parties in parliament was by now frantic, as various alignments and combinations were canvassed, everything hanging on the passing into law of the finance bill. For the first time, the Northern League had voted to oppose official government policy, supporting the creation[38] of a special parliamentary commission to examine the whole issue of broadcasting, posing a direct threat to Berlusconi's media holdings. But the Northern League was internally divided, with upwards of 40 of its MPs unwilling to cross the floor if this meant banding together with the PDS. The National Alliance was also wary lest Berlusconi was tempted to forge a centre ground alliance in order to stay in office. Dini had made an appeal for responsibility, and to ease the budget's path the Northern League and the PDS withdrew the bulk of their tabled amendments, letting the projected L48 000b worth of reductions stand and bringing some temporary stability to market trading.

Even so, the *lira* had dropped to 1042 to the deutschmark, affected by the news that further austerity measures, not excluding tax-raising ones (which Berlusconi had always proscribed), would be necessary in the spring. The PDS and Communist Refoundation in the meantime were busying themselves by composing separate motions of censure, attacking the 'presidentialist' tendencies of the coalition. Bossi, the instigator of a motion that had already attracted the backing of the PPI, was confident that they could raise the 316 votes required to bring the government down.[39] The problem was to bring this about without precipitating an election, which the Northern League and the opposition parties were opposed to as long as the electoral law remained unchanged and the prime minister had not relinquished control of his television network.

Berlusconi's response to the fragmenting of his parliamentary position was to try to hold the advantage, announcing that a vote of confidence would be held in the Chamber of Deputies the day after the budget was passed, and that if he lost he would then, and only then, resign. In an extraordinary speech at the Manzoni theatre in Milan on 19 December, and in a prerecorded video circulated to television stations, he raised the stakes by calling on his supporters in the country – over the heads of parliament, the parties and the President – to take to the streets in a 'new resistance' to peacefully demonstrate against the subverting of the democratic will, demanding to know how it was that the losers of the March election could end up in government while the victors, ousted by a 'red coup', were forced into opposition. Members of *Forza Italia!* should, he said, go and remind Northern League MPs that they owed their election to his party's voters. 'Deception must not pay; injustice must not come to pass'.

The words were not, ill-advisedly, chosen carefully enough. 'We seem to be rehearsing a civil war', the leader of the PPI Rocco Buttiglione remarked. D'Alema believed that Berlusconi has confirmed 'his anti-democratic vocation'. Even members of Berlusconi's own party were uneasy at where this kind of call might end up, while small-scale pro-government crowds assembled in Turin, Milan and Rome. Scalfaro was said to have found the speech 'stupefying'. Berlusconi's histrionics had had the effect of muddling his own role as head of government with his position as leader of a party, while denying that there could be any other legiti-mate source of authority or constitutional counterweight to a direct appeal to the people. It took the President to point out that Italy, for good historical reasons, was a representative and not a direct democracy, so that the popular will expresses itself in parliament.[40]

Final approval of the budget by the Senate (by 140 votes to 93) and the Chamber (232 votes to 166 with 31 abstentions) cleared the decks for the set-piece no-confidence debate on 21 December, which the government demanded should be televised live. To general surprise (since the government was already known to be outnumbered),[41] Berlusconi opened, at-tacking the 'election robbery' of the opposition and the 'split personality' of Bossi, and invoking 'the sovereignty of the people'. He urged that if the majority fell apart, there would be no alternative but to go for another election. After half an hour's delay, Bossi replied in kind, denouncing Berlusconi's 'Peronist' ambitions and lack of a sense of the state.

Only Fini steered clear of personal insults, pointing out that the crisis was different from all previous ones because the gov-ernment was not beaten but was being betrayed, contrary to the wishes of a good part of public opinion. Once again, Scalfaro was unhappy at the way the prime minister was trying to tie his hands; to hold an election in such circumstances would be 'catastrophic'.[42] The following morning, however, having made his case but wanting to avoid the humiliation of inevitable defeat, Berlusconi went to the *Quirinale*, and – after just 226 days in office – formally tendered his resignation, pre-sumptuously suggesting an election date in March. On a day of high symbolism, the prime minister's brother was given a suspended jail sentence for making illicit payments to the old Christian Democrat party.

CONCLUSION

One of the hallmarks of the majoritarian form of government is that the parties to an electoral contest pre-agree to accept the outcome, which confers on the victors the undisputed right to govern. Where the verdict of the voters is especially conclusive, it is not unusual for the winning side to argue that they have been empowered or 'mandated'. It was a measure of the infirmity of the short-lived Pole of Freedom government that its right to rule was never universally conceded, and that this was to be the principal point of contention when the government fell, or was forcibly expelled, from power.

Throughout his premiership, Berlusconi had harked back to the all-conquering mandate bestowed on his government by the general election of March 1994 and, by implication, the popular referendum of April 1993 which had made it possible. To go against this was, he argued, to flout the democratic will. Repudiating the election returns might be legal, but according to Berlusconi it was certainly not legitimate. The prime minister's many adversaries consistently held that election to office did not equate with unrestricted power, and that there were conventional limits to the exercise of a prime minister's power, one of which was that a government endures only so long as it is able to control a parliamentary majority. Failure to fulfil this basic requirement was not a thwarting of the popular will by parliament, but its democratic expression through parliament. The very fact of the government's downfall illustrated what its opponents had been saying all along about the 'unnatural' nature of the original governing coalition.[43]

In what was a bitterly contested struggle, there were sharply opposing arguments, turning on radically different concep-tions of democratic politics. The first had to do with Berlusconi himself. One of his claims was that he and his followers were entirely new to politics – 'we are a new kind of people, outside corruption', he boasted in April 1994. His coalition brought together those forces excluded from or antagonistic towards the old political order, and in particular those new productive social classes who had felt alienated by 'Roman rule'. Berlusconi played on his entrepreneurial success, creating and marketing a company-party with which to carry out his electoral campaign. It was true that he had his own business affairs to consider and protect, but he saw no contradiction because he identified his defence of free enterprise with the economic well-being of the country. In time this supposed harmony of interests broke down – too many decisions were taken with which he looked to have an interested stake, and too many judicial findings undermined his clean image. His failure to clarify the position compromised his attempt to govern in the common good, even though he attributed this difficulty to the machinations of others. His desperate televised appeals betrayed an adventurer's exasperation with the inescapable requirements of democratic leadership.

A second argument concerned his government's efforts to establish its governing authority. Berlusconi promised to bring stability and coherence, providing a new policy direction and effecting real change. He hoped to put a stop to the crisis-ridden cycle of the recent past. But, from the beginning, there were problems. His cabinet team took the traditionally long time to fall into place, and lacked centralised co-ordination or a clear unity of purpose. Proclaimed objectives, like the privatisation programme, ground to a halt. Old-style patronage resurfaced, so that it was unclear whether they intended to de-politicise the state or to occupy it.[44] Intolerance was shown towards other pluralist centres of power – a parliamentary opposition which would not let the government govern, conspiring lobbies, the 'twisting' media. Furthermore agencies of renewal, such as the magistracy, the Bank of Italy, the Presidency, were treated like relics of the old system. The upshot was a caricature of strong majority government: new, largely majoritarian voting but bereft of the culture of political responsibility to go with it.[45] The irony was that the Berlusconi government ended in similar circumstances to so many other postwar Italian governments, engulfed by allegations of corruption, budget battles, factional infighting and social strife – in short, the same old ungovernability. The major difference this time was that the situation was far more precarious, because the old political class and its negotiated understandings had been swept away.

The third and final point bore on the possibility and practicality of constitutional change, following on from the half-reform of 1993–4. By asserting a mandate to govern, Berlusconi was ascribing to the electorate a sovereign power which should override all other constraints, firmly pinning the responsibility for the making and unmaking of governments on the voters. He was, in this sense, anticipating a future, reformed constitution – including a directly-elected president of a plebiscitary kind – to which his supporters aspired. This was evidently in contradistinction to the constitution-in-being, based (at least formally) on the conventional expectation that elected representatives were not there to express a party mandate but to serve the nation, which had the ultimate call on their loyalties. The complexion of past governments had often been determined, without electoral ratification, by parliamentary manouevre. But this was not just a procedural stand-off. It was also a dispute about fundamentals, and about the future prospects of bipolar politics, provoking each party to demonise the other side by accusing it of undemocratic behaviour. In so doing they were projecting their differences onto the institutions of the state, which did not appear to be at all well-equipped to withstand such open and divisive contestation. The disorderly transition to a Second Republic might be underway, but with the rules of the First still well operating.[46]

Notes

1. The five-part government coalition (*pentapartito*) was famously a coalition of power rather than of policy. M. Cotta argues that the parties of the *pentapartito* did not programmatically fix the policy agenda and put forward specific proposals; they tended to react to problems brought about by external pressures which demanded action, which they then tackled in the light of their own preferences. See M. Cotta, 'Il governo di partito in Italia: crisi e transformazione dell'assetto tradizionale' in M. Caciagli *et al.* (eds), *L'Italia Fra Crisi e Transizione* (1994) p.125.

2. The right-wing alliance was voted into office on a platform of lower taxes and more jobs, speaking a language of federalism and national unity.

3. This is the description of Berlusconi given by Eugenio Scalfari, the editor of the daily *La Repubblica*.

4. A point brought home by his unceremonious rush to select a cabinet without even waiting for the President to nominate him as prime minister-designate.

5. Fini praised Mussolini, calling him 'the greatest statesman that Italy has known', which excited and alarmed international opinion about the likelihood of members from the MSI becoming ministers.

6. Irene Pivetti (1963–). Journalist. First elected to parliament in 1992. Strongly Roman Catholic, believing that Catholicism is the only true, revealed religion.

7. Carlo Scognamiglio (1944–). Economist. Rector of LUISS. private university in Rome. Former Liberal MP who transferred to the Union of the Democratic Centre, the smallest of Berlusconi's five coalition partners.

8. 'Queste cose le decido io', *Panorama*, 20 May 1994, p.12.

9. Both of which had said during the election that they would not support his coalition.

10. The fifth article of the Italian Constitution states that the Italian Republic 'one and indivisible, acknowledges and promotes local autonomies'.

11. After all, both AN and the Northern League, in their different ways, renounced the founding principle of anti-fascist national unity of the First Republic.

12. Roberto Maroni (1955–). Former left-wing extremist and jazz enthusiast. Lawyer for Avon Cosmetics. Floor leader of the Northern League in the Chamber of Deputies (1992–94). One of those whom Scalfaro was said to have been particularly concerned about.

13. Lamberto Dini (1931–). IMF executive. Manager (an important intermediary in the IMF loan to the Andreotti government in 1976) and then Director-General of the Bank of Italy. Passed over for the Governorship when Ciampi became prime minister in April 1993. became prime minister in January 1995.

14. Europe's uneasiness towards extreme right-wing elements in Berlusconi's government is perhaps understandable. For example, one AN MP, Mirko Tremaglia, had been calling for the renunciation of the treaty of Osimo, signed with the former Yugoslavia in 1975, reopening the border issue between Italy and Slovenia by reviving Italy's historic claim to the Istrian peninsular.

15. These include former presidents of the republic and other distinguished personalities, not necessarily from the world of politics.

16. S. Noiret, 'Faut-il avoir peur d'un nouveau fascisme a l'italienne?', in *Le Soir*, 25 July 1994, p.2, quoting Marc Lazar.

17. This last finally occasioned the resignation of the PDS party secretary Achille Occhetto.

18. Fini had spoken of a 'radical renewal' of the *nomenklatura*, but 'without vendettas'. *L'Italiasettimanale*, the extreme right-wing weekly

newspaper, published a hit-list of officials it wanted to see purged, among whom were included Giancarlo Caselli and Luciano Violante.

19. On the restructuring of the RAI, see G. Mazzoleni 'The RAI: restructuring and reform', in C. Mershon and G. Pasquino (eds), *Italian Politics: A Review*, Vol. 9 (1995).

20. M. Frei, 'The long reach of Silvio Berlusconi', in *British Journalism Review* (1994) pp.29–33.

21. M-C. Decamps, 'Nouvelles tensions entre M. Berlusconi et la television d'Etat', in *Le Monde*, 2 July 1994, p.4.

22. 'Quello strano assenso di Scalfaro', in *L'Europeo*, 27 July 1994, p.17.

23. Leaked details of the financial presentation given to the banks the previous March by Franco Tato, the administrator of Fininvest, putting the consolidated debts of the group at L3900bn, were carried by *La Repubblica* on 22 July 1994.

24. Andreotti was accused of the still more serious charge of 'mafia acts', as his former ally, Nino Drago, was arrested in Catania, and Antonio Gava and Vincenzo Scotti (the latter the minister of the interior in Andreotti's last government) were jointly implicated in collusion with the Neapolitan *Camorra*.

25. On the importance of the separation of powers within the liberal culture, and an assessment of the independence of the judiciary in the Italian constitution, see the excellent analysis by Pasquale Pasquino, *Uno e Trino* (1994).

26. G. Amato 'Il dilemma del principio maggioritario', *Quaderni Costituzionali* (1994) pp.171–86. A slightly altered version of this article is published in English as 'The dilemmas of the majoritarian system', in R. Leonardi and R.Y. Nanetti (eds), *Italy: Politics and Policy* (1996) pp.73–87.

27. Ibid. p.84.

28. Ibid. p.86.

29. Ibid. p.86.

30. A. Faujas, 'Le gouvernement Berlusconi cajole les PME', in *Le Monde*, 28 June 1994, p.III.

31. On 10 June the Court overturned a 1983 law which had put a cap on increases in second pensions, ordering an estimated L32 500b in arrears to be paid out to some 600 000 people, blowing a huge hole in the finances of the national pension fund, the *Istituto Nazionale della Previdenza* (INPS). Dependants outnumbered the economically active, and one-half of all pensioners were below the age of 60.

32. The government was also locked in combat with the Bank of Italy over the choice of a new director-general in succession to Dini, the Bank wanting to promote his deputy, the government wishing to exercise its right to control appointments by bringing in an outsider. The government eventually gave way in November.

33. M. Campanella, 'Getting the core: a neo-institutionalist approach to the EMU', in *Government and Opposition*, summer 1995, p.361. It is worth noting that some European governments were resentful of the competitive boost that devaluation had brought to the Italian economy.

34. Martino, although strongly critical of the Maastricht treaty, was not hostile to a single currency; what he objected to was the movement by stages to monetary union, which left the weaker economies, like that of Italy, wide open to speculators.
35. The most that Berlusconi would admit (in an interview with the *International Herald Tribune* on 12 August) was that bribes had been paid by Fininvest to win contracts, but that his group had been the 'victims of extortion' and that the sums involved anyway amounted to no more than 'a litre of water in the Mediterranean'.
36. 'Self-pity of "suffering" Berlusconi' in *The Sunday Telegraph*, 27 November 1994, p.28.
37. Martinazzoli had won in Brescia on a PPI–PDS ticket, defeating the Northern League's minister for industry Vito Gnutti.
38. In the aftermath of a Constitutional Court ruling that the Mammí law of 1990 was unconstitutional.
39. There were unconfirmed claims by the Northern League that *Forza Italia!* had been offering bribes to Northern League MPs to stick with the existing coalition.
40. *La Repubblica*, 22 December 1994, p.6.
41. All told, a total of 320 Deputies had signed up to the three separate no-confidence motions.
42. *La Repubblica*, 23 December 1994, p.3.
43. In a televised interview on RAI1 on December 21, the leader of the PDS D'Alema explained that the problems with Berlusconi's government stem from Berlusconi's pre-electoral agreements. In the last analysis, there was not a single electoral pact on the right, but two separate pacts, one between Bossi and Berlusconi, and the other between Berlusconi and Fini. In other words there was never a pledge between Bossi and Fini. When Bossi was interview on the same programme, he said that Berlusconi spoke like a Thatcherite, but behaved like a fascist.
44. P. McCarthy, *L'Italie dans la Tourmente* (1995) p.132.
45. A thesis sustained by O. Massari in *Italia, Democrazia Maggioritaria? Sfide e Percoli della Transizione* (1995) pp.82–91.
46. M. Sheridan, 'Charmed life of the great seducer', in *The Independent*, 23 December 1994, p.7. P. Allum provides a useful checklist of the main features of the non-majoritarian parliamentary system in 'Les élections Italiennes de Mars 1994 – la transition continue', in the special edition of *Peuples Méditerranéens* of April–June 1994, pp.166–8.

10 The Dini Government – 'A Government of Truce'

In circumstances wholly reminiscent of the First Republic, the Second Republic began the New Year without a government or any recognisable sense of political direction. With Berlusconi's government enduring only 225 days, President Scalfaro was not keen to call yet another general election less than one year after the previous one, but the intense war of words between opposing party blocs made it difficult to find a solution acceptable to a majority in parliament. After a lengthy period of consultations with all the political leaders, Scalfaro decided that the only feasible short-term course of action was to form a non-party government, formed by technocrats rather than politicians. Lamberto Dini, the Treasury minister in the previous Berlusconi government, was offered the premiership. In the words of Scalfaro, it would be 'a government of truce'.

A 'TECHNOCRATIC' GOVERNMENT

Dini was one of Italy's most respected technocrats. The same could not, unfortunately, be said for the other members of his government, the majority of whom did not have international reputations or prestigious careers behind them. They came instead from the public administration, prompting the *International Herald Tribute* to suggest that Dini's government was a government of 'low profile professionals'.[1]

Notwithstanding the fact that no ministerial posts were given to parliamentarians, reinforcing the view that it was going to be a non-political government, Dini's team had problems being accepted by the political class. In particular, his refusal to commit himself to an election date angered Berlusconi, who liked to boast that he had 'invented' Dini; when Dini asked for a vote of confidence in parliament, he was paradoxically supported by the left and rejected by his supposed allies on the right. In the end, however, the vote of confidence in Dini's government was a justified outcome given the continuing confusion of party political alignments. *Forza Italia!* began pressing for a more widely-based government, although not all of its MPs had joined in the demand for an immediate general election. The PPI, which had helped to precipitate Berlusconi's downfall, split into two after Rocco Buttiglione (general secretary of the PPI) renewed a cooperation accord with *Forza Italia!* in advance of the regional elections of 23 April, a position not shared by the PPI's national council. Bossi had to fight off a strong attack at the Northern League conference in February, as many supporters of the Northern League were not pleased by his decision to abandon the Pole of Freedom governing coalition, bringing Berlusconi's episode as Prime Minister to an abrupt and premature end. Communist Refoundation was strongly critical of Dini, but at the last minute backed away from voting against him, realising it would otherwise have no electoral allies. In the end, Dini owed his survival in the first place to the fact that his government, by delaying the holding of another election, suited all the anti-Berlusconi forces.

FOUR OBJECTIVES

From the outset, Dini made it clear that he would pursue a number of limited aims, and would go as soon as these had been accomplished, but that he would also go if any of them were blocked by parliament.

Dini's political programme was based around four key objectives.[2] First, to pursue a radical reform of the pension scheme. Secondly, to draft a new mini-budget that would compensate for the inadequacies of the previous budget passed by the Berlusconi government. Thirdly, to draft a new budget for 1996, with the specific aim to cut down Italy's heavy national debt. Fourthly, to draft an emergency decree that would regulate electoral propaganda on television prior to the next elections, establishing the semblance of a *par condicio* between opposing camps during the run up to the election.

Dini was well aware that the key to his government's success was in the reforming of the pension scheme. By international standards, Italy still had a generous pension provision, and by 1994 the ratio of pension spending to GNP reached 14 per cent. In 1995 the national pension fund required state transfers of L72 000bn, covering approximately a quarter of its outgoings.³ The pension scheme was clearly a major strain on the Italian economy, weighing heavily on the budget deficit, slowing down the growth of the economy, and preventing the country from meeting the Maastricht convergence criteria. Furthermore demographic trends suggested that the burden would be an increasing one for future generations.

In order to tackle the thorny problem of a pensions reform, Dini operated on two fronts. First, he cracked down on fraudulent claims for invalidity pensions. Considering that invalidity pensions account for 26 per cent of all pension spending, there was probably a substantial saving to be made here. Not only were many invalidity pension holders claiming unlawfully from more than one authority, but there were thousands of bizarre cases such as people claiming to be blind while holding a driving licence, or even holding jobs as private chauffeurs. Secondly, he passed a reform of the pension scheme, introducing amongst other things incentives for private pension schemes, and making cuts in seniority pensions. Before being passed, this reform had to be approved by the unions, who had been the principal stumbling block behind the failure of the pension reform by the Berlusconi government. The *Istituto Nazionale della Previdenza Sociale*, the national pension fund, estimated savings of L23 600bn by 1998 and L108 100bn by 2005.

Trade union agreement to the reform of the state pensions system, secured without the social unrest of the previous autumn, was a landmark decision,⁴ even though not everyone was persuaded by Dini's achievements. For example, the industrialists' organisation *Confindustria* argued that Dini's reform was too gradual, indeed it has been suggested that this will not be the last reform of the pension scheme.⁵ Nevertheless after many months of political stalemate, it was imperative to take action. That Dini consequently managed to make some progress on all four fronts, owing to the reform of the pension scheme, was entirely due to his skill in finding the exact point at which conflicting views were in balance.

THE JUNE REFERENDUM

On 11 June 1995, the Italian people were asked to vote on 12 new, separate referenda. This was the eleventh occasion since 1946 that a round of referenda was being called, with the number of issues being voted on showing clearly a steep increase: in the 1990s, 24 separate issues were put to the electorate, compared to eleven in the 1980s and three in the 1970s.[6] As we pointed out in Chapter 6, the referendum tactic had played an important part in unblocking the path to electoral reform in the early 1980s. But the constant resort to referenda to settle what were some highly technical issues indicated that a popular vote – however illogical or ill-informed – still enjoyed a legitimacy which parliament could no longer match, illustrating the extent of the breakdown of trust in representative government. It is not a coincidence that the two European countries which have made most use of the referendum since 1945 are Italy and Switzerland, where the direct participation of the people in political affairs is highly valued, at the expense of other liberal values (see Table 10.1).

The 12 referenda of June 1995 touched on a vast variety of issues, ranging from the serious issue of union representation – ending the automatic deduction of union contributions from pay packets – to the mundane issue of regulating shops' opening hours. We want to concentrate on the three crucial referenda issues which had to do with abrogating sections of the Mammí law of 1990 (from the name of the minister who proposed it), which regulated the Italian broadcasting system. There are six main channels in Italy: Canale5, Italia1, and Rete4 are private, and they belong to Fininvest (now Mediaset), the company owned by Silvio Berlusconi. RAI1, RAI2 and RAI3 are public. The Mammí law legitimated the private broadcasting monopoly of Fininvest.

The aims of this referendum were the following:

1.   To reduce to one the number of channels that a private company can own.
2.   To reduce to one the number of advertising breaks within a television movie picture.
3.   To abolish the monopoly of RAI and Fininvest for advertising distribution.

Table 10.1   Number of referenda issues voted for between 1945 and
1995 in Western Europe

Countries	Referenda
Austria	2
Belgium	1
Denmark	14
France	12
Germany	0
Greece	4
Iceland	0
Ireland	17
Italy	40
Luxembourg	0
Netherlands	0
Norway	2
Portugal	0
Spain	5
Sweden	4
Switzerland	298
United Kingdom	1

Source: Adapted from M. Gallagher, 'Conclusion', in M. Gallagher
and P.V. Uleri (eds), *The Referendum Experience in Europe* (1996).

In the final outcome, all three referenda issues were rejected,
as shown on Table 10.2 below.

Although the main proposal, which would have forced
Berlusconi to give up two of his three national channels,
was defeated by 57 per cent to 43 per cent, the President of
the Constitutional Court insisted that Berlusconi would
still be obliged to 'remedy' the situation because of an
earlier Court ruling. This had found the relevant paragraph
of Mammí's law unconstitutional, as a consequence of
which a private company could not any longer own three
channels. Parliament was supposed to change the law by
August 1996.[7]

Table 10.2   Results of the three referenda on the Mammí law

Referenda issues	Yes	No
1	43%	57%
2	44.3%	55.7%
3	43.6%	56.4%

The results of these referenda were a political life-line for Berlusconi, whose leadership of the right-wing Pole of Freedom was under increasing threat from Gianfranco Fini of *Alleanza Nazionale.* Since Dini became Prime Minister, Berlusconi had suffered a number of setbacks. Investigations about corruption persevered, and Berlusconi was charged for three bribes given between 1989 and 1992 to the tax authorities to ensure favourable tax inspection of three subsidiaries of his Fininvest empire. There is no doubt that the payments were made, especially as his brother Paolo Berlusconi had admitted as much. Silvio Berlusconi's defence was that the bribes were a 'rare and isolated episode' of which he had no personal knowledge. Furthermore, and in keeping with his well-publicised view that there was an invidious conspiracy against him, he depicted the investigation as a politically motivated act of malice inspired by Antonio di Pietro, the most prominent member of the *Mani pulite* pool. The judges responded by stating that he 'could not have not known' about the payment of kickbacks by Fininvest to the *Guardia di Finanza* (tax police). Berlusconi's trial opened on 17 January 1996.[8]

The investigations by the judges were not the only problems facing Berlusconi and his Pole of Freedom right-wing coalition. In April 1995, in a by-election in Padova, the candidate representing the Pole of Freedom lost to the candidate from the centre-left coalition, and in the regional elections later the same month, the left carried off 9 of the 15 contested regions, with the PDS winning 24.9 per cent of the votes against *Forza Italia!*'s 21.4 per cent, even though Berlusconi continued to insist that the exit polls had got it right.

DINI RESIGNS

Contrary to all expectations, but disclaiming any ambitions of his own, Dini succeeded in calming the political game. Economic prospects also improved somewhat. Confidence returned, interests rates fell, and Dini set in train a three-year programme for debt reduction which he hoped would fix the problem 'for good'. The sacrifices to be made for a single European currency were, he felt, not impossible, but they should not be pressed to the point of a social rupture. The pensions reform was passed by parliament in early August. His only outstanding failure was in being unable to secure the projected re-entry of the lira into the EMS by the end of the year. For the first time, on the back of these successes, he began to show some signs of political ambition, proposing in particular a package of constitutional changes.

Without a secure majority, however, Dini could not expect to last indefinitely. His government had worked out a number of urgent reforms, but once his budget for 1996 had been got through parliament in December, an election seemed imminent. At the end of a three-day debate in the Chamber of Deputies, on 11 January, Dini announced his decision to resign, claiming that the Government over which he had presided had exhausted its duties. This was the second time in a fortnight Dini had offered his resignation. He had previously tendered his resignation to Scalfaro on 30 December, which the President refused to accept.

Dini's decision to resign forthwith in January, rather than suffer a vote of no confidence in parliament, was a shrewd political move on his part. In so doing, he made sure that, if a successor could not be found, he would stay in office as caretaker prime minister right up until the election, whenever that might be. The names of other political personalities were floated, but it proved impossible for Berlusconi and D'Alema to agree on any common programme of action now that Dini's own mandate was exhausted. On February 16, having been left with no other option, Scalfaro finally decided to dissolve parliament and hold a general election on 21 April – no less than the third general election in five stormy years.

Although Dini resigned on 11 January 1996, it was important for him to stay on as caretaker Prime Minister for the months prior to the next elections. This was because Italy was to hold the the European Presidency from January to June 1996, and Dini saw this as a unique opportunity for Italy to win back some of the influence and respect lost over the past couple of years. Dini was a well-known European enthusiast, and a zealous advocate of further economic integration, considering it inconceivable, for example, to extend the January 1999 deadline for European monetary union (EMU), even if Italy failed to make the grade when the EU picks the first members in early 1998. Dini was determined to keep the 'EMU train' moving, and his objective to bring down Italy's heavy national debt was in part motivated by the desire to convince his European partners that Italy merited a place among the inner core countries.

On the 29th of March, in Turin, the Intergovernmental Conference was held. The aim of this summit was to agree on ways to reform EU institutions, better coordinate foreign and defence policy and plan for voting ahead of future enlargement of the EU to include new members from Central and Eastern Europe. In an interview to Alan Friedman,[9] Dini said that the main objectives of the Turin summit were to bring the EU and the idea of unity closer to the average citizen, to make the revision of the Maastricht treaty the highest political priority, to pay particular attention to the growing problem of unemployment, and to reform key institutions, including the role of the European Parliament and the Commission, to achieve a qualified majority voting for the future, and to rethink the Common Agricultural Policy.

RUN UP TO THE ELECTIONS

Dini was at the centre of the election campaign, when to the surprise of many he announced his intention to form a centrist party, *Rinnovamento Italiano*, to give stability and governability to the country. The move stunned the centre-right coalition, which accused Dini of planning to align himself with the centre-left. Berlusconi was particularly critical, saying that Dini, hitherto seen as above party politics, was like a referee who suddenly chose to play for one of the teams. In fact many commentators rejected Berlusconi's condemnation

of Dini,[10] although some speculated that behind Dini's decision to form his own party lay the tacit encouragement of
President Scalfaro who, like Dini, wanted to see an end to 'revolving-door' governments by introducing constitutional
reforms, including a referendum on installing a French-style
presidency.

As election day approached, Dini openly endorsed the
views of the centre-left coalition. He said he hoped to win
the election with the help of the left to save Italy from 'the
danger of right-wing extremism' and 'to bring the moderates
back where they belong'.[11] Dini held the view that he could
attract a sufficient number of moderate votes to be a force
within the centre left, although he declined to say whether he
hoped to supplant Romano Prodi, the centre left's candidate
for Prime Minister.

As caretaker Prime Minister, Dini knew that whatever the
result of the election, he was going to chair the June EU
summit in Florence, and he played this card during the election campaign to his benefit. Respected for his administrative
ability and his handling of the economy, both at home and
abroad, Dini had won the trust of the Italian electorate. He
claimed his economic policies had helped Italy to move
closer to the criteria for a single currency, by reducing
inflation and the budget deficit. He also believed that Italy
could still be one of the countries joining in with monetary
union, since a monetary union that does not include two or
three of the larger countries, such as Italy, would not be very
significant.[12]

CONCLUSION

Dini's 'government of truce' perfectly expressed the democratic paradoxes: a Prime Minister recruited from the ranks of
Forza Italia! but sustained in office by the centre-left; a wholly
unelected government held up as the only generally acceptable political settlement; a stop-gap solution of unexpected
longevity. It was a government of transition during a phase
of transition,[13] but it achieved more lasting changes than many
had expected, and its efforts did not go without electoral
reward.

Notes

1. Quoted in G. Pasquino, 'Il governo di Lamberto Dini', in M. Caciagli and D.I. Kertzer (eds), *Politica in Italia* (1996) p.162.
2. Ibid.
3. J. Simkins, 'A story of too little reform too late?', in *Financial Times*, July 4 1996, Survey, p.IV.
4. See M. Braun, 'I sindacati confederali e il governo Dini: il grande ritorno del neo-corporativismo?', in M. Caciagli and D.I. Kertzer (eds), *Politica in Italia – i Fatti dell'anno e le interpretazioni. Edizione 1996* (1996).
5. See O. Castellino, 'La riforma delle pensioni: forse non sarà l'ultima', in M. Caciagli and D.I. Kertzer (eds) op. cit. (1996).
6. P.V. Uleri and R. Fideli, 'I referendum non piovono dal cielo: la consultazione referendaria di giugno', in M. Caciagli and D.I. Kertzer (eds) op. cit. (1996).
7. In fact, no decision had been reached by this deadline, and at the end of August 1996, Prime Minister Prodi decided to postponed the ruling for a further six months until February 1997.
8. See *The Times*, 15 January 1996.
9. *International Herald Tribune*, 25 March 1996, p.5.
10. See G. Bocca, 'Meglio Dini oggi, che Fini domani', *Uomini and Business*, March 1996.
11. Quoted in *The Times*, 6 April 1996.
12. While some economists did not paint such a rosy picture of the Italian economy as Dini, there was a clear sense that the international financial markets would have preferred a government of the centre-left as opposed to a government of the centre right. See G. Turani, 'Un paese sull'orlo di una crisi di nervi', *Uomini and Business*, March 1996.
13. G. Pasquino, op. cit. (1996) p.175.

11 The General Election of April 1996

The general election of April 1996 was an historic watershed. For the first time since Italy became a Republic in 1948, a left-wing government was voted into office. In many ways the outcome represents, at long last, the coming of age of Italian democracy. The significance of the result was not only that the left emerged victorious, although this was unprecedented. The striking aspect was the experience of something which all other liberal democracies have long taken for granted: the peaceful changeover of power. This is the single most significant aspect of the Italian election.

LIBERAL DEMOCRACY AND POLITICAL ALTERNATION

In order to appreciate the magnitude of the results of the April 1996 election, and the consequences for Italian democracy, it is necessary to take a brief detour through the more theoretical literature on liberal democracy. Winston Churchill once said that liberal democracy is the worst form of government in the world, except for all the others. There is much wisdom in this witticism. While many would agree that liberal democracy is indeed special,[1] it is a more difficult task to ascertain what exactly it is about liberal democracy that is so appealing.

We want to suggest that the comparative advantage of liberal democracy over other forms of government lies in its ambition to reconcile diversity with peaceful coexistence. As Norberto Bobbio points out, the difficult challenge liberalism is facing is 'how to make it possible for various freedoms to coexist without encroaching on each other'.[2] This endeavour to reconcile diversity with peaceful existence has been dismissed by many critics of liberalism as quixotic, or the equivalent of squaring a circle. Yet to many sympathisers of liberalism, it is this paradox which is most precious about the liberal tradition. Liberalism values pluralism and conflict as much as it values stability and harmony. These are values worth fighting for.

Of course, not all liberals would agree with our characterisation of the liberal project.[3] For the sake of the argument, let us accept as valid the view that liberal democracy sets out to secure peaceful cohabitation between different people with diverse beliefs and conceptions of the good life. Even if we agree on the premises of the liberal project, we find that liberalism is faced with a second momentous challenge, namely, how to translate this ideal into political reality? This is the challenge that many Western political theorists (not only of a liberal persuasion) have been troubled with, at least since the time of Plato.

As we argued in the introduction, democracy is essentially defined in procedural terms, and a political system is held to be democratic if its institutional arrangements enjoy popular consent. It follows that a number of institutional prerequisites are necessary for fostering this reconciliation between diversity and peaceful coexistence, including the free and fair election of officials; an inclusive suffrage; the right to run for office; freedom of expression; access to alternative sources of information; and the right of free association.

In the postwar period, as the political culture of liberal democracy has become more widely prevalent, one finds that apart from the political institutions listed above, there is another feature which has distinguished liberal democracy from other forms of government, namely, the peaceful and legitimate transfer of power by opposing political parties alternating in office. Of course, we are not suggesting that political alternation is a necessary condition of liberal democracy. And it certainly is not a sufficient condition. Nevertheless it is peculiar that, but for the exception of Italy and Japan,[4] in all liberal democracies political alternation has been a way of life, with different parties or coalitions of different ideological shades succeeding one-another in government.

There is an important reason why political alternation may be desirable, which has to do with the success of liberal democracy taking root as the dominant political culture. Political alternation is worth having because of its' repercussion on popular conceptions of political legitimacy. In non-liberal democracies, the ruling party's claim to legitimacy is often supported by the use of force, stamping out democratic alternatives. On the other hand, in liberal democracies legitimacy is rooted in the consent or agreement of all those who have to live under it.[5] In order to generate consent, legitimacy in a liberal state is tied to certain procedures which are widely (if not unanimously) accepted. The idea is that once democratic procedures are in place, and are seen as legitimate, the outcome of these procedures is also deemed legitimate.

Political alternation is desirable because it reinforces the view that no one has a divine right to rule, or alternatively that everyone has an equal right to rule as long as the rules of the game are respected. It follows that lack of political alternation may have a detrimental influence on the way people perceive the legitimacy of the state. The view that in a liberal democracy legitimacy is associated with widely accepted procedures, rather than predetermined outcomes – that democracy, in short, is a *method* – finds in the experience of political alternation a valiant accomplice. Furthermore, accepting political alternation as a legitimate consequence of living in a liberal democracy may foster the inclination to accept and trust a plurality of views, which feeds back into the main aspiration of liberal democracy as a political culture, reconciling diversity with harmony.[6]

We have tried to suggest that there are philosophical reasons why the results of the 1996 election are encouraging. For the first time since the end of the fascist era, Italy has experienced legitimate, peaceful political alternation. This will no doubt strengthen the weak roots of liberal democracy in Italy, a fact that any sympathiser of the liberal tradition ought to cheer without reservations.

THE RESULTS OF THE 1996 ELECTION: ACCIDENT OR DESIGN?

That the Left has won the 1996 elections cannot be disputed. As Figures 11.1 and 11.2 below show, the Olive Tree centre–left alliance plus the more extreme Left-wing Communist Refoundation have an outright majority in both houses of parliament, 319 out of 630 in the Chamber of Deputies and 167 out of 315 in the Senate.

Figure 11.1   Results of 1996 and 1994 elections in terms of seats in the Chamber of Deputies

1996		1994	
OLIVE TREE	284	PROGRESSIVES	202
COMMUNIST REFOUNDATION	35	COMMUNIST REFOUNDATION	11
POLE OF FREEDOM	246	POLE OF FREEDOM + POLE OF GOOD GOVERNMENT	366
NORTHERN LEAGUE	59	PACT FOR ITALY	46
OTHERS	6	OTHERS	5
TOTAL	630	TOTAL	630

Figure 11.2   Results of 1996 and 1994 elections in terms of seats in the Senate

1996		1994	
OLIVE TREE	157	PROGRESSIVES	122
COMMUNIST REFOUNDATION	10	PACT FOR ITALY	31
POLE OF FREEDOM	116	POLE OF FREEDOM + POLE OF GOOD GOVERNMENT	155
NORTHERN LEAGUE	27	PANNELLA LIST	1
SOCIAL MOVEMENT	1	OTHERS	6
PANNELLA-SGARBI LIST	1		
OTHERS	3		
TOTAL	315	TOTAL	315

1996: Olive Tree (Democratic Party of the Left, Dini List, For Prodi [Italian Popular Party, South Tyrol People's Party, Italian Republican Party, Democratic Union], Greens); Pole of Freedom (Forza Italia, National Alliance, Christian Democratic Centre, Union of the Centre). 1994: Progressives (Democratic Party of the Left, Socialist Party, Socialist Rebirth, Communist Refoundation, Greens, Democratic Alliance, The Network, Christian Social); Pole of Freedom (Forza Italia, Northern Leagu CVVVe, Christian Democratic Centre, Union of the Centre, Pannella List); Pole of Good Government (Forza Italia, National Alliance, Christian Democratic Centre, Union of the Centre); Pact for Italy (The Segni Pact, Italian Popular Party).

Source: 1996: *La Stampa*, 23 April 1996. 1994: adapted from S. Burgess, 'The New Italy and the General Election of March 1994', *Representation*, Vol.32, No.118, 1994.

The Left's majority in both houses of parliament is due to an increase of 151 representatives compared to 1994 (106 in the Chamber of Deputies and 45 in the Senate). On the basis of the these results, one would expect to find that the gains of the Left in terms of parliamentary seats were caused by a parallel increase in overall votes gained by the Left. In fact, that was not the case. If we compare how the Right and Left performed under the proportional system (in the Chamber of Deputies) in 1994 and 1996, we see that there has been virtually no swing to the Left. The two major parties on the Right (*Forza Italia!* and AN) secured 34.5 per cent of the votes in 1994 and 36.3 per cent in 1996, while the two major parties on the Left (Democratic Party of the Left and Communist Refoundation) secured 26.4 per cent of the votes in 1994 and 29.7 per cent in 1996. Yet compared to 1994, the centre–left alliance won 155 more seats in parliament, equivalent to an increase of 16.4 per cent. Overall, the Olive Tree alliance plus Communist Refoundation won 16 232 000 votes while the Pole of Freedom (plus Pannella-Sgarbi) won 16 481 000 votes.[7]

This incongruity between number of votes and percentage of seats won should not be dismissed simply as a quirky statistical curiosity. Instead it has a lot to do with the electoral system, which ought to be the starting point of any explanation of these results. There are at least two reasons why we should focus on the distortions in the translations of votes into seats caused by the electoral system. First of all, because the coming of age of Italian democracy may be nothing more than the artificial offspring of a highly disputed electoral system. In other words, the numerical break-down of the results shows that the Italian people had very little to do with promoting political alternation, which suggests that the maturing of liberal democracy in Italy was more a case of accident than design. The other reason is because the internal logic of the electoral system may hold the key to a better understanding of the results, in particular it may shed some light on the reasons behind the success of the Left, and failure of the Right, in winning parliamentary seats.

There is no doubt that the electoral system is the key to a comprehensive explanation of the 1996 electoral results. It follows that before proceeding any further in our analysis, it is necessary to recall the basic features of the rules according to which the 1996 elections were fought. The Italian parliament has 945 elected members, 630 seating in the Chamber of Deputies and 315 in the Senate. The parliamentarians, or *deputati*, in the Chamber of Deputies are chosen according to two separate systems. 75 per cent of the *deputati*, equivalent to 475 seats out of 630, are chosen on a simple majority constituency basis, or first-past-the-post system, while the remaining 155 seats are allocated proportionally on a national basis. Each voter is asked to fill-in two separate voting slips, one for the majoritarian seat and the other for the proportional seats. What is important to emphasise is that by having two separate voting slips, the voters had the option of a split-ticket, voting for one coalition in the majoritarian part of the election but for another party (perhaps not from that coalition) in the proportional part of the election. For example, a voter could vote simultaneously for the centre-left Olive Tree alliance and for Berlusconi's *Forza Italia!*.

The Senate is also elected according to two separate systems, with 75 per cent of the seats (or 232 seats out of 315) allocated via a majoritarian system in regional constituencies, while the remaining 25 per cent (or 83 seats) according to a proportional list. Yet unlike for the Chamber of Deputies, this time the voter has only one voting slip to fill in, which counts for both the majoritarian and the proportional allocation.

If we compare the break-down of the votes won by the Right and by the Left in 1994 and 1996 in the Chamber of Deputies (see Tables 11.1 and 11.2), we see that while in 1994 the Right did considerably better under the majoritarian system compared to the proportional system, the tables were reversed in 1996. In 1994 the right-wing alliance[8] won 63.7 per cent of the 475 seats allocated according to majoritarian rules, but only 35.6 per cent in 1996. Of the 155 seats allocated according to a proportional list, the parties in the right-wing alliance[9] won 41.3 per cent seats in 1994 and 49.6 per cent in 1996.

The opposite is true for the Left, who in 1996 did much better under the first-past-the-post system compared to 1994. In 1994 the left-wing alliance[10] won only 34.5 per cent of the 475 seats allocated according to majoritarian rules, but 55 per cent in 1996. Of the 155 allocated according to a proportional list, the parties on the Left[11] won 31.6 per cent of the seats in 1994 and 37.4 per cent in 1996.

Table 11.1   The Right in the Chamber of Deputies

	% of seats in majoritarian system	% of seats in proportional system
1994	63.7	41.3
1996	35.6	49.7

Table 11.2   The Left in the Chamber of Deputies

	% of seats in majoritarian system	% of seats in proportional system
1994	34.5	31.6
1996	54.9	37.4

These statistics are revealing. It means that in order to explain the success of the Left (where the success is measured in terms of parliamentary seats), we must try to explain why the Left was more attractive to the electorate in the part of the election where the *deputati* were chosen according to the majoritarian system. Needless to say, this is an extremely difficult task, thus what follows is, at best, speculative. But at this early stage in the proceedings one cannot hope to do better than put forward an hypothesis that, in the spirit of Popper's logic of scientific discovery, will in due time be falsified.

There are two possible reasons that may explain why the Left did better under the first-past-the-post system in 1996. First of all, it could be argued that compared to 1994, the Left came across as less of a threat. In 1996 the Left went into the election with two leaders, one for the PDS, the other for the centre-left alliance.[12] In other words, in 1996 the leader of the Democratic Party of the Left, D'Alema, was not the leader of the Olive Tree

alliance. Psychologically this may have made a significant difference. The electorate knew that had the Left won the election, as
it did, D'Alema would not have been the Prime Minister. The
fact that the leader of the Olive Tree alliance, Romano Prodi,
was an ex-member of the DC was probably more reassuring to an
electorate that always had problems trusting the Left. Coming
across as less of a threat may have induced the voters to give the
Left the benefit of the doubt under the first-past-the-post system.

Secondly, the Left was probably being rewarded for having
supported the Dini government during difficult times over the
last twelve months. As shown in Chapter 10, in 1995 Italy was
going through difficult times, and it became clear that after
many months of change and uncertainty, it was time for some
stability. The Dini government was forced to pass through parliament a number of unpopular reforms, which no-one liked
but that many felt were necessary to restore Italy's financial
status. During Dini's premiership, the Democratic Party of the
Left was always constructive and supportive, while the Right
was single-mindedly destructive and critical. It may be that the
electorate felt that while the Left had the interest of the
country at heart, the Right was prepared to cause havoc for its
own electoral gains, hence in the eyes of the electorate the
former deserved to be rewarded while the latter was going to
be punished.

So far we have suggested two reasons why the Left may have
been more attractive to the electorate. In what follows, we
want to suggest possible reasons why in 1996 the Right did
more poorly under the first-past-the-post system compared to
1994. First of all, the votes on the Right were fragmented.
Here we are not only referring to Bossi's Northern League,
who this time decided to run on its own. Thus in 1996 the
Northern League was not attached to either the right-wing alliance as it was two years ago, or the centre-left coalition. Had
Bossi agreed to join the right-wing coalition, today we would
probably have a right-wing government.[13]

Apart from Bossi's noncompliance, the right-wing alliance
was also damaged by the creation of smaller parties which,
while small, took decisive votes away from it. More specifically
there are two splinter-parties that did considerable damage to
the right-wing alliance. First, the extreme right-wing party
Movimento Sociale-Fiamma Tricolore, led by Pino Rauti.[14] They

won 338 000 votes, or 0.9 per cent votes under the proportional system in the Chamber of Deputies, and although this was not sufficient to secure a seat, it took votes away from Fini's National Alliance and thus from the Pole of Freedom. In the Senate, Rauti's party successfully elected one senator (2.3 per cent). The other party that did some damage to the right-wing alliance was Dini's *Rinnovamento Italiano*. Dini's party probably won more votes than many expected (4.3 per cent in the Chamber of Deputies), yet one could speculate that had he not started his own party, his votes would probably have gone to the right-wing alliance. Hence Dini, like Rauti, took important votes away from the right-wing Pole of Freedom.

Secondly, there was a major difference between the right-wing alliance of 1994 as opposed to 1996. Two years ago, during the election campaign this alliance came across as compact and unified. After the election the plot changed, indeed the explosive tensions within the alliance could not be hidden for very long. Inevitably the incompatibility between the three leaders forced Berlusconi to resign after only seven months as Italy's 52nd Prime Minister. Yet it must be said that during the campaign Bossi, Fini and Berlusconi were able to present a united front, which led many to believe in the durability of this alliance. The same cannot be said for the Pole of Freedom during the 1996 campaign, in fact the right-wing alliance, even without Bossi, came across as less united than its opposing alliance on the centre-left. Indeed Fini and Berlusconi were both acting as leaders of the Pole of Freedom alliance. As Angelo Panebianco[15] rightly points out, the problem with the Pole of Freedom was not that due to the growing popularity of Fini's *Alleanza Nazionale* the Pole of Freedom shifted towards more extreme positions. Instead the problem lies in Berlusconi's *Forza Italia!*, which suffers from a lack of leadership, insufficient structure and organization, and inadequate political culture. Considering that *Forza Italia!* is pivotal to the success of the Pole of Freedom, these problems within *Forza Italia!* may well have determined the fortunes of the alliance.

Finally, it must be said that compared to the Olive Tree alliance, the candidates chosen to represent the right-wing Pole of Freedom were, at best, mediocre. Being politically inexperienced and generally little known can be an handicap in an election fought under the first-past-the-post electoral system. Of course, it could be argued that Berlusconi managed to pull it off two years ago. That is true. Yet the political context was very different in April 1996 compared to March 1994. In 1994, the electorate was looking for new faces, new ideas, new parties, in part as a protest against the politicians of the First Republic. This is why Berlusconi was able to play the trump card of 'novelty' with success in 1994. But this trump card can only be played once. In 1996, the electorate was not out to castigate anyone. After many years of transition, it was time for stable government. The electorate probably felt that it was time once again to trust its political representatives. But trust is not something that can be won overnight. Trust is a precious asset which is built over time. And in terms of trust, the choice of candidates can make a difference.

As an example of how the calibre of a candidate can make a difference in a majoritarian system, consider the case of Tana de Zulueta. Correspondent for *The Economist*, Tana de Zulueta has become a highly regarded public figure, feared by the Right, indeed it is said that Berlusconi would avoid television debates where she was present. Having acquired Italian citizenship, Tana de Zulueta decided to run for the Senate in the highly competitive constituency of Rome 1. Although she did not win, she came second by only 28 votes, which is a remarkable achievement considering that she entered the race only a few weeks before the election date.

WINNERS AND LOSERS

The left-wing Olive Tree alliance was not the only winner of the 1996 election, just as the right-wing Pole of Freedom alliance was not the only loser. There were others, which ought to be duly acknowledged. Let us begin with the two other winners of the 1996 Italian election.

First of all, as we argued in the outset of this chapter, Italian liberal democracy was a winner. Even if the results of the election were accidental, the political culture of liberal democracy will come out stronger as a result of this election, no matter how it was achieved. Second, the highly-criticised electoral system was a winner. Thanks to this electoral system, Italy has a chance for political stability. In fact it was the electoral system that manufactured a parliamentary majority out of very little.

The merits and vices of the present electoral system have been debated at length over the last few years.[16] After the election, the debate became even more accentuated. On the pages of the Italian daily *Il Corriere della Sera*, two of Italy's most prominent political scientists exchanged blows on this question. On one side, Renato Mannheimer argues that notwithstanding its limitations, this time the electoral system has delivered the goods: 'From minor variations in the (political and territorial) distribution of votes, the electoral system was able to produce a parliamentary majority. This is exactly what a majoritarian system is supposed to do'.[17]

On the other side Giovanni Sartori responds by arguing that, in fact, the electoral system is a shambles and that contrary to what Mannheimer believes, it should not be praised. According to Sartori, we should distinguish between a majoritarian electoral system that *can* produce a majority in parliament, and the normative consideration of whether this artificial fabrication is indeed desirable. Far from being a virtue of the present electoral system, the fact that a majority of votes translates into a minority of seats in parliament, as was the case in this election, is a disturbing reality. Yes, the first-past-the-post electoral system has the ability to strengthen an electoral majority, but it should not be praised for creating one artificially.[18]

On this debate between Mannheimer and Sartori we want to side with Mannheimer. In order to make this point, we want to return to the prior analysis of the break-down of the vote, which shows that the centre-left alliance did better than the right-wing alliance in the part of the election where the *deputati* in the Chamber of Deputies were chosen according to the first-past-the-post system. It is here that the virtues of the electoral system can best be appreciated.

It is a well-known fact that the first-past-the-post electoral system fosters a bipolarization of electoral forces. Of course some would argue that this is undesirable. Leaving that issue aside, one of the advantages of an election fought between two political forces, one representing the government and the other representing the opposition, is that each election becomes a sort of referendum on the performance of the party or parties in government. In other words, if the voters liked what the government did during its time in office, the party in government will be voted again. If not, the opposition will be given a chance.

This is the second election fought according to first-past-the-post rules, and the logic of this system is slowly filtering through. To some extent, the 1996 election was going to be a referendum on the performances of the two governments since March 1994: the Berlusconi government and the Dini government. It should not be forgotten that in the space of five years Italy has had three general elections (1992, 1994 and 1996), and the electorate was growing weary of so much uncertainty. In 1994 the Right had its chance, but it was unable to deliver what most Italians were eager for: stability. In the last analysis, the collapse of the Berlusconi government in December 1994, brought about by skirmishes within the governmental coalition itself, was alarmingly reminiscent of the way politics was conducted in the First Republic. It is not surprising that, as a result of Berlusconi's disappointing record in office, in 1996 the electorate was prepared (albeit with some reservations) to give a chance to the Left. Thus in the majoritarian part of the election the Left did better than the Right, and the reservations of the electorate came in the form of the votes cast in favour of the right-wing alliance in the proportional part of the election.

So much for the winners of the elections, what about the losers? For the record, it is important to acknowledge the fact that in the most recent elections women did more poorly than hoped, which is a regrettable reality. As a result of the 1996 elections, women make up only 9 per cent of parliament, or 85 women out of 945 seats (60 in the Chamber of Deputies and 25 in the Senate).[19] Furthermore, today there are fewer women in parliament compared to two years ago, when 124 women were voted in parliament (95 in the Chamber of Deputies and 29 in the Senate). The fact that in terms of sex equality Italian politics has such a poor record is perhaps not surprising, considering that Italian liberal democracy is well behind respect other Western countries. It is also a potent reminder that in terms of embracing the political culture of liberal democracy, Italy still has a long way to go.

CONCLUSION: WHAT DOES THE FUTURE HOLD?

In the immediate aftermath of the election, in an article in the daily *La Stampa,* Bobbio refers to Italian democracy becoming unblocked.[20] The anomaly of democracy Italian style, whereby one of Italy's two largest parties had always been in power while the second-largest party had always been in opposition, seems to be a thing of the past. In the last two elections, two different coalitions have emerged as winners, the right-wing coalition in 1994 and the centre-left coalition in 1996. According to Bobbio, this is a turning point for the evolution of Italian democracy. It is true that, as we have tried to argue in this chapter, Italian democracy has come to age notwithstanding the Italian people (rather than thanks to the Italian electorate!). But this should not worry us too much. What is important is that political alternation has finally taken place, which is the best thing that could have happened to Italian democracy.

The future looks bright for liberal democracy in Italy. Can the same be said for Romano Prodi and his centre-left coalition? Will Prodi's government last longer than Berlusconi's government in 1994? In order to answer these questions, two issues must be taken into consideration. First, the uneasy relationship between the Democratic Party of the Left (the heir of the old Communist Party) and the unreconstructed marxist group of Communist Refoundation, especially as the Olive Tree alliance needs the votes of Communist Refoundation to have a majority in both the Chamber of Deputies and the Senate. Although Communist Refoundation was formally not part of the Olive Tree alliance, it made an informal agreement with the other left-wing parties (known as *desistenza*) not to cause waves during the electoral campaign, as it did in 1994 concerning the taxing of state bonds (BOTs). Furthermore the Olive Tree alliance and Communist Refoundation agreed not to compete against each other in certain constituencies, instead Communist Refoundation would put up its candidates only against the candidates of *Lista Dini.* There are three protagonists in this balancing act: Bertinotti (leader of Communist Refoundation), D'Alema (leader of the Democratic Party of the Left) and Prodi (Prime Minister and leader of the Olive Tree alliance). It would be foolish to predict at such an early stage in the proceedings how these three key men will respond to the challenges ahead of them.

Being the first time that the Left is in government, there is no history from which to consult and learn.

Rather than indulge in empty speculation, which would be impossible to substantiate, what we feel is more fruitful is to suggest how one should study the relationship between D'Alema's Democratic Party of the Left and Bertinotti's Communist Refoundation. We believe that in pursuing this research agenda, rational choice theory is an invaluable tool of analysis. What must be established is not only the 'horizontal' bargaining power that each party has within the coalition,[21] but also the 'vertical' relations that determine intraparty dynamics.[22] The latter is particularly important. The idea is that especially in the case of Communist Refoundation, intraparty politics may be the key to whether it will co-operate with the other parties in the centre-left coalition. It follows that we should relax the assumption that a party operates as a unitary actor, and concentrate on the dynamics within the party itself.

The second issue which will determine the longevity of Prodi's term in office concerns the power relations *within* the centre-left alliance. As Warner and Varese[23] argue, the potential withdrawal of support for the government by Communist Refoundation is not the only problem facing Prodi's government. In fact Prodi faces the prospect of an uneasy relationship *within* the Olive Tree alliance. The prime minister himself, Romano Prodi, lacks a true power base in any of the parties making up the Olive Tree alliance. The fact that Prodi cannot count on any party for his support is a major potential weakness, aggravated by the fact that within the cabinet there are highly independent and ambitious figures like the former *Mani pulite* magistrate and now minister of public works Antonio Di Pietro (see Chapter 4), the ex-prime minister and now foreign minister Lamberto Dini, and of course Massimo D'Alema, who as leader of the PDS is leader of the largest party within the Olive Tree alliance. Prodi's leadership skills will be tested over the next few years, especially as the key protagonists within the Prodi government hold bargaining power. In terms of understanding the longevity of Prodi's centre-left government, we believe these questions assessing the bargaining powers within each party (and especially within Communist Refoundation), as well as between the parties in the Olive Tree alliance, form the most pressing and rewarding research agenda.

Notes

1. See for example B. Barry, 'Is Democracy Special?', in B. Barry, *Democracy, Power and Justice* (1989).
2. N. Bobbio, *The Future of Democracy* (1987) p.106. The growing concerns of multiculturalism have made this an even more pressing question, see for example W. Kymlicka, *Multicultural Citizenship* (1996).
3. See for example J. Gray, *Liberalisms* (1989).
4. The political monopoly of the Japanese liberal-democratic party (Jiminto), which endured for 38 years, came to an end in 1993.
5. See J. Waldron, 'Theoretical Foundations of Liberalism', in *The Philosophical Quarterly* (1987).
6. On the importance of trust in fostering cooperative relations, see D. Gambetta (ed.), *Trust* (1988). In particular, on the affinity between liberalism and trust, see the chapter by N. Luhmann 'Familiarity, Confidence, Trust: Problems and Alternatives', p.99.
7. This refers to the votes for the Chamber of Deputies. The Democratic Party of the Left won 7 897 000 votes, and Forza Italia 7 715 000 votes. See *Il Corriere della Sera*, 23 April 1996.
8. In 1994 this included Forza Italia, National Alliance, Northern League, Christian Democratic Centre, Union of the Centre, Pannella List. In 1996 it included Forza Italia, National Alliance, Christian Democratic Centre, Union of the Centre.
9. In 1994 this includes Forza Italia, National Alliance and Northern League. In 1996 it includes Forza Italia, National Alliance, and Christian Democratic Centre – Union of the Centre.
10. In 1994 this included Democratic Party of the Left, Socialist Party, Socialist Rebirth, Communist Refoundation, Greens, Democratic Alliance, The Network, Christian Social. In 1996 it included Democratic Party of the Left, Dini List, Greens, For Prodi (Italian Popular Party, South Tyrol People's Party, Italian Republican Party, Democratic Union).
11. In 1994 this included the Democratic Party of the Left and Communist Refoundation. In 1996 it included the Democratic Party of the Left, Communist Refoundation, Dini List, Greens, For Prodi (Italian Popular Party, South Tyrol People's Party, Italian Republican Party, Democratic Union).
12. After the 1994 electoral fiasco, Occhetto's wisdom of standing as leader of the PDS and of the Left-wing Progressives Alliance was put into question. See for example G. Pasquino, 'Un leader nuovo? no, ce ne servono due' and G. Bosetti, 'Professionisti del presente', both in *Reset* (1994).
13. See S. Warner and F. Varese 'The Italian general election of 1996', in *Electoral Studies* (forthcoming).
14. The radical neo-fascist Italian Social Movement was formally dissolved in 1995, being replaced by Fini's moderate 'post-fascist' *Alleanza Nazionale*. Notwithstanding its electoral success, Fini's leadership was strongly criticized for disowning the fascist tradition. Therefore in view of the 1996 elections Pino Rauti set up his own neo-fascist party,

Movimento Sociale-Fiamma Tricolore. For an account of the relationship between Fini's National Alliance and the old Italian Social Movement, see C. Ruzza and O. Schmidtke, 'Towards a Modern Right: Alleanza Nazionale and the "Italian Revolution"', in S. Gundle and S. Parker (eds), *The New Italian Republic: From the Fall of the Berlin Wall to Berlusconi* (1996). For the view that there is no substantial difference between Fini's National Alliance and the old Italian Social Movement, see P. Ignazi, 'Alleanza Nazionale', in I. Diamanti and R. Mannheimer (eds), *Milano a Roma: Guida all'Italia Elettorale del 1994* (1994).

15. A. Panebianco, 'Doppio errore per il Polo', *Il Corriere della Sera*, 3 May 1996.

16. Steven Warner and Diego Gambetta, *La Retorica della Riforma* (1994), and D. Gambetta and S. Warner, 'The rhetoric of reform revealed', *Journal of Modern Italian Studies* (1995).

17. R. Mannheimer, 'Nessun vento di sinistra sulle elezioni', *Il Corriere della Sera*, 29 April 1996.

18. G. Sartori, 'Un paese senza gambe', *Il Corriere della Sera*, 6 May 1996.

19. The Left elected 40 of the 60 women in the Chamber of Deputies (33 in the Olive Tree alliance and 7 in Communist Refoundation), and 18 of the 25 in the Senate (17 in the Olive Tree alliance and 1 in Communist Refoundation). See *Il Corriere della Sera*, 25 April 1996.

20. N. Bobbio 'L'alternanza sblocca la democrazia', *La Stampa*, 23 April 1996.

21. See M. Laver and N. Schofield, *Multiparty Government: The Politics of Coalition in Europe* (1990).

22. See R. Mulé, 'Party competition and the hierarchy of goals', in J. Lovenduski and J. Stanyer (eds), *Contemporary Political Studies 1995, Volume I* (1995).

23. S. Warner and F. Varese, op. cit. (forthcoming).

Conclusion: Italy in Transition

Theory devoid of empirical detail is all too often dry and un-historical, yet the mere reciting of events often tends to be un-theorised. One of the main purposes of the preceding chapters has been to bridge this gap between description and analysis. More specifically, our aim has been to delineate the dynamics of change in Italy since 1989 in the form of a contin-uous historical narrative, while at the same time suggesting some explanatory interpretations for these events.

It only remains to pull together all the strings in our analy-sis, and draw some conclusions on the state of the Italian polity after the last eight turbulent years. There are three recurring themes in our study: the uniqueness of Italian democracy; the phenomenon of particracy; and the lack of a liberal culture in Italian democracy. In what follows we will provide a recapitulation of our views on these three different, though concurring, themes.

IS ITALIAN DEMOCRACY SPECIAL?

It has long been commonplace to observe that Italy is an ex-ceptional, even anomalous country, so exceptional as to be all but incomparable, even when judged alongside its closest Western European neighbours. Italy's historically late unification, weak governing structure, rival power centres, and its sharp geographical and social cleavages all combined to create the impression of an extraordinary political order. The unbroken post-war dominance of the Christian Democrat party contributed to the singular paradox of Italy's 'stable instability'.[1]

The belief that Italy is different has, indeed, found some confirmation in the upheavals over the last decade. As we argued in Chapter 1, Italy was not only among the first of the Western liberal democracies to be struck by the after-effects of

244

the fall of the Berlin Wall and closer European integration. The political impact of these historic changes on the domestic scene was also the most extreme. While in other parts of Western Europe presidents and prime ministers were toppled, and governments forced out of office, in Italy there was the breaking up of the entire party system. The subsequent exacerbation of pre-existing internal strains and pressures – the regional challenge of the Northern League, for example, or the struggle over the future financing of the welfare state – has even led some commentators to think of Italy as 'a unique geopolitical laboratory' forging a post-modern path that other nations are likely to follow.[2] In a new answer to the old question, the recent transformation in Italian politics has simply reinforced the idea of its characteristic distinctiveness.

The special nature of recent changes in Italian politics points to a further unusual aspect, namely, the comparative rarity with which an already functioning democracy has undergone a dramatic democratic evolution. Recent political literature is replete with works about the collapse of authoritarian and totalitarian government, the transition to and consolidation of democratic regimes, and even about how democracies can founder.[3] Yet there are very few instances of a modern, mass liberal democracy re-inventing itself: in Europe, only the creation of the Fifth Republic in France after 1958 seems to qualify. Italy constitutes one of those rare examples where a complete reshaping of party politics has occurred without this demolishing the entire constitutional framework or paving the way for tyranny.[4]

For this reason, it will not suffice to fall back upon the adage that all democracies are democratic, but that each is democratic in its own way. It could be argued that Italy, by dint of the rapid and absolute changeover from the old politics to the new, is perhaps beyond compare. That said, the very fact of being able to form such a judgement implies some kind of a comparativist perspective. One needs a working concept of democracy in the abstract before one can then apply it to specific cases. As Jean Blondel maintains, a generalised model is not going to be discovered one fine morning, but it is equally false to think that each country is so uniquely different that there is no point in comparing.[5] The anomalous is not necessarily incomprehensible. What is it that has made, and continues to make, Italian-style democracy so distinctive? Can we give a normative evaluation of Italian-style democracy?

There is a great deal of disagreement about whether Italy is properly regarded as 'the oldest of the new democracies or the newest of the old'.[6] This is not only a matter of categorisation. It relates to two major themes of our work, namely the changing nature of particracy in all aspects of Italian social and political life, and a reconsideration of the historical strength or otherwise of a liberal democratic tradition in Italy.

A THEORY OF THE PARTY STATE

One of the distinctive aspects of Italian democracy since the war has been the central and hegemonic role of political parties in the political system. The prominence of political parties in Italian social and political life is unique compared to other Western democracies. According to Mauro Calise political parties held monopolistic control over the governmental process.[7] As we discussed in the introduction, this phenomenon is known as particracy, a type of political system separate and distinct from the other well-established forms of government: presidential or parliamentary.

After 1989, and perhaps unexpectedly, the era of particracy underwent a major crisis. As Italian democracy began the slow and painful process of large-scale change, the most radical changes concerned the traditional parties and the party system itself. Over the last ten years, the crisis of the parties is reflected in the changes in party names and symbols, in the splits within and mergers between parties, and in the new types of party organisation and party elite turnover.[8] Because political parties were for so long pivotal to the functioning of Italian politics, it is not surprising that these radical changes in the political parties and the party system coincided with the crisis of Italy's First Republic. What is more difficult to explain is the timing of this crisis, and what it tells us about the nature of particracy in Italy.

The conventional understanding for the proclaimed downfall of the First Republic has been that the ending of the Cold War, allied to the growing pressures arising from closer European integration, did away with the old ideological polarisation of Italian party politics, unleashing new forces of change. Further developments, such as the stepping up of the war against the mafia, formed part of the same post-Cold War thesis, which largely placed the emphasis upon the reshaping of party alignments.

This post-Cold War thesis is not entirely convincing. There is no demonstrable link between the forming of the party-state and the Cold War balance of power, so that the disappearance of the latter cannot explain the demise of the former. Furthermore it is difficult to be persuaded by the view that the integrationist effects of the European Union were all that important either, especially not after the withdrawal of the *lira* from the ERM in September 1992. Indeed as we saw in Chapter 2, the post-Cold War thesis is heavily qualified by several students of electoral trends who consider the result of the 1992 general election to be the explicable outcome of a number of longer-term shifts in voting behaviour that, in fact, predated the collapse of Communism in Eastern Europe. Amongst the key factors one finds the changing social and economic fabric of society,[9] as well as the weakening of traditional social cleavages and sub-cultures.

There is, of course, an entirely different explanation for the proclaimed downfall of the First Republic, grounded on an appreciation of the systemic nature of politico-economic corruption.[10] In Chapter 4, we argued that political parties played a key role in the evolution of the market of production, providing the institutional framework necessary for the smooth operation of corrupt transactions. The collapse of the party system can therefore be seen as a consequence of the breakdown in the equilibrium generated by the market of corruption.

Switching the focus of analysis away from the aftermath of the end of the Cold War, pointing instead towards the market of corruption, has important implications for the way we define the concept of particracy. While acknowledging that the unblocking of party power and ideology had been one of the principal factors in the dismantling of the old Italy, those who search for an explanation of the downfall of the First Republic in the collapse of the market of corruption do not construe the concept of *particracy* quite so narrowly. The main political parties were not just – or no longer – 'catch-all' parties concerned with the aggregation and representation of different interests. They had become 'cartel-parties', manned by business-politicians colluding with organised crime and the world of industry in a clientelistic–consociational contract involving the co-optation of diverse social groups in a visible and clandestine network of mutual exchange, utilising the resources of the state to buy consent.

This network of regularised transactions fell apart with the financial strains (debt, fraud) which set in in the late eighties and which had reduced the capacity of the parties to maintain their clientelistic relations. Illegal pay-offs had exploded. The price of kickbacks became too dear for many private entrepreneurs to endure. As the market of corruption became unsustainable, all those people who for many years had benefitted from corrupt transaction decided they had had enough. The moment people realised that playing the game of corruption did not pay off any longer, was the moment they spontaneously turned against the old particratic rule.

In Stefano Guzzini's revised interpretation, the idea of particracy does not just describe a novel form of government – as Calise has it – but a fully-fledged theory of the state, in which the parties have been transformed into an organised and integral part of the institutions of state itself, legitimising their role by reaching down into civil society. The more the parties came to rely on a support system of institutionalised illegality, the more they had to depend on those means to make up for the loss of authority, creating a vicious circle of disaffection which eventually, and inevitably, caused the exercising mechanisms of public power to self-destruct.

The debate about which conceptual model best encapsulates the political economy of postwar Italy has been a debate without end, and sceptics might maintain that there are problems with the notions both of consociationalism and clientelism which are certainly not overcome by amalgamating them together. All democratic states are characterised by a complex interchange of interests and pressures which vary in emphasis and over time, and which yield only to empirical inquiry.[11] Guzzini has the merit of relating the party–state idea not only to a particular institutional arrangement but to the wider economic and social system of power, linking the emergence of political mediators who had developed personal, non-ideological ties in the market for corruption, to the common modernising trends to be found in other advanced welfare democracies.

Perhaps Guzzini's excluding of *any* Cold War impact is much too sweeping, since he took no account of the extensive and long-established co-involvement of state companies in the military and defence industries, highlighted for example by the corrupt dealings of the Italian Agusta helicopter company (owned by EFIM) with the Belgian armed forces in 1988. Nevertheless he provides a conceptualisation of the Italian state which goes a long way towards accounting for the apparent and baffling paradox of a strong party system combined with a high incidence of illicit activity.

TOWARDS A LIBERAL DEMOCRACY?

If we accept Guzzini's analysis – particracy not as a type of government but a form of state – then a crisis in Italy's party system is synonymous with a crisis of the Italian state. For social scientists moments of institutional crisis are invaluable. It is during these rare times that a social scientist can view the inner dynamics of a system with unprecedented clarity. It is therefore in the perspective of a crisis of the Italian state that we must assess the extent to which Italian-style democracy is desirable from a normative perspective, and whether a different (liberal) culture is being enabled to flourish.

There is no doubt that particracy feeds into a specific conception of democratic polity. Particracy promotes a type of democracy not based on the liberal distinction between the public and the private sphere. Disguised under the banner of a communitarian ethic, or appealing to the distinguished tradition of civic humanist republicanism, the collapse of the dichotomy between state and civil society is justified by lauding the virtues of active citizenship, enriching people's lives through political participation. In other words, according to civic republicanism, active political participation has an intrinsic value for the participants themselves.[12]

The unconditional intervention of the state in the affairs of civil society, undertaken by political parties interested in promoting their interests, is a dangerous game to play.[13] The simultaneous operation of political parties in the public sphere of government and the private sphere of civil society inevitably encourages the violation of the ethics of impartiality. Favouritism, privilege and prejudice become the norm as party-people build their power networks: as we discussed in Chapter 4, party officials build their careers on the exchange of favours for votes. The extent to which clientelistic relations proliferated in Italy is, no doubt, a result of particracy. The allocation of jobs in the public administration in the South is an index of patronage. According to Sabino Cassese, between 1973 and 1990 about 350 000 people (out of 600 000) were recruited into the civil service without regular procedures.[14] Under particracy, patronage and personal contacts replaces meritocracy and need as the dominant distributive criterion, reflecting a total disregard for individual needs and individual rights. The reality of particracy reinforces the view that there is a chronic lack of liberal culture in Italy, as suggested by Alexander Passerin d'Entrèves more than 20 years ago.

Passerin d'Entrèves argued that the polis, or state, should be approached and considered on three levels: the level of force or might, the level of legality or power, and the level of legitimacy or authority. He then added that 'on all three accounts, something seems to have gone wrong in Italy after unification'.[15] To a large number of Italians, the state is primarily a matter of force rather than of consent, of coercion rather than of conviction. What many Italians fail to see is that force is not enough:

> Yet I cannot help thinking that a kind of cheap, second-rate Machiavellianism is still ingrained in the mind of many Italians, which may account for their proclivity always to emphasize the seamy side of political life, as if self-interest were its only determining factor. This leads to a pessimistic, or, more exactly, to a cynical view of the State, based on the assumption that politics is a matter of getting the upper hand and that all men, if not potential criminals, are at any rate would-be profiteers or tax-evaders.[16]

What we need to ask ourselves is to what extent have things changed since Alexander Passerin d'Entrèves reproached the Italian people of second-rate Machiavellianism. So far the signs are not reassuring.

The current debate on constitutional reform is indicative. The Italian constitution of the First Republic, as it now stands, has its merits. First of all, although it is fashionable to deny it, there is in fact no continuity between the fascist era and the First Republic.[17] After the new constitutional order was established following the demise of fascism, Italy became a founding member of both NATO and the European Economic Community. There was a remarkable increase in welfare and prosperity, especially during the phase of the 'economic miracle' between 1958 and 1963. Finally, notwithstanding the circumstance of continuous, routinised crisis, the Italian polity developed a political framework habituated to self-sustaining democratic procedures.[18] This democratic heritage is still, evidently, a living one. Important turning points since 1989, exemplified by the new judicial activism, the backlash against mafia crime and the popular involvement of the referendum movement, apparently indicated an encouraging capacity of the institutions of government to respond to public pressure. Whether that constitutional framework, devised when Italy was still a largely agricultural, non-industrialised nation, is equipped to cope with the new challenges that have emerged in the wake of recent transformations is now widely questioned. It appears that the rules of the game are in need of revision, and political parties will inevitably play a big part in formulating any constitutional review. But the question remains: how is the constitution going to be reformed?

Some of the recent debates on constitutional reform would seem to indicate that Passerin d'Entréves' views are still as valid today as they were twenty years ago. There is for example a school of thought that believes that a constitution should not embody the wishes of the entire people, but instead should be the expression of the will of the majority. This is the view entertained by Gianfranco Miglio, who believes that a constitution is something that the victorious majority can impose on the defeated minority.[19] If parties can change the constitution to suit their interests, than particracy not only will survive, but will become even stronger. The views expressed by Miglio are a far cry from the beliefs intrinsic to the liberal tradition in which the constitution is seen in terms of a contract stipulated to safeguard the rights of *all* subjects within a polity. The contractual nature of constitutionalism is vindicated by Luigi

Ferrajoli, who sees the constitution as a pact designed to keep the peace and secure the coexistence of extremes, and therefore as an agreement amongst all the players involved.[20]

If the concept of a majoritarian constitution can be seen as an attempt to resurrect particracy in Italy, the opposite backlash against particracy is also alarming. It is important to emphasise that doing away with particracy does not mean doing away with the party system *tout court*. As Bobbio reminds us, all modern democracies require political parties to organise and aggregate the electorate. The alternative of a democracy built around political parties is a democracy built around persons, who are more likely to be elected on the basis of their sympathy and television appeal, than on their merit, programmes or electoral platform. A modern, mass democracy needs its political parties. In the last analysis, stability depends on it: if there are going to be as many parties in parliament as there are MPs, it will be impossible to create a stable, working parliamentary majority.[21]

Political cultures are not created overnight, and liberal culture is not an exception. It will take many years before people (including politicians) become acquainted with the new political procedures, and the corresponding expectations these procedures unleash. It takes time before people become educated of the values of fairness, impartiality, reciprocity and trust. It is not surprising that the reformist hopes of a post-Cold War democratic upsurge did not materialise. In fact, as we have tried to show in this book, since 1989 new and more disturbingly illiberal phenomena have ensued. The rise of the Northern League (as discussed in Chapters 2), with it populist appeal, endorses a communitarian rather than a liberal conception of democracy. Similarly Silvio Berlusconi's government was characterised by strong illiberal tendencies, shown by his attempt to control the mass media and the judiciary (see Chapter 9). Finally, upon the fall of the Berlusconi government in December 1994, that each side could accuse the other of anti-democratic behaviour was a revealing sign of the mutual lack of tolerance and trust. The old political order was purged, but this did not automatically lead to the revitalising of democratic life or the reassertion of democratic principles.

In order for a liberal political culture to have a chance of prospering, the first fundamental step is the occurrence of political alternation. This step was taken for the first time in 1996, with the electoral victory of the centre-left coalition. Political alternation is important because it fosters trust between people of the same community, and trust (like social cooperation) is a valuable commodity in any society.[22] Furthermore, and more importantly, the peaceful changeover of power, *sine effusione sanguinis* (without bloodshed), encourages a belief in individual rights and impartiality.

Once it is accepted that power can change hands, opposition becomes possible (because it is no longer seen as treasonable or subversive) and government is moderated (because the powerful of today may not be the powerful of tomorrow). Alternation does not, or rather has not yet, redefined the boundaries between the state, business and civil society. But upon this solid grounding, a new social order which upholds liberal values might now be established.

Notes

1. Italy has had 50 different governments between June 1945 and June 1992, all centred around the DC.
2. L. Caracciolo, 'L'Italie, un laboratoire unique', in *Le Monde*, 18 December 1993, p.10; J. Hooper, 'Testing to destruction', in *The Guardian*, 6 January 1995, p.22. See also M. Lazar, 'Existe-t-il un "made in Italy" politique?', *Revue Politique et Parlementaire* (1993).
3. See A. Prezeworski, *Sustainable Democracy* (1995).
4. See M. Calise, 'The Italian particracy: beyond president and parliament', *West European Politics* (1993); N. Bobbio, quoted in *Le Monde*, 26 January 1995, p.15, refers to the breaking of the historical law according to which a badly governed democracy finishes up inevitably as an authoritarian state.
5. J. Blondel, 'Plaidoyer pour une conception œcuménique de l'analyse politique comparée', in *Revue Internationale de Politique Comparée* (1994) pp.5–18. See also T. Mackie and D. Marsh, 'The comparative method', in D. Marsh and G. Stoker (eds), *Theory and Methods in Political Science* (1995).
6. S. Barnes, 'L'Elettorato Italiano e la teoria della democratizzazione', in M. Caciagli *et al.* (eds), *L'Italia fra Crisi e Transizione* (1994) p.15.
7   See M. Calise, op. cit. (1993).
8. See L. Morlino, 'Crisis of Parties and Change of Party System in Italy', in *Party Politics* (1996).
9. See A. Bagnasco, *L'Italia in Tempi di Cambiamento Politico* (1996).

10. S. Guzzini, 'The "long night of the First Republic": years of clientelis- tic implosion in Italy', *Review of International Political Economy* (1995). French translation S. Guzzini, 'La longue nuit de la premiere république – l'implosion clienteliste en Italie', in *La Revue Française de Science Politique* (1994).
11. J. La Palombara, '"Clientela e parentela" rivisitato', in M. Caciagli *et al.* (eds), op. cit. (1994) p.36.
12. See W. Kymlicka and W. Norman, 'Return of the citizen: a survey of recent work on citizenship theory', *Ethics* (1994).
13. For a sharp critique of republican citizenship, which looks at the ques- tion of constitutional politics, see E. Christodoulidis, '"A new constitu- tional reality for civil society"? Some cautionary remarks on republican citizenship', in R. Bellamy, V. Bufacchi and D. Castiglione (eds), *Democracy and Constitutional Culture in the Union of Europe* (1995).
14. S. Cassese, 'Hypotheses on the Italian Administrative System', *West European Politics* (1993).
15. A. Passerin d'Entrèves, 'New reflections on the history of Italy', *European Studies Review* (1974) p.204.
16. Ibid., p.195.
17. On the lack of continuity, see N. Bobbio, *Tra Due Repubbliche: Alle Origini della Democrazia Italiana* (1996) pp.130–9.
18. We are using here the language employed by D. Rustow to explain 'Transitions to democracy: towards a dynamic model', in *Comparative Politics* (1970) pp.337–63.
19. In the words of Miglio, 'It is wrong to say that a constitution must embody the wishes of the entire people. A constitution is a pact that the victorious powers impose on the defeated side. It [the constitu- tion] can be changed, and in fact this possibility is provided for within the constitution itself, as part of Article 138, which deals expressly with the question of constitutional change. All that is required is half the votes in Parliament plus one. What is my dream? That the Northern League and Forza Italia obtain half plus one. Half of the Italians frame the constitution for the other half as well. After that, it's just a question of maintaining law and order on the streets', quoted in L. Ferrajoli, 'Democracy and the Constitution in Italy', *Political Studies* (1996) pp.461–2.
20. See ibid. (1996). On the connection between constitutions and con- tracts, see the excellent work by Dario Castiglione 'Contracts and Constitutions', in R. Bellamy, V. Bufacchi and D. Castiglione (eds), *Democracy and Constitutional Culture in the Union of Europe* (1995).
21. See N. Bobbio, op. cit. (1996) pp.119–24.
22. See R. Putnam, *Making Democracy Work* (1993).

Bibliography

Agosta, A., 'Maggioritario e proporzionale', in I. Diamanti and R. Mannheimer (eds), *Milano a Roma: guida all'Italia elettorale del 1994*, Roma: Donzelli (1994).

Alexander, H.E. (ed.), *Comparative Political Finance in the 1980s*, Cambridge: Cambridge University Press (1989).

Allievi, S., *Le Parole della Lega*, Milano: Garzanti (1992).

Allum, P., *Italy: Republic without Government*, London: Weidenfeld & Nicolson (1973).

Allum, P., 'The Liga Veneta', *ASMI Newsletter*, Spring 1993.

Allum, P., 'Chronicle of a Death Foretold: The First Italian Republic', *The Italianist*, 13, 1993.

Allum, P., 'Il Mezzogiorno', in I. Diamanti and R. Mannheimer (eds), *Milano a Roma: guida all'Italia elettorale del 1994*, Roma: Donzelli (1994).

Almond, G.A. and Verba, S., *The Civic Culture: Political Attitudes and Democracy in Five Nations*, Princeton, NJ: Pronceton University Press (1963).

Almond, G.A. and Verba, S. (eds), *The Civic Culture Rivisited*, Boston: Little, Brown (1980).

Amato, G. 'Il dilemma del principio maggioritario', *Quaderni Costituzionali*, Vol.14, No.2, 1994.

Amato, G. 'The dilemmas of the majoritarian system', in R. Leonardi and R. Nanetti (eds), *Italy: Politics and Policy*, Aldershot: Dartmouth (1996).

Andreoli, M., *Andavano in Piazza Duomo*, Milano: Sperling & Kupfer (1993).

Andvig, J.C. and Moene, K.O., 'How corruption may corrupt', *The Journal of Economic Behaviour and Organisation*, Vol. 13, 1990.

Arlacchi, P., *Gli Uomini del Disonore*, Milano: Mondadori (1992).

Avineri, S. and de-Shalit, A. (eds), *Communitarianism and Liberalism*, Oxford: Oxford University Press (1992).

Bagnasco, A., *L'Italia in tempi di Cambiamento Politico*, Bologna: Il Mulino (1996).

Bardi, L. and Morlino, L., 'Italy: tracing the roots of the great transformation', in R. Katz and P. Mair (eds), *How Parties Organise*, London: Sage (1994).

Barnes, S., 'L'elettorato italiano e la teoria della democratizzazione', in M. Caciagli, F. Cazzola, L. Morlino and S. Passigli (eds), *L'Italia fra Crisi e Transizione*, Bari: Laterza (1994).

Barry, B., *Sociologists, Economists and Democracy*, London: Macmillan (1970).

Barry, B., 'On analogy', *Political Studies*, Vol.XXIII, No.2–3, 1975.

Barry, B., 'Is it better to be powerful or lucky?', in *Democracy, Power and Justice: Essays in Political Theory*, Oxford: Clarendon (1989).

Barry, B., 'Is democracy special?' in *Democracy, Power and Justice: Essays in Political Theory*, Oxford: Clarendon (1989).

Barry, B., 'How not to defend liberal institutions', *British Journal of Political Science*, Vol.20, Part 1, January 1990.

Barry, B., *Justice as Impartiality*, Oxford: Oxford University Press (1995).

Bedani, G., 'A Masterpiece of Electoral Engineering', public lecture presented at the University of Manchester, May 1995.

Beetham, D., *Max Weber and the Theory of Modern Politics*, Camprodge: Polity Press (1985).

Beitz, C., *Political Equality*, Princeton, NJ: Princeton University Press (1989).

Bellamy, R., *Liberalism and Modern Society*, Cambridge: Polity Press (1992).

Bellamy, R., Bufacchi, V. and Castiglione, D. (eds), *Democracy and Constitutional Culture in the Union of Europe*, London: Lothian (1995).

Belotti, V., 'Il patto per l'Italia', in I. Diamanti and R. Mannheimer (eds), *Milano a Roma: guida all'Italia elettorale del 1994*, Roma: Donzelli (1994).

Berlinguer, G., *I Duplicanti Politici in Italia*, Bari: Laterza (1991).

Blondel, J., 'Plaidoyer pour une conception œcuménique de l'analyse politique comparée', in *Revue Internationale de Politique Comparée*, April 1994.

Bobbio, L., 'Dalla destra alla destra, una strana alternanza', in P. Ginsborg (ed.), *Stato dell'Italia*, Milano: Il Saggiatore/Mondadori (1994).

Bobbio, N., *The Future of Democracy*, Cambridge: Polity Press (1987).

Bobbio, N., *Democracy and Dictatorship: The Nature and Limits of State Power*, Cambridge: Polity Press (1989).

Bobbio, N., *Liberalism and Democracy*, London: Verso (1990).

Bobbio, N., *Left and Right: The Significance of a Political Distinction*, Cambridge: Polity (1996).

Bobbio, N., *Tra Due Repubbliche: alle origini della democrazia italiana*, Roma: Donzelli (1996).

Bocca, G., *L'Inferno – profondo sud, male oscuro*, Milano: Mondadori (1992).

Bogdanor, V. (ed.), *Constitutions in Democratic Politics*, Aldershot: Gower (1988).

Bozzo, Baget G., *Cattolici e Democristiani*, Milano: Rizzoli (1994).

Braun, M. 'I sindacati confederali e il governo Dini: il grande ritorno del neo-corporativismo?', in M. Caciagli and D. Kertzer (eds), *Politica in Italia – i fatti dell'anno e le interpretazioni. Edizione 1996*, Bologna: Il Mulino (1996).

Bufacchi, V. 'The success of mani pulite: luck or skill?', in R. Leonardi and R. Nanetti (eds), *Italy: Politics and Policy*, Aldershot: Dartmouth (1996).

Bufacchi, V., 'The coming of age of Italian democracy', *Government and Opposition*, Vol.31, No.3, summer 1996.

Bull, Cento A., 'The politics of industrial districts in Lombardy: replacing Christian Democracy with the Northern League', *The Italianist*, Vol.13, 1993.

Bull, M. 'Whatever happened to Italian communism? explaining the dissolution of the largest communist party in the west', *West European Politics*, Vol.14, No.4, October 1991.

Bull, M. 'The unremarkable death of the Italian Communist Party', in F. Sabetti and R. Catanzaro (eds), *Italian Politics: A Review*, Vol.6, London: Pinter (1991).

Bull, M. 'The PDS, the Progressive Alliance and the crisis', *Modern Italy*, Vol.1, No.1, Autumn 1995.

Bull, M., 'The great failure? The Democratic Party of the Left in Italy's transition', in S. Gundle and S. Parker (eds), *The New Italian Republic?: From the Fall of the Berlin Wall to Berlusconi*, London: Routledge (1996).

Bull, M. and Newell, J. 'Italian politics and the 1992 elections: from "stable instability" to stability and change', *Parliamentary Affairs*, Vol.46, No.2, April 1993.

Bull, M. and Newell, J. 'Italy changes course? the 1994 elections and the victory of the right', *Parliamentary Affairs*, Vol.48, No.1, January 1995.

Burgess, S. 'All change: the Italian electoral referendum of April 1993', *Representation*, Vol.32, No.118, Summer 1994

Burgess, S. 'The new Italy and the general election of March 1994', *Representation*, Vol.32, No.118, Summer 1994

Busch, A. 'the crisis in the ESM', *Government and Opposition*, Vol.29, No.1, winter 1994.

Caciagli, M. 'Italie 1993: vers la seconde république?', *La Revue Française de Science Politique*, Vol.43, No.2, 1993.

Caciagli, M. Cazzola, F., Morlino, L. and Passigli, S. (eds), *L'Italia fra Crisi e Transizione*, Bari: Laterza (1994).

Caciagli, M. and Kertzer, D. (eds), *Politica in Italia – i fatti dell'anno e le interpretazioni. Edizione 1996*, Bologna: Il Mulino (1996).

Calise, M., 'Remaking the Italian party system: how Lijphart got it wrong by saying it right', *West European Politics*, Vol.16, No.4, October 1993.

Calise, M., 'The Italian particracy: beyond president and parliament', *Political Science Quarterly*, Vol.109, No.3, Special Issue 1994a.

Calise, M., *Dopo la Partitocrazia*, Torino: Einaudi (1994b).

Calvi, G., 'Italie: une société sans état?', *Futuribles*, December 1990.

Calvi, G. and Vannucci, A., *L'Elettore Sconosciuto – analisi socioculturale e segmentazione degli orientamenti nel 1994*, Bologna: Il Mulino (1995).

Campanella, M., 'Getting the core: a neo-institutional approach to the EMU', *Government and Opposition*, Vol.30, No.3, Summer 1995.

Carducci, M., 'Un nuovo modello di organizzazione dell'opposizione parlamentare: "il governo ombra del PCI"', *Politica del Diritto*, Vol.21, 1990.

Carlucci, A., *Tangentomani – storie, affari e tutti i documenti sui barbari che hanno saccheggiato Milano*, Milano: Baldini & Castoldi (1992).

Cassese, S., 'Hypotheses on the Italian Administrative System', *West European Politics*, Vol.16, No.3, July 1993.

Castellino, O. 'La riforma delle pensioni: forse non sarà l'ultima', in M. Caciagli and D. Kertzer (eds), *Politica in Italia – i fatti dell'anno e le interpretazioni. Edizione 1996*, Bologna: Il Mulino (1996).

Castiglione, D. 'Contracts and constitutions', in R. Bellamy, V. Bufacchi and D. Castiglione (eds), *Democracy and Constitutional Culture in the Union of Europe*, London: Lothian (1995).

Christodoulidis, E. '"A new constitutional reality for civil society?" some cautionary remarks on republican citizenship', in R. Bellamy, V. Bufacchi and D. Castiglione (eds), *Democracy and Constitutional Culture in the Union of Europe*, London: Lothian (1995).

Chubb, J., *Patronage, Power and Poverty in Southern Italy – A Tale of Two Cities*, Cambridge: Cambridge University Press (1982).

Chubb, J. and Vannicelli, M., 'Italy: a web of scandals in a flawed democracy', in A. Markovits and M. Silverstein (eds), *The Politics of Scandals – Power and Process in Liberal Democracies*, New York: Holmes & Meier (1988).

Ciaurro, G.F., 'Public financing of parties in Italy', in H.E. Alexander (ed.), *Comparative Political Finance in the 1980s*, Cambridge: Cambridge University Press (1989).

Colombo, G., 'The new code of criminal procedure', in F. Sabetti and R. Catanzaro (eds), *Italian Politics: A Review*, Vol.6, London: Pinter (1991).

Corbetta, P. and Parisi, A., 'The referendum of the electoral law for the Senate: another momentous April', in C. Mershon and G. Pasquino (eds), *Italian Politics – Ending the First Republic*, Vol.9, Boulder, Colorado: Westview Press (1995).

Cotta, M., 'Il governo di partito in Italia: crisi e transizione dell'asetto tradizionale', in M. Caciagli *et al.* (eds) *L'Italia fra Crisi e Transizione*, Bari: Laterza (1994).

Craxi, B., *Il Caso C.*, Milano: Critica Sociale (1994).

Criscitiello, A., 'Majority summits: decision-making inside the cabinet and out: Italy, 1970–1990', *West European Politics*, Vol.16, No.4, October 1993.

Daalder, H. and Mair, P. (eds), *Western European Party Systems – Continuity and Change*, London: Sage (1983).

Dahl, R., *Democracy and its Critics*, New Haven: Yale University Press (1993).

D'Alberti and Finocchi, R. (eds), *Corruzione e Sistema Istituzionale*, Bologna: Il Mulino (1994).

Daniels, P. 'Italy and the Maastricht Treaty', in S. Hellman and G. Pasquino (eds), *Italian Politics: A Review*, Vol.8, London: Pinter (1993).

Davigo, P., 'I limiti del controllo penale sulla corruzione e i necessari rimedi preventivi', in D'Alberti and R. Finocchi (eds), *Corruzione e Sistema Istituzionale*, Bologna: Il Mulino (1994).

della Porta, D., 'Milan: immoral capital', in S. Hellman and G. Pasquino (eds), *Italian Politics: a review*, Vol.8, London: Pinter (1993).

della Porta, D., *Lo Scambio Occulto – casi di corruzione politica in Italia*, Bologna: Il Mulino (1992).

della Porta, D. 'Political parties and corruption: reflections on the Italian case', *Modern Italy*, Vol.1, No.1, 1995.

della Porta, D. and Vannucci, A., 'Politics, the mafia and the market for corrupt exchange', in C. Mershon and G. Pasquino (eds), *Italian Politics – Ending the First Republic*, Vol.9, Boulder, Colorado: Westview Press (1995).

Diamanti, I., *La Lega: geografia, storia e sociologia di un nuovo soggetto politico*, Roma: Donzelli (1993).

Diamanti, I., 'La politica come marketing', *Micromega*, 2, 1994.

Diamanti, I. and Mannheimer, R., 'Introduzione', in I. Diamanti and R. Mannheimer (eds), *Milano a Roma: guida all'Italia elettorale del 1994*, Roma: Donzelli (1994).

Diamanti, I. and Mannheimer, R. (eds), *Milano a Roma: guida all'Italia elettorale del 1994*, Roma: Donzelli (1994).

Di Franco, G. and Gritti, R. (eds), *L'Italia al Voto – analisi delle elezioni amministrative del 1993 e delle prospettive del sistema politico italiano*, Roma: Edizioni Associate (1994).

Donovan, M., 'Party strategy and centre domination in Italy', in P. Mair and G. Smith (eds), *Understanding Party System Change in Western Europe*, London: Cass (1990).

Donovan, M., 'A party system in transformation: the April 1992 Italian election', *West European Politics*, Vol.15, No.4, October 1992.

Donovan, M., 'The politics of electoral reform in Italy', *The International Political Science Review*, Vol.16, No.1, January 1995.

Donovan M., 'The referendum and the transformation of the party system', *Modern Italy*, Vol.1, No.1, 1995.

Donovan, M., 'Corruption in Italy: a dominant reality', Working Paper, *Centre for Mediterranean Studies*, Bristol University.

Downs, A., *An Economic Theory of Democracy*, New York: Harper & Row (1957).

Dunleavy, P., *Democracy, Bureaucracy, and Public Choice*, London: Harvester Wheatsheaf (1991).

Dunn, J., 'In the thicket of the theories of the state', *Government and Opposition*, Vol.22, No.4, Autumn 1987.

Dyson, K., *Party, State and Bureaucracy*, Beverly Hills, California: Sage (1977).

Edwards, A. and Roberts, G., *A New Dictionary of Political Analysis*, London: Edward Arnold (1991).

Elster, J., *Ulysses and the Sirens*, Cambridge: Cambridge University Press (1984).

Elster, J., *Nuts and Bolts for the Social Sciences*, Cambridge: Cambridge University Press (1989).

Ewing, K.D., *Money, Politics and Law: A Study of Campaign Finance Reform in Canada*, Oxford: Oxford University Press (1992).

Farrell, J., 'Berlusconi and Forza Italia: new forces for old?', *Modern Italy*, No.1, Vol.1, autumn 1995.

Fedele, M., *Democrazia Referendaria – l'Italia dal primato dei partiti al trionfo dell'opinione pubblica*, Roma: Laterza (1994).

Ferdinand, P., 'The party's over – market liberalisation and the challenges for one-party and one-party dominant regimes: the cases of Taiwan and Mexico, Italy and Japan', *Democratization*, Vol.1, No.1, spring 1994.

Ferrajoli, L., 'Democracy and the constitution in Italy', in *Political Studies*, Vol.44, No.3, Special Issue 1996.

Ferraresi, F., 'A secret structure codenamed Gladio', in S. Hellman and G. Pasquino (eds) *Italian Politics: A Review*, Vol.7, London: Pinter (1992).

Foot, J., 'The "Left opposition" and the crisis: Rifondazione Comunista and La Rete', in S. Gundle and S. Parker (eds), *The New Italian Republic?: From the Fall of the Berlin Wall to Berlusconi*, London: Routledge (1996).

Follini, M., *C'era una Volta la DC*, Bologna: Il Mulino (1994).

Frei, M., 'The long reach of Silvio Berlusconi', *British Journalism Review*, Vol.5, No.3, 1994.

Furlong, P., 'Government stability and electoral systems: the Italian example', *Parliamentary Affairs*, Vol.44, No.1, January 1991.

Furlong, P., *Modern Italy: Representation and Reform*, London: Routledge (1994).

Fusaro, C., 'Media, sondaggi e spese elettorali: la nuova disciplina', *Rivista Italiana di Scienze Politiche*, Vol.24, December 1994.

Gallagher, M., Conclusion in M. Gallagher and P.V. Uleri (eds) *The Referendeem Experience in Europe* Basingstoke: Macmillan (1996).

Gallagher, T., 'Regional nationalism and party system change: Italy's Northern League', *West European Politics*, Vol.16, No.4, October 1993.

Galli, C., 'La cultura politica', in S. Vertone (ed.) *La Cultura degli Italiani*, Bologna: Il Mulino (1994).

Galli, G., *Storia del Partito Armato*, Milano: Rizzoli (1986).

Gambetta, D. (ed.) *Trust*, Oxford: Blackwell (1989).

Gambetta, D., *The Sicilian Mafia – the Business of Private Protection*, Cambridge, Mass.: Harvard University Press (1993).

Gambetta, D., 'Inscrutable markets', *Rationality and Society*, Vol.6, No.3, July 1994.

Gambetta, D. and Warner, S., 'The rhetoric of reform revealed (or: if you bite the ballot it may bite back)', *Journal of Modern Italian Studies*, 1, (3), (1996).

Gardiner, A., 'Defining corruption', *Corruption and Reform*, Vol.7, No.2, 1992.

Ginsborg, P., *A History of Contemporary Italy: Society and Politics, 1943–1988*, Harmondsworth: Penguin (1990).

Ginsborg, P. (ed.), *Stato dell'Italia*, Milano: Il Saggiatore/Mondadori (1994).

Ginsborg, P., 'La sinistra, la crisi, la sconfitta', in P. Ginsborg (ed.), *Stato dell'Italia*, Milano: Il Saggiatore/Mondadori (1994).

Ginsborg, P., 'Italian political culture in historical perspective', *Modern Italy*, Vol.1, No.1, Autumn 1995.

Ginsborg, P., 'Comment expliquer la crise italienne?', *Politix*, Vol.30, 1995.

Ginsborg, P., 'Explaining Italy's crisis', in S. Gundle and S. Parker (eds), *The New Italian Republic? From the Fall of the Berlin Wall to Berlusconi*, London: Routledge (1996).

Glees, A., 'The Flick affair: a hint of corruption in the Bonn Republic', *Corruption and Reform*, Vol.2, 1987.

Goldstone, J.A., 'Revolutions, theories of' in D.Miller (ed.), *The Blackwell Encyclopaedia of Political Thought*, Oxford: Basil Blackwell (1987).

Goodin, R. and Pettit, P. (eds), *A Companion to Contemporary Political Philosophy*, Oxford: Blackwell (1993).

Gray, J., *Liberalisms*, London: Routledge (1989).

Green, D. and Shapiro, I., *Pathologies of Rational Choice Theory*, New Haven: Yale University Press (1994).

Guarnieri, C., 'The political role of the Italian judiciary', *Deconstructing Italy* (forthcoming).

Guarnieri, C., *Magistratura e Politica in Italia*, Bologna: Il Mulino (1993).

Gundle, S. and O'Sullivan, N., 'The mass media and the political crisis', in S. Gundle and S. Parker (eds), *The New Italian Republic?: From the Fall of the Berlin Wall to Berlusconi*, London: Routledge (1996).

Gundle, S. and Parker, S. (eds), *The New Italian Republic?: From the Fall of the Berlin Wall to Berlusconi*, London: Routledge (1996).

Guimbard, C., *Où va l'Italie?*, Paris: Presses de l'Université de Paris-Sorbonne (1994).

Guzzini, S., 'La longue nuit de la première république – l'implosion clienteliste en Italie', *La Revue Française de Science Politique*, Vol.44, No.6, December 1994.

Guzzini, S., 'The "long night of the First Republic": years of clientelistic implosion in Italy', *Review of International Political Economy*, Vol.2, No.1, winter 1995.

Haakossen, K., 'Republicanism', in R. Goodin and P. Pettit (eds), *A Companion to Contemporary Political Philosophy*, Oxford: Blackwell (1993).

Heidenheimer, A.J. Johnston, M. and Levine, V.T. (eds), *Political Corruption: A Handbook*, 2nd edn, New Brunswick: Transaction (1989).

Held, D. (ed.), *Political Theory Today*, Cambridge: Polity Press (1991).

Held, D. (ed.), *Prospects for Democracy*, Special Issue, *Political Studies*, Vol.XL, (1992).

Hellman, S. and Pasquino, G. (eds), *Italian Politics: A Review*, Vol.7, London: Pinter (1992).

Hellman, S. and Pasquino, G. (eds), *Italian Politics: A Review*, Vol.8, London: Pinter (1993).

Hine, D. 'Italy: condemned by its constitution?', in V. Bogdanor (ed.), *Constitutions in Democratic Politics*, Aldershot: Gower (1987).

Hine, D. 'The new Italian electoral system', *Association for the Study of Italy Newsletter*, Autumn 1993.

Hine, D., *Governing Italy: The Politics of Bargained Pluralism*, Oxford: Oxford University Press (1993).

Hine, D. 'Party, personality and the law: the political culture of corruption in Italy', in P.N. Jones (ed.), *Party, Parliament and Personality*, London: Routledge (1995).

Hollis, M., *The Philosophy of Social Science*, Cambridge: Cambridge University Press (1995).

Hollis, M. *Reason in Action: Essays in the Philosophy of Social Science*, Cambridge: Cambridge University Press (1996).

Hyman, E., *A Dictionary of Modern Revolution* London: Allen Lane (1973).

Iacopini, R. and Bianchi, S., *La Lega Ce l'Ha Crudo!* Milano: Mursia (1994).

Ionescu, G., *Politics and the Pursuit of Happiness*, London: Longman (1984).

Ignazi, P., *Il Polo Escluso: profilo del Movimento Sociale Italiano*, Bologna: Il Mulino (1989).

Ignazi, P., *Dal PCI al PDS*, Bologna: Il Mulino (1992).

Ignazi, P. 'La force des racines – la culture politique du mouvement social italien au seuil du gouvernement', *La Revue Française de Science Politique*, Vol.44, No.6, December 1994.

Ignazi, P. 'Alleanza Nazionale', in I. Diamanti and R. Mannheimer (eds), *Milano a Roma: guida all'Italia elettorale del 1994*, Roma: Donzelli (1994).

Katz, R., 'The 1993 parliamentary electoral reform', in C. Mershon and G. Pasquino (eds), *Italian Politics: A Review*, Vol.9, Boulder, Colorado: Westview Press (1995).

Katz, R. and Mair, P. (eds), *How Parties Organise*, London: Sage (1994).

Kilz, H.W. and Preuss J., *Flick – die gekaufte republik*, Reinbek: Rowohlt (1984).

Kymlicka, W., *Contemporary Political Philosophy: An Introduction*, Oxford: Oxford University Press (1990).

Kymlicka, W., *Multicultural Citizenship*, Oxford: Oxford University Press (1996).

Kymlicka, W. and Norman, W., 'Return of the citizen: a survey of recent work on citizenship theory', *Ethics*, Vol.104, No.2, 1994.

Laitin, D., 'The civic culture at thirty', *The American Political Science Review*, Vol.89, No.1, March 1995.

Landau, M., 'On the uses of metaphor in political analysis', *Social Research*, Vol.28, No.3, Autumn 1961.

Lange, P. and Tarrow, S. (eds), *Italy in Transition: Conflict and Consensus*, London: Cass (1980).

Lange, P. and Regini, M. (eds), *State, Market and Social Regulation – New Perspectives on Italy*, Cambridge: Cambridge University Press (1989).

La Palombara, J., *Democracy, Italian Style*, New Haven: Yale University Press (1987).

La Palombara, J., 'Structural and institutional aspects of corruption', *Social Research*, Vol.61, No.2, Summer 1994.

La Palombara, J. '"Clientela a parentela" rivisitato', in M. Caciagli *et al.* (eds), *L'Italia fra Crisi e Transizione*, Bari: Laterza (1994).

Laver, M. and Schofield, N., *Multiparty Government: The Politics of Coalition in Europe*, Oxford: Oxford University Press (1990).

Lazar, M. 'Italie: pour comprendre la Ligue', *La Revue Française de Science Politique*, Vol.43, No.6, 1993.

Lazar, M., 'Existe-t-il un "made in Italy" politique?', *Revue Politique et Parlamentaire*, Vol.95, No.968, Nov-Déc 1993.

Leonardi, R. and Wertman, D., *Italian Christian Democracy – the politics of dominance*, Macmillan: Basingstoke (1989).

Leonardi, R. and Nanetti, R. (eds), *Italy: Politics and Policy*, Aldershot: Dartmouth (1996).

Lewin, L., *Self-Interest and Public Interest in Western Politics*, Oxford: Oxford University Press (1991).

Little, W. and Posada-Carbo, E. (eds), *Political Corruption in Europe and Latin America*, London: Institute of Latin American Studies (1996).

Locke, R., 'Eppure si tocca: the abolition of the scala mobile', in C. Mershon and G. Pasquino (eds), *Italian Politics: A Review*, Vol.9, Boulder, Colorado: Westview Press (1995).

Luhmann, N., 'Familiarity, confidence, trust: problems and alternatives', in D. Gambetta (ed.), *Trust*, Oxford: Blackwell (1989).

Luttwak, E., 'Screw you', *London Review of Books*, Vol.15, No.16, August 1993.

Mastropaolo, A., 'Perché é entrata in crisi la democrazia italiana? Un'ipotesi sugli anni ottanta', in M. Caciagli *et al.* (eds), *L'Italia fra Crisi e Transizione*, Bari: Laterza (1994).

Machiavelli, N., *The Prince*, translated by G. Bull, Harmondsworth: Penguin (1961).

Mackie, T. and Marsh, D., 'The comparative method', in D. Marsh and G. Stoker (eds), *Theory and Methods in Political Science*, Basingstoke: Macmillan (1995).

Macpherson, C.B., *The Life and Times of Liberal Democracy*, Oxford: Oxford University Press (1977).

Mair, P. and Smith, G. (eds), *Understanding Party System Change in Western Europe*, London: Cass (1990).

Mannheimer, R. (ed.), *La Lega Lombarda*, Milano: Feltrinelli (1991).

Mannheimer, R., 'The electorate of the Lega Nord', in G. Pasquino and P. McCarthy (eds), *The End of Post-War Politics in Italy – the Landmark 1992 Elections*, Boulder, Colorado: Westview (1993).

Mannheimer, R., 'Forza Italia' in I. Diamanti and R. Mannheimer (eds), *Milano a Roma*, Roma: Donzelli (1994).

Markovits, A. and Silverstein, M. (eds), *The Politics of Scandals – Power and Process in Liberal Democracies*, New York: Holmes & Meier (1988).

Marsh, D. and Stoker, G. (eds), *Theory and Methods in Political Science*, Basingstoke: Macmillan (1995).

Massari, O., *Italia, Democrazia Maggioritaria? sfide e pericoli della transizione*, Genova: Costa and Nolan (1995).

Mazzoleni, G. 'The RAI: restructuring and reform', in C. Mershon and G. Pasquino (eds), *Italian Politics – Ending the First Republic*, Vol.9, Boulder, Colorado: Westview Press (1995).

McCarthy, P. 'The referendum of 9 June', in S. Hellman and G. Pasquino (eds), *Italian Politics: A Review*, Vol.7, London: Pinter (1992).

McCarthy, P. 'Inching towards a new regime', in G. Pasquino and P. McCarthy (eds), *The End of Post-War Politics in Italy – The Landmark 1992 Elections*, Boulder, Colorado: Westview (1993).

McCarthy, P. 'The Italian communists divide – and do not conquer', in G. Pasquino and P. McCarthy (eds), *The End of Post-War Politics in Italy – the Landmark 1992 Elections*, Boulder, Colorado: Westview (1993).

McCarthy, P., *L'Italie dans la Tourmente*, Paris: Presses de Saerices Po (1995).

McCarthy, P., *The Crisis of the Italian State: from the Origins of the Cold War to the Fall of Berlusconi*, Basingstoke: Macmillan (1995).

McCarthy, P., 'Forza Italia: the new politics and old values of a changing Italy', in S. Gundle and S. Parker (eds), *The New Italian Republic*, London: Routledge (1996).

Merlini, C., 'Italy and Europe', in J. Story (ed.), *The New Europe – Politics, Government and the economy since 1945*, Oxford: Blackwell (1993).

Mershon, C. and Pasquino, G. (eds), *Italian Politics: A Review*, Vol.9, Boulder, Colorado: Westview Press (1995).

Mill, J.S. 'On Liberty', in *Utilitarianism, On Liberty and Considerations on Representative Government*, London: Everyman (1972).

Miglio, G., *Verso una Nuova Costituzione*, Milano: Giuffrè (1983).

Miglio, G., *Per una Costituzione per i Prossimi Trent'Anni*, edited by M. Staglieno, Bari: Laterza (1990).

Miglio, G., *Come Cambiare: le mie riforme*, Milano: Mondadori (1992).

Miglio, G., 'Towards a federal Italy', *Telos*, No.90, Winter 1991–2.

Mingione, E., 'Italy: the resurgence of regionalism', *International Affairs*, Vol.69, No.2, April 1993.

Morlino, L., 'Crisis of parties and change of party system in Italy', *Party Politics*, Vol.2, No.1, Jan.1996.

Mueller, D., *Public Choice II*, Cambridge: Cambridge University Press (1989).

Mulé, R., 'Electoral behaviour in Italy', *European Journal of Political Research*, Vol.23, 1993.

Mulé, R. 'Party competitionand the hierarchy of goals', in J. Lovenduski and J. Stanyer (eds), *Contemporary Political Studies 1995*, Vol. I, The Political Studies Association of the United Kingdom (1995).

Mullhall, S. and Swift, A., *Liberals and Communitarians*, Oxford: Blackwell (1992).

Nascimbeni, E. and Pamparana, A., *Le Mani Pulite*, Milano: Mondadori (1992).

Natale, P., 'Lega Lombarda e insediamento territoriale', in R. Mannheimer (ed.), *La Lega Lombarda*, Milano: Feltrinelli (1991).

Nelken, D., 'A legal revolution? the judges and Tangentopoli', in S. Gundle and S. Parker (eds), *The New Italian Republic*, London: Routledge (1996).

Neppi Modona, G. 'Tangenti e Mani pulite: dopo le indagni i processi', in P. Ginsborg (ed.), *Stato dell'Italia*, Milano: Il Saggiatore\Mondadori (1994).

Newell, J. and Bull, M., 'The Italian referenda of April 1993: real change at last?', *West European Politics*, Vol.16, No.4, October 1993.

Nye, J.S., 'Corruption and Political Development: A Cost-Benefit Analysis', in A.J. Heidenheimer, *et al.* (eds), *Political Corruption: A Handbook*, New Brunswick: Transaction (1989).

Okin, S.M., *Justice, Gender and the Family*, New York: Basic Books (1989).

Okin, S.M., 'Gender, the public and the private', in D. Held (ed), *Political Theory Today*, Cambridge: Polity Press (1991).

Ottomani, M., *Brigate Rozze: a sud e a nord del senatore Bossi*, Napoli: Tulio Pironti (1992).

Padovani, M., *Men of Honour – the truth about the mafia*, London: Fourth Estate (1992).

Pamparana, P., *Il Processo Cusani*, Milano: Mondadori (1994).

Panebianco, A., *L'Italia che Non c'é*, Milano: Rizzoli (1995).

Panebianco, A., *Il Prezzo della Libertà*, Bologna: Il Mulino (1995).

Pappalardo, A., 'La nuova legge elettorale in parlamento: chi, come e perché', *Rivista Italiana di Scienze Politiche*, Vol.24, No.2, August 1994.

Parisi, A. and Pasquino, G., 'Changes in Italian electoral behaviour: the relationships between parties and voters', *West European Politics*, Vol.2, No.3, October 1979.

Parker, S. 'Electoral reform and political change in Italy, 1991–1994', in S. Gundle and S. Parker (eds), *The New Italian Republic*, London: Routledge (1996).

Partridge, H., 'Can the leopard change its spots? Sleaze in Italy', *Parliamentary Affairs*, Vol.48, No.4, October 1995.

Pasquino, G., 'Unregulated regulators, parties and party government', in P. Lange and M. Regini (eds), *State, Markets and Social Regulation – a New Perspective on Italy*, Cambridge: Cambridge University Press (1989).

Pasquino, G., 'The De Mita government crisis and the powers of the president of the republic: which form of government?', in F. Sabetti and R. Catanzaro (eds), *Italian Politics: A Review*, Vol.5, Pinter: London (1991).

Pasquino, G., 'Programmatic renewal and much more: from the PCI to the PDS', *West European Politics*, Vol.16, No.1, Jan.1993.

Pasquino, G., 'Introduction: A Case of Regime Crisis' in G. Pasquino and P. McCarth (eds) *The end of Post-War Politics in Italy. The Landmark 1992 Election* Boulder Colorado: Westview (1993).

Pasquino, G. (ed.), *Votare un Solo Candidato: le conseguenze politiche della preferenza unica*, Bologna: Il Mulino (1993).

Pasquino, G., 'The birth of the "Second Republic"', *The Journal of Democracy*, Vol.5, No.3, July 1994.

Pasquino, G. 'Un leader nuovo? no, ce ne vogliono due', *Reset*, No.7, June 1994.

Pasquino, G. (ed.), *L'Alternanza Inattesa: le elezioni del 27 Marzo 1994 e le loro conseguenze*, Messina: Rubbettino Editore (1995).

Pasquino, G., 'Il governo di Lamberto Dini', in M. Caciagli and D. Kertzer (eds), *Politica in Italia – i fatti dell'anno e le interpretazioni. Edizione 1996*, Bologna: Il Mulino (1996).

Pasquino, G. and McCarthy, P. (eds), *The End of Post-War Politics in Italy – the Landmark 1992 Elections*, Boulder, Colorado: Westview (1993).

Pasquino, G. and Vassallo, S., 'The government of Carlo Azeglio Ciampi', in C. Mershon and G. Pasquino (eds), *Italian Politics – Ending the First Republic*, Vol.9, Boulder, Colorado: Westview Press (1995).

Pasquino, P., *Uno e Trino*, Milano: Anabasi (1994).

Passerin d'Entréves, A., 'New Reflections on the History of Italy', *European Studies Review*, Vol.4, No.3, 1974.

Pateman, C., *Participation and Democratic Theory*, Cambridge: Cambridge University Press (1970).

Pateman, C., 'Feminist critique of the public/private dichotomy', in *The Disorder of Women*, Cambridge: Polity Press (1989).

Phillips, A. 'Must feminists give up on liberal democracy?', in D. Held (ed.) *Prospects for Democracy*, Special Issue, *Political Studies*, Vol.XL, (1992).

Piccone, P. 'Federal Populism in Italy', *Telos*, No.90, Winter 1991–92.

Pizzorno, A., 'La corruzione nel sistema politico', introduction to D. della Porta *Lo Scambio Occulto – casi di corruzione politica in Italia*, Bologna: Il Mulino (1992).

Poche, B., 'La Ligue Nord face à l'état italien: entre la décomposition territoriale et la recomposition institutionnelle', *La Revue Politique et Parlamentaire*, Vol.95, No.968, Nov–Déc. 1993.

Popper, K., *Unended Quest: An Intellectual Autobiography*, La Salle and London: Open Court (1982).

Pozzi, E. and Rattazzi, S., *Farsi Eleggere: la campagna elettorale nella seconda repubblica*, Milano: Il Sole 24 Ore (1994).

Prezeworski, A., *Sustainable Democracy*, Cambridge: Cambridge University Press (1995).

Putnam, R., *The Beliefs of Politicians: Ideology, Conflict, and Democracy in Britain and Italy*, New Haven: Yale University Press (1973).

Putnam, R., *Making Democracy Work*, Princeton: Princeton University Press (1993).

Rawls, J., *A Theory of Justice*, Cambridge, Mass.: Harvard University Press (1971).

Rhodes, M., 'The "long wave" subsides: The PSI and the demise of craxismo', in S. Hellman and G. Pasquino (eds), *Italian Politics: a Review*, Vol.8, London: Pinter (1993).

Rhodes, M., 'Reinventing the left: the origins of Italy's progressive alliance', in C. Mershon and G. Pasquino (eds), *Italian Politics – Ending the First Republic*, Vol.9, Boulder, Colorado: Westview Press (1995).

Rhodes, M. 'The Italian left between crisis and renewal', in R. Leonardi and R. Nanetti (eds), *Italy: Politics and Policy*, Aldershot: Dartmouth (1996).

Ricolfi, L., *L'Ultimo Parlamento*, Roma: La Nuova Italia Scientifica (1993).

Ricolfi, L., 'Politica senza fede: l'estremismo di centro dei piccoli leghisti', *Il Mulino*, Jan–Feb 1993.

Ricolfi, L. 'Elezioni e mass media. Quanti voti ha spostato la TV', *Il Mulino*, Nov–Dec 1994.

Rizzo, A., *Big Bang – il cambiamento italiano nel cambiamento mondiale*, Bari: Laterza (1993).

Romano, S., *Guida alla Politica Estera Italiana*, Milano: Rizzoli (1993).

Rustow, D., 'Transitions to democracy: towards a dynamic model', *Comparative Politics*, Vol.2, No.3, April 1970.

Ruzza, C. and Schmidtke, O., 'Towards a modern right: Alleanza Nazionale and the "Italian revolution"', in S. Gundle and S. Parker (eds), *The New Italian Republic*, London: Routledge (1996).

Sabetti, F. and Catanzaro, R. (eds), *Italian Politics: A Review*, Vol.5, London: Pinter (1991).

Salvadori, M., *Storia d'Italia e Crisi di Regime*, Bologna: il Mulino (1994).

Sani, G., 'The political culture of Italy: continuity and change', in G. Almond and S. Verba (eds), *The Civic Culture Revisited*, Boston: Little, Brown (1980).

Sani, G., 'Dai voti ai seggi', in I. Diamanti and R. Mannheimer (eds), *Milano a Roma: guida all'Italia elettorale del 1994*, Roma: Donzelli (1994).

Santino, U. and La Fiura, G., *L'Impresa Mafiosa*, Milano: Franco Angeli (1990).
Sartori, G., *Seconda Repubblica? Si, ma Bene*, Milano: Rizzoli (1992).
Sassoon, D., *Contemporary Italy*, London: Longman (1986).
Savelli, G., *Che Cosa Vuole la Lega*, Milano: Longanesi (1992).
Saward, M., 'Direct democracy revisited', *Politics*, Vol.13, No.2, October 1993.
Scarpino, S., *Tutti a Casa, Terroni*, Milano: Leonardi (1992).
Schumpeter, J., *Capitalism, Socialism and Democracy*, London: Unwin (1954).
Scoppola, P., *La Repubblica dei Partiti – profilo storico della democrazia in Italia (1945–1990)*, Bologna: Il Mulino (1991).
Seton-Watson, C., 'Recent Italian foreign policy', *Rivista*, Jan–Feb. 1991.
Sidoti, F., 'The Italian political class', *Government and Opposition*, Vol.28, No.3, Summer 1993.
Sjoblom, G., 'Political change and political accountability: a proportional inventory of causes and effects', in H. Daalder and P. Mair (eds), *Western European Party Systems – Continuity and Change*, London: Sage (1983).
Smith, G., 'The functional properties of the referendum', *The European Journal of Political Research*, Vol.4, No.1, Special issue, March 1976.
Spence, A.M., *Market Signalling*, Cambridge, Mass.: Harvard University Press (1974).
Spotts, F. & Wieser, T., *Italy: A Difficult Democracy*, Cambridge: Cambridge University Press (1987).
Story, J. (ed.), *The New Europe – Politics, Government and the Economy Since 1945*, Oxford: Blackwell (1993).
Swedberg, R. *Joseph A. Schumpeter – His Life and Work*, Cambridge: Policy Press (1991).
Tong, R., *Feminist Thought*, London: Unwin Hyman (1989).
Tretiack, P., *La Vie Blindée*, Paris: Seuil (1992).
Turone, S., *Politica Ladra: storia della corruzione in Italia, 1861–1992*, Milano: Mondadori (1992).
Uleri, P.V. and Fideli, R., 'I referendum non piovono dal cielo: la consultazione referendaria di giugno', in M. Caciagli and D. Kertzer (eds), *Politica in Italia – i fatti dell'anno e le interpretazioni. Edizione 1996*, Bologna: Il Mulino (1996).
Urban, J.B., 'Gorbachev's state visit to Italy and the Vatican', in F. Sabetti and R. Catanzaro (eds), *Italian Politics: A Review*, Vol.5, London: Pinter (1991).
Valentini, C. 'Alleanza Nazionale: la componente "storica" del Polo della Libertà', in P. Ginsborg (ed.), *Stato dell'Italia*, Milano: Il Saggiatore/Mondadori (1994).
Vannucci, A., 'La realtà economica della corruzione politics: analisi di un caso', *Stato e Mercato*, No.34, Aprile 1992.
Vannucci, A., 'Il mercato della corruzione', PhD thesis, Pisa: Scuola Superiore S. Anna, 1994
Veltri, E., *Da Craxi a Craxi*, Bari: Laterza (1993).
Vertone, S. (ed.), *La Cultura degli Italiani*, Bologna: Il Mulino (1994).
Vimercati, D., *I Lombardi alla Nuova Crociata*, Milano: Mursia (1990).
Volcansek, M., 'Decision-making Italian style: the new code of criminal procedure', *West European Politics*, Vol.13, No.4, October 1990.
Waldron, J., 'Theoretical foundations of liberalism', *The Philosophical Quarterly*, Vol.37, No.147, 1987.

Walsh, J.I., 'International constraints and domestic choices: economic convergence and exchange rate policy in France and Italy', *Political Studies*, Vol.42, June 1994.

Waquet, J-C., 'Some considerations on corruption, politics and society in 16th and 17th century Italy', in W. Little and E. Posada-Carbo (eds), *Political Corruption in Europe and Latin America*, London: Institute of Latin American Studies (1996).

Warner, C., 'The new catholic parties: the Popolari, Patto Segni and CCD', in R. Leonardi and R. Nanetti (eds), *Italy: Politics and Policy*, Aldershot: Dartmouth (1996).

Warner, S. and Gambetta, D., *La Retorica della Riforma: fine del sistema proporzionale in Italia*, Torino: Einaudi (1994).

Warner, S. and Varese, F., 'The Italian General Election of 1996', *Electoral Studies*, (forthcoming).

Waters, S., 'Tangentopoli and the emergence of a new political order in Italy', *West European Politics*, Vol.17, No.1, January 1994.

Wertman, D., 'The Christian Democrats: a party in crisis', in G. Pasquino and P. McCarthy (eds), *The End of Post-War Politics in Italy – the Landmark 1992 elections*, Boulder, Colorado: Westview (1993).

Wertman, D., 'The last year of the Christian Democrat party', in C. Mershon and G. Pasquino (eds), *Italian Politics – Ending the First Republic*, Vol.9, Boulder, Colorado: Westview Press (1995).

Willan, P., *Puppet Masters – the Political Use of Terrorism in Italy*, London: Constable (1991).

Zamagni, S., 'Sul processo di generazione della corruzione sistemica', in L. Barca and S. Trento (eds), *L'Economia della Corruzione*, Bari: Laterza (1994).

Index

272

Index